VICTORIA & VANCOUVER ISLAND

ANDREW HEMPSTEAD

Contents

Although every effort was made to make sure the information in this book was accurate when going to press, research was impacted by the Covid-19 pandemic and things may have changed since the time of writing. Be sure to confirm specific details, like opening hours, closures, and travel guidelines and restrictions, when making your travel plans. For more detailed information, see p. 222.

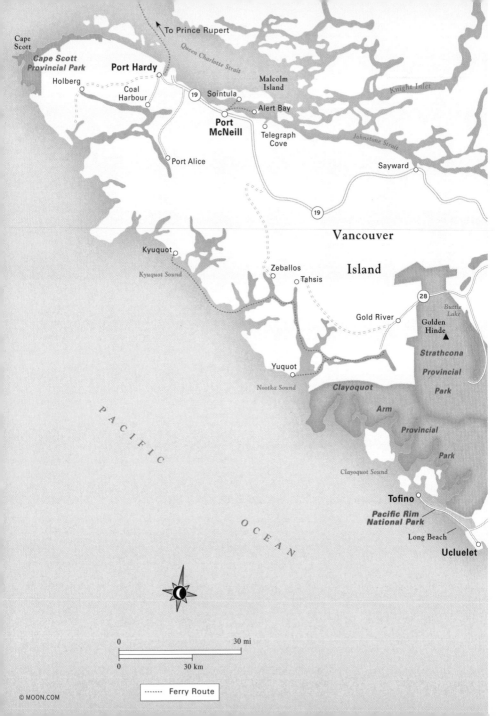

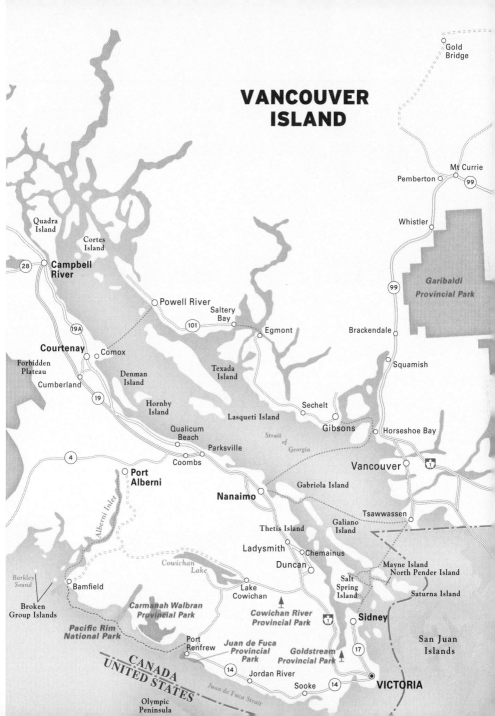

VANCOUVER ISLAND

Gold Bridge

Mt Currie

Pemberton (99)

Whistler

Quadra Island

Cortes Island

(28) **Campbell River**

Powell River

Saltery Bay

Egmont

(101)

Garibaldi Provincial Park

(99)

Brackendale

(19A)

Courtenay

Comox

Texada Island

Squamish

Forbidden Plateau

Cumberland

Denman Island

(19)

Hornby Island

Sechelt

Lasqueti Island

Gibsons

Horseshoe Bay

Qualicum Beach

Strait of Georgia

Parksville

(4)

Coombs

Port Alberni

Nanaimo

Gabriola Island

Vancouver

(1)

Alberni Inlet

Thetis Island

Tsawwassen

Galiano Island

Ladysmith

Chemainus

Duncan

Mayne Island
North Pender Island

Barkley Sound

Cowichan Lake

Salt Spring Island

Saturna Island

Bamfield

Lake Cowichan

Broken Group Islands

Carmanah Walbran Provincial Park

Cowichan River Provincial Park

Sidney

(17)

San Juan Islands

Pacific Rim National Park

Port Renfrew

Juan de Fuca Provincial Park

Goldstream Provincial Park

(14)

VICTORIA

CANADA
UNITED STATES

Jordan River

Sooke

(14)

Juan de Fuca Strait

Olympic Peninsula

DISCOVER

Victoria &
Vancouver Island

Although Vancouver Island is just a small speck on the map of Canada, its size belies its diversity. A chain of rugged mountains divides the island into two distinct sides: dense rain-drenched forest and remote surf- and wind-battered shores on the west, and well-populated, sheltered, beach-fringed lowlands facing the Strait of Georgia to the east.

Victoria, the island's largest city and the capital of British Columbia, lies on the island's southern tip. Its many cosmopolitan charms include colorful gardens and afternoon tea. It has the mildest climate of any Canadian capital, which provides a beautiful harborside setting for an array of cultural, dining, and shopping choices.

Outside the city, complete one of the great coastal hikes. Try your hand at stand-up paddleboarding or sea kayaking through protected fjords. Explore the rural oases of the Southern Gulf Islands. Surf along the rugged west coast. Share the thrill of hooking a giant salmon or the bizarre scenario of sleeping in a treetop sphere. Whatever adventures you choose, Vancouver Island won't disappoint you.

Clockwise from top left: west coast forest; Strathcona Provincial Park; humpback whale breaching off the coast of Victoria; water taxi and Fisherman's Wharf in Victoria; sand dollar on Qualicum Beach; Fairmont Empress.

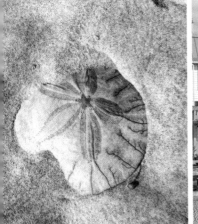

8 TOP
EXPERIENCES

1 **Go Whale-Watching:** Of the island's many whale-watching spots, none is better than **Robson Bight** (page 181), where orcas gather in large numbers.

∧
∧ ∧
∧ ∧ ∧

2 **Wander through Butchart Gardens:** Generally regarded as one of the world's premier gardens, Butchart is a colorful wonderland of rare and exotic flowers, shrubs, and trees (page 44).

3 **Sip Afternoon Tea:** Victoria is the place to indulge in this exceedingly British tradition. Try one of the low key **tearooms** scattered around the city, or go upscale at the **Fairmont Empress** (page 56).

4 **See Art and Architecture:** Victoria is a feast for the eyes, from the impressive **Craigdarroch Castle** (page 38) and historical **Parliament Buildings** (page 34) to stunning **fine art** from around the world at the **Bateman Gallery** (page 36) and the **Art Gallery of Greater Victoria** (page 38).

<<<

5 **Cast a Line:** Fish from **Discovery Pier at Campbell River**, search out a river, or **charter a boat** for day to reel in some salmon (page 166).

>>>

6 **Island Hop:** Explore the **wilderness of Saturna Island** (pictured, page 90), relax on the **beaches of Hornby Island** (page 152), or learn about **Indigenous culture at Alert Bay** (page 179).

>>>

∧
∧
∧

7 **Get on the Water:** Float down the Cowichan River on an inflatable **tube** (page 102), **kayak** around the Southern Gulf Islands (page 87), or **ride the waves** off Tofino (page 137).

8 **Hit the Trail:** Take a stroll along the beaches of **Saturna Island** (page 90), explore **Pacific Rim National Park** (page 134), or plan on a multi-night backpack on the **West Coast Trail** (pictured, page 97).

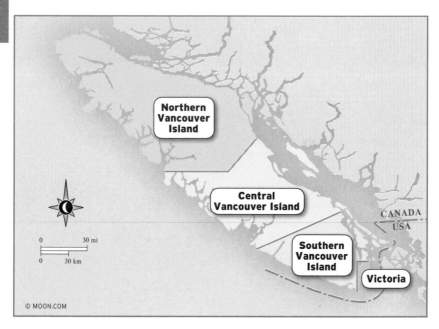

© MOON.COM

Where to Go

Victoria

The capital of British Columbia is a study in **urban elegance.** Well-preserved old buildings line inner-city streets. **Restored historical areas** house trendy shops, offices, and restaurants. **Totem poles** sprout from shady parks. **Double-decker buses** and **horse-drawn carriages** compete for the summer tourist trade.

Southern Vancouver Island

North of the capital, the bustling harborside town of **Sidney** is a gateway to the idyllic **Southern Gulf Islands.** A **winding coastal highway** leads to Port Renfrew, where backcountry enthusiasts begin the long-distance **West Coast Trail.** Or admire **totem poles** in Duncan and float down the **Cowichan River** on an inflatable tube.

Central Vancouver Island

The central section of Vancouver Island extends from **Nanaimo,** a 90-minute drive from Victoria, north to the **Comox Valley,** and up and over the Vancouver Island Ranges to the west. Along the east coast of the **Strait of Georgia** are **Oceanside resort towns,** while the interior is dotted with **waterfalls** and stands of **old-growth forest.** The west coast is dominated by **wild, untamed beaches** bookended by fishing-turned-tourist towns, Ucluelet and Tofino.

Northern Vancouver Island

Northern Vancouver Island is the largest but least populated region of the island. The gateway city is **Campbell River,** famous for **salmon fishing.** Beyond lies **forested wilderness** and a **wild and rugged coastline.** Take a **coastal cruise,** join a **whale-watching trip,** or explore islands that have been inhabited by **First Nations** for thousands of years.

When to Go

Vancouver Island can be visited year-round, with some outdoor activities possible in the dead of winter in Victoria.

Tourist attractions and hotels are busiest during the **July-August high season.** Many towns celebrate the season with festivals (such as Nanaimo's **World Championship Bathtub Race** and Parksville's **sand-sculpting competition**).

My favorite time to visit is **April-June.** Days are long and warm enough to enjoy the outdoors (expect temperatures a few degrees cooler in Vancouver than across the water in Victoria), but crowds are at a minimum, and lodging rates are reduced. The roses at Butchart Gardens don't flower until July, but I can live without that.

During the **October-March low season,** attractions shorten their hours (some close completely), and lodging prices are reduced drastically. Winters are relatively mild. This is storm-watching season on the island's west coast. Up north, **steelhead fishing** draws anglers to Campbell River, while dedicated **skiers and snowboarders** head to alpine resort Mount Washington, near Courtenay.

Before You Go
PASSPORTS AND VISAS

To enter Canada, a **passport** is required of citizens and permanent residents of the United States. For further information, see the website http://travel.state.gov. For current **entry requirements** to Canada, check the Citizenship and Immigration Canada website (www.cic.gc.ca).

All other foreign visitors must have a valid passport and may need a **visa** or visitors permit, depending on their country of residence and the vagaries of international politics. At present, visas are not required for citizens of the United States,

---

In March, cherry blossoms come alive with color throughout Victoria.

Port Alberni lighthouse

fish market in the waterfront town of Sidney

British Commonwealth countries, or Western Europe. The standard **entry permit** is for **six months,** and you may be asked to show onward tickets or proof of sufficient funds to last you through your intended stay.

TRANSPORTATION

Visitors to Vancouver Island have the option of arriving by **air** or **ferry.** The main gateway city for flights to Vancouver Island is Victoria, although many visitors fly into Vancouver, which is the Canadian point of entry for flights originating in Asia and the South Pacific, and then travel over to the island by ferry or **floatplane.**

Ferries run year-round from mainland British Columbia and Washington State to Vancouver Island, and also link over a dozen smaller islands with Vancouver Island. They also run north from the northern tip of the island to Prince Rupert, on British Columbia's northwest coast.

While Vancouver Island has scheduled bus service, driving, whether it be your own vehicle or a rental car, is the best way to get around. Distances are not great, and gas stations are located at regular intervals.

Best of Vancouver Island

Two weeks on Vancouver Island is enough time to enjoy the very best that the island has to offer—to get a taste of Victoria's major sights, head over to the west coast, travel as far north as Alert Bay, and spend a couple of days in the Southern Gulf Islands. This tour combines the very best of these regions and includes all the major natural and historic attractions. It assumes you have your own vehicle or will be reserving one for pickup at Victoria International Airport. If you only have one week, limit your time on the Southern Gulf Islands and skip northern Vancouver Island.

Victoria

DAY 1

Three days is enough time to get a taste of Victoria's compact downtown core. Head south from the airport and loop around the **scenic route to Oak Bay** to reach Victoria's Inner Harbour and your downtown accommodations.

A modern lodging like the **Parkside Hotel & Spa** or the historic **Fairmont Empress** will keep you within walking distance of the action-packed Inner Harbour. Get dinner at a downtown restaurant (try personal favorite **Agrius** for island-sourced organic ingredients). Then wander the beautiful Inner Harbour promenade, which is illuminated at night.

DAY 2

Start your day with a walk along the harborfront to the **Bateman Gallery** and then to the historical streets of **Old Town.** Admire the historical architecture of **Market Square** and the eclectic collection of goods at **Capital Iron.** Choose a Bastion Square restaurant such as **Rebar** for lunch. Spend a full afternoon at colorful **Butchart Gardens.** In the evening, head to **Café Brio** for excellent Italian fare, and end your day with a drink at the **Lido Waterfront Bar.**

Victoria's Inner Harbour from the Fairmont Empress terrace

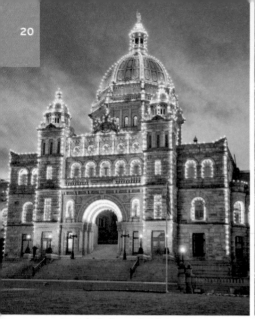

evening at the Parliament Buildings

Butchart Gardens

DAY 3

Catch a cab to Government House. Admire the surrounding native gardens and then wind your way on foot back down to the harbor via imposing Craigdarroch Castle and the Art Gallery of Greater Victoria. Enjoy a stroll through historic Point Ellice House, which is easily reached by water taxi from the Inner Harbour. For dinner, choose between casual seafood at Red Fish Blue Fish, or transport yourself to the Himalayas at The Mint.

Exploring Vancouver Island

DAY 4: TOFINO

Head north out of the capital, making a stop at the photogenic waterfalls of Goldstream Provincial Park. Then continue across the island on Highway 4 to Tofino, which takes less than three hours. Spend some time enjoying the surf, whether watching the waves or riding them (local outfitter Live to Surf offers lessons that make it easy). Take a relaxing afternoon walk along Long Beach. You are spoiled for dining choices in Tofino. Try some of the best fish tacos this side of the Caribbean at the Tacofino food truck. Or go more formal with the Pointe Restaurant at the Wickaninnish Inn, which offers sweeping ocean views—and is also the town's premier lodging.

DAY 5: PORT ALBERNI TO PARKSVILLE

Head back to Port Alberni along Highway 4, allowing two hours of driving time. Take a tour aboard vintage passenger-only ferry MV *Frances Barkley,* which cruises down the remote Alberni Inlet. Upon your return to Port Alberni, drive another hour east along Highway 4 through Cathedral Grove to Ocean Sands Resort in Parksville, where you'll stay the night. All units have full kitchens; take advantage by cooking your own dinner.

DAY 6: WHALE-WATCHING AT TELEGRAPH COVE

Drive north along Highway 19 to Telegraph Cove, around four hours from Parksville. Stop at Horne Lake Caves for an underground tour along the way. Arrive at your Telegraph Cove historic boardwalk lodging (which you've reserved in advance for two nights). Take an afternoon whale-watching excursion to **Robson Bight,** one of the best places in the world to view orcas. End the day with fish-and-chips at the **Killer Whale Café.**

DAY 7: FIRST NATIONS AT ALERT BAY

Make the short 15-minute drive north along Highway 19 and Port McNeill. Leave your vehicle and jump aboard a ferry to **Alert Bay.** This small settlement on Cormorant Island is a hotbed of First Nations history. It's easy to spend a full day visiting the local museum, searching out some of the world's tallest totem poles, and hiking to an intriguing black-water swamp. After your return ferry to the mainland, head back to your Telegraph Cove lodging.

DAY 8: SALMON FISHING
IN CAMPBELL RIVER

Allow just over two hours to drive back down along Highway 19 to **Campbell River** and oceanfront **Painter's Lodge,** where an experienced guide will take you out into waters renowned for the best salmon fishing in the world.

DAY 9: CUMBERLAND AND COMOX

Depending on your frame of mind, spend the morning exploring the coal-mining history of **Cumberland,** golfing in **Crown Isle,** or enjoying a relaxing lunch at a waterfront restaurant in **Comox.** Then continue south to Nanaimo, about a 90-minute drive on Highway 1. If it is sunny, spend your afternoon exploring **Newcastle Island.** On a rainy day, the local museum and downtown core have plenty to hold your interest. Check into the **Buccaneer Inn** and make reservations at one of the many inviting Nanaimo restaurants, such as **Nest Bistro.**

DAYS 10-13: SOUTHERN GULF ISLANDS

Head south from Nanaimo with a ferry schedule in hand and work out a three-day itinerary through the Southern Gulf Islands. Highlights include **Galiano Island,** with the sandy

carved eagle on a viewing dock in Alert Bay

First Nations Sites

In the 12,000 years that anthropologists surmise human beings have inhabited Vancouver Island, a variety of cultures have evolved, each with its own unique and distinguishing features. The very earliest people left behind few traces of their presence, but today, island visitors can immerse themselves in First Nations history at the following destinations and attractions:

- Victoria's **Thunderbird Park** holds a collection of towering totem poles. While you're in the capital, **Eagle Feather Gallery** and **Cowichan Trading** are two excellent opportunities for First Nations shopping.

- **Duncan** is a small town with a big collection of historic and contemporary totem poles scattered throughout downtown.

- **Petroglyph Provincial Park,** south of Nanaimo, protects one of the island's oldest known archeological sites. The rock carvings here are dated at 3,000 years old.

- **Quadra Island** has been home to the Kwakwaka'wakw people for generations. You can learn about them at the Nuyumbalees Cultural Centre and then spend the night surrounded by their distinctive architecture at **Cape Mudge Resort.**

totem poles in Thunderbird Park

- **Nootka Sound** is best known as the location for a historic treaty signed by the Spanish, British, and First Nations, but today is the site of two First Nations villages almost totally unaffected by the outside world.

- **Alert Bay** is home to a thriving community of Kwakwaka'wakw people, who welcome visitors to the **U'mista Cultural Centre** and the world's tallest totem poles.

shoreline of **Montague Harbour Provincial Park; Salt Spring Island,** with the inviting shops and cafés in **Ganges;** and **Saturna Island,** with its unhurried hiking trails.

DAY 14: HOMEWARD BOUND
Watch the Southern Gulf Islands disappear in the distance as your ferry heads toward Swartz Bay. Allow enough time to say goodbye to Victoria, perhaps with a return visit to Butchart Gardens for tea. Allow 30 minutes of driving time between the gardens and Victoria International Airport, your departure point for your journey homeward.

Getaway to Adventure

Vancouver Island is a major destination for outdoor enthusiasts. Adventure seekers can mix and match their favorite activities for a 10- or 12-day island odyssey.

DAY 1: CAMPING ON SIDNEY SPIT
Both Victoria International Airport and the Swartz Bay ferry terminal are a short hop from your first overnight adventure: the rustic beachfront campsites on **Sidney Spit,** accessible only by water taxi from Sidney.

DAY 2: HIKING ON SATURNA ISLAND
Head to the Swartz Bay ferry terminal and you're off again—this time to **Saturna Island,** the least visited of Southern Gulf Islands. Enjoy hiking trails (the short trail around **Narvaez Bay** is a highlight), deserted rocky coves, and even a low-key winery. There's no camping on the island, and only limited accommodations, so make sure you have reservations at **Saturna Lodge.**

DAY 3: KAYAKING OFF GALIANO ISLAND
After breakfast at the **Saturna Cafe,** island-hop from Saturna to **Galiano Island.** Go kayaking along the shore of **Montague Harbour Provincial Park.** Arriving back on Vancouver Island at Crofton, drive to Campbell River, and then west to your overnight lodging at **Gold River.**

DAY 4: CRUISING NOOTKA SOUND
Today is spent **cruising Nootka Sound** aboard the MV *Uchuck,* which departs just south of Gold River. You'll stop at remote fishing lodges and logging camps along a stretch of coast rarely visited by the average tourist. Upon arriving back at the dock, it takes 90 minutes of driving to retrace your route back to the island's east coast. Check into the totally groovy **Free Spirit Spheres,** west of Courtenay, for the night.

family playing in the sand on Sidney Spit

hiking the West Coast Trail

surfing lesson in Tofino

DAY 5: SURFING IN TOFINO

It's a three-hour drive between Courtenay and the west coast, along Highway 4, so wake up early. Make your first stop at **Cathedral Grove** to admire the colossal old-growth forest. **Surfing in Tofino** is made easy by Live to Surf, who will outfit you with a wetsuit and surfboard for an hour or so of fun in the local breakers. Take a lesson if you've never surfed before. **Pacific Sands Beach Resort** is designed especially for outdoorsy types like yourself.

DAY 6: DIVING IN THE STRAIT OF GEORGIA

The shallow waters off **Nanaimo** are renowned for artificial reefs created by ships that have been sunk especially for **wreck diving.** Tell the experts at Nanaimo Dive Outfitters that you want to try a dive, and let them choose a site that best suits your experience, whether it be the 442-foot-long *Saskatchewan* or the popular **snorkeling with seals** option. Nanaimo's **Buccaneer Inn** is the best divers' hangout. If you've had enough adventure for one trip, head homeward. Hardcore hikers will want to venture on, heading through the Cowichan Valley to Port Renfrew (allow two hours from Nanaimo).

DAYS 7-12: THE WEST COAST TRAIL

Experienced backcountry hikers won't want to miss the rugged and remote **West Coast Trail.** This self-sufficient four- to six-day coastal trek starts at Port Renfrew, west of Victoria, and ends near the remote village of Bamfield. The majority of hikers leave their vehicle at one end of the trail and return to their starting point by scheduled shuttle. If you don't have the time for the famed West Coast Trail, get a taste for the adventure in **Juan de Fuca Provincial Park,** where short trails lead to wild west coast beaches.

Family Camping Trip

So you're planning a camping trip to Vancouver Island and bringing along the kids? Not a problem—there's plenty to do and see for all age groups, but just remember that what you want them to see is probably a lot different from what they want to do.

DAY 1: CAMPING AT
GOLDSTREAM PROVINCIAL PARK

On the ferry trip between the mainland and Vancouver Island, find an outside seat on the starboard side and watch the Vancouver skyline and Coast Mountains disappear into the distance. Once in the provincial capital of Victoria, a **double-decker bus tour** is popular with all ages. Catch a water taxi to **Fisherman's Wharf** for an early dinner at **Barb's Fish & Chips,** hoping that the resident seals make an appearance. Set up camp at **Goldstream Provincial Park.**

DAY 2: SALMON FISHING
IN CAMPBELL RIVER

By driving north to Campbell River along Highway 1 then 19 (under four hours from Goldstream) early in the trip, all the heavy driving has been done. Ideal rest stops en route include the **murals of Chemainus** and the sand at **Miracle Beach Provincial Park.** Once in Campbell River, have the family try **salmon fishing** off Discovery Pier. Catch a ferry to **Quadra Island,** set up camp at **We Wai Kai Campsite,** and spend the evening exploring **Rebecca Spit Marine Provincial Park.**

DAY 3: COURTENAY

It takes under an hour to travel south from Campbell River along Highway 19 to **Courtenay,** where a family-friendly tour of **Horne Lake Caves** adds a different element to the vacation. The campground adjacent to the caves has a good beach with freshwater swimming.

Horne Lake Caves Provincial Park

Goldstream Provincial Park

Parksville Beach

DAY 4: HORNBY ISLAND

The ferry fun continues on Day 4, with a short hop out to Denman Island from Buckley Bay just south of Courtenay and then another to Hornby Island, where the campground at Tribune Bay is right beside a white sandy beach and within walking distance of a funky collection of shops and cafés.

DAY 5: OCEANSIDE

The beach scene continues a 20-minute drive south of Buckley Bay at the Oceanside resort towns of Parksville and Qualicum Beach, where safe swimming in warm water draws crowds throughout summer. A good camping choice here is Rathtrevor Beach Provincial Park, which is right on a sandy beach, but more importantly, within easy biking distance of Riptide Lagoon mini golf.

DAY 6: LAKE COWICHAN

It's a short drive from Oceanside to Lake Cowichan, south along Highway 19 and then west on Highway 18, which is the starting point for tubing down the Cowichan River. Continue west to Juan de Fuca Provincial Park; unlike the remote wilderness of the West Coast Trail, the beach camping here requires nothing more than a short walk through old-growth forest.

DAY 7: VICTORIA AND HOMEWARD

On your final day, it takes under two hours to drive back to your starting point, Victoria, from Juan de Fuca Provincial Park. If time allows, once back in the capital, head into downtown Victoria and check out the beautiful Parliament Buildings and art galleries, or wander through Beacon Hill Park searching for peacocks.

Victoria

Many people first see the city of Victoria from

the Inner Harbour as they arrive by boat, the way people have done for over 160 years. Ferries, fishing boats, and seaplanes bob in the harbor, with a backdrop of manicured lawns
and flower gardens, quiet residential suburbs, and striking urban architecture. Despite the pressures that go with city life, easygoing Victorians still find time for a stroll along the waterfront, a round of golf, or a night out at a fine-dining restaurant. Discovering Victoria's roots has been a longtime favorite with visitors, but some locals find the "more English than England" reputation tiring. Yes, there's a tacky side to some traditions, but high tea, double-decker bus tours, and

Look for ★ to find recommended sights, activities, dining, and lodging.

Highlights

★ **Fairmont Empress:** You don't need to be a guest at this historical hotel to admire its grandeur. Plan on eating a meal here for the full effect (page 34).

★ **Maritime Museum of British Columbia:** Check out British Columbia's seafaring past at this fun and informative museum (page 34).

★ **Bateman Gallery:** View over 160 paintings by one of the world's preeminent wildlife artists at this grandiose waterfront building (page 36).

★ **Craigdarroch Castle:** To get a feeling for the wealth of the city in the Victorian era, take a tour of this extravagant castle (page 38).

★ **Scenic Route to Oak Bay:** Whether by car, bike, or foot, you'll experience the natural splendor of Victoria along this route (page 39).

★ **Goldstream Provincial Park:** Laced with hiking trails, Goldstream Provincial Park is a great escape from the city. If you're visiting in late fall, a trip to the park is worthwhile to view the spectacle of spawning salmon (page 43).

★ **Butchart Gardens:** Even if you have only one day in Victoria, make time to visit one of the world's most delightful gardens (page 44).

exploring formal gardens remain some of the true joys in Victoria.

Victoria (pop. 370,000) has an abundance of created and natural attractions. Once you've visited must-sees like the Bateman Gallery and Butchart Gardens, you can devote your time to outdoor pursuits such as whale-watching, a bike ride through Oak Bay, or something as simple as enjoying afternoon tea in an old-fashioned tearoom. You will be confronted with oodles of ways to trim a bulging wallet in Victoria. Some commercial attractions are worth every cent, whereas others are routine at best, though the latter may be crowd-pleasers with children, which makes them worth considering if you have little ones in tow.

PLANNING YOUR TIME

Many visitors to Victoria spend a few nights in the city as part of a longer vacation that includes the rest of Vancouver Island. At an absolute minimum, plan on spending two full days in the capital, preferably overnighting at a character-filled bed-and-breakfast. Regardless of how long you'll be in the city, much of your time will be spent in and around the Inner Harbour, a busy waterway surrounded by the city's top sights, including the gracious Fairmont Empress and the impressive Bateman Gallery. Beyond the harbor, devote at least a half day to wandering through historical Craigdarroch Castle, taking in the ocean and mountain panorama along the scenic route to Oak Bay, and enjoying the classic English surroundings of Point Ellice House. Victoria's most visited attraction is Butchart Gardens, an absolutely stunning collection of plants that deserves at least half a day of your time. Away from downtown are the natural highlights of old-growth forest and waterfalls at Goldstream Provincial Park.

The best way to get to know Victoria is on foot. All of the downtown attractions are within a short walk of one another, and the more remote sights are easily reached by road or public transit. In summer, various tours are offered, giving you the choice of seeing Victoria by horse-drawn carriage, bus, boat, bicycle, limo—you name it. But if you still feel the need to have a car readily available, you'll be pleased to know that parking is plentiful just a few blocks from the Inner Harbour.

Sights

The epicenter of downtown Victoria is the foreshore of the Inner Harbour, which is flanked by the parliament buildings, the city's main museum, and the landmark Fairmont Empress Hotel. Government Street leads uphill from the waterfront through a concentration of touristy shops and restaurants, while parallel to the west, Douglas Street is the core of a smallish central business district.

INNER HARBOUR

Initially, the harbor extended farther inland. Before the construction of the massive stone causeway that now forms the marina, the area on which the impressive Empress now stands was a deep, oozing mudflat. Walk along the lower level and then up the steps in the middle to come face-to-face with an unamused Captain James Cook; the bronze statue commemorates the first recorded British landing in 1778 on the territory that would later become British Columbia. Above the northeast corner of the harbor is the Victoria Visitor Centre (812 Wharf St., 250/953-2033, www. tourismvictoria.com), the perfect place to start your city exploration. Be sure to return

Previous: Fairmont Empress on the Inner Harbour; Royal Victoria Yacht Club; totem pole in Butchart Gardens.

Victoria and Vicinity

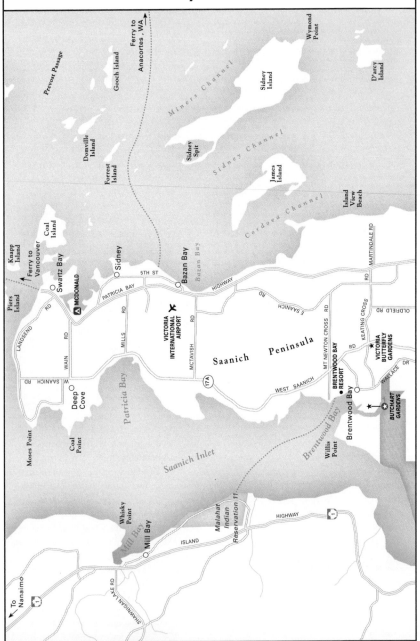

Prevost Passage

Gooch Island

Ferry to
Anacortes, WA

Wymond
Point

Sidney
Island

D'arcy
Island

Miners Channel

Domville
Island

Forrest
Island

Sidney
Spit

Sidney Channel

James
Island

Cordova Channel

Island
View
Beach

Coal
Island

Knapp
Island

Ferry to
Vancouver

Swartz Bay

Sidney

5TH ST

Bazan Bay

Bazan Bay

MARTINDALE RD

Piers
Island

△ McDONALD

PATRICIA BAY

HIGHWAY

RD

RD

RD

OLDFIELD RD

LANDSEND RD

RD

WAIN RD

MILLS

PATRICIA BAY RD

MCTAVISH

✈
VICTORIA
INTERNATIONAL
AIRPORT

Saanich   Peninsula

E SAANICH RD

MT NEWTON CROSS RD

KEATING CROSS RD

★ VICTORIA
BUTTERFLY
GARDENS

W SAANICH RD

Deep
Cove

Patricia Bay

17A

WEST   SAANICH

BRENTWOOD BAY
RESORT ●

RD

WALLACE DR

★ ⊛
BUTCHART
GARDENS

Brentwood Bay

Moses Point

Coal
Point

Saanich Inlet

Brentwood Bay

Willis
Point

Whisky
Point

Mill Bay

Mill Bay

Malahat Indian Reservation 11

HIGHWAY

⊞

ISLAND

⊞

To
Nanaimo

SHAWNIGAN LAKE RD

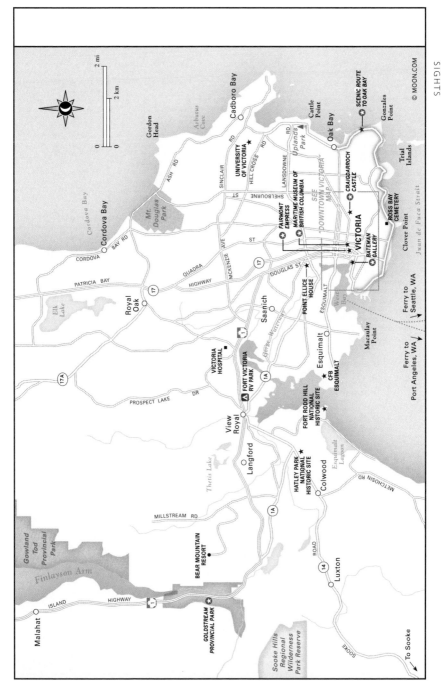

© MOON.COM

Victoria

CAPITAL
IRON

STORE

HERALD ST

ST

Upper Harbour

CHINATOWN
ARCH

OCEAN
RIVER
SPORTS

WAI LAI
YUEN ▼

DON MEE ▼

SWIFT ST

ST

FISGARD ST

FAN TAN ALLEY

TYEE RD

HARBOUR RD

TUG EATERY ▼

SOUR PICKLE
CAFÉ ▼

HABIT
COFFEE ▼

ST

0   100 yds

0   100 m

SWAN'S
HOTEL ●

PANDORA ST

Market
Square

▼ HEY HAPPY

ESQUIMALT ST

JOHNSON ST BRIDGE

STORE ST

WHARF ST

WADDINGTON ALLEY

IL TERRAZZO ●

HI-VICTORIA ●

DELTA HOTELS
VICTORIA
OCEAN POINTE
RESORT ●

VICTORIA
REGENT ●

YATES ST

LIDO/
FINN'S ▼

COMMERCIAL ALLEY

ST

KIMTA RD

THE LOCAL ▼

REBAR ▼

Bastion
Square

LANGLEY

To Spinnakers
Brew Pub
←

SONGHEES

DARCY'S
PUB ▼

RD

RED FISH
BLUE FISH ▼

ST

Victoria   Harbour

Laurel Point

FLYING OTTER
GRILL ▼

Centennial
Park

INNER HARBOUR
CENTRE ■

VICTORIA
VISITOR
CENTRE [i]

Inner Harbour

INN AT
LAUREL POINT ●

BATEMAN
GALLERY ✪

COAST VICTORIA
HARBOURSIDE HOTEL ●

ST

PENDRAY INN
& TEA HOUSE ●

QUEBEC ST

BELLEVILLE ST

FERRY
TERMINALS ■

Quadra
Park

DAYS INN ON
THE HARBOUR ●

ST

★

KINGSTON ST

PENDRAY ST

ST

MONTREAL ST

KINGSTON

OSWEGO ST ●

ST

HOTEL GRAND
PACIFIC ●

MENZIES ST

SUPERIOR ST

OSWEGO

Parliament
Buildings

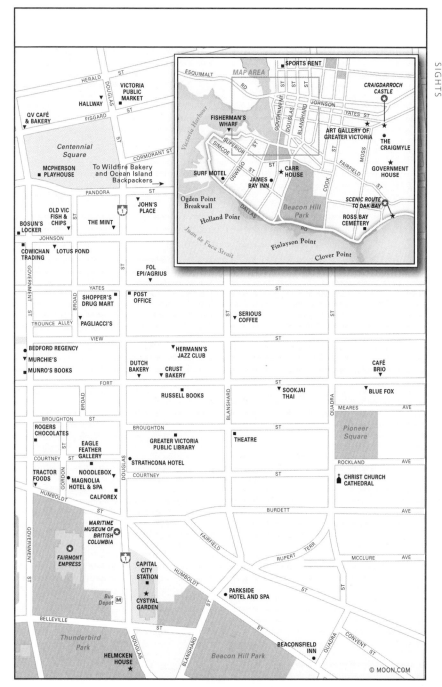

© MOON.COM

to the Inner Harbour after dark, when the parliament buildings are outlined in lights and the Empress Hotel is floodlit.

★ Fairmont Empress

Overlooking the Inner Harbour, the pompous 1908 **Fairmont Empress** (721 Government St., 250/384-8111 or 800/257-7544, www.fairmont.com) is Victoria's most recognizable landmark. Its architect was the well-known Francis Rattenbury, who also designed the BC parliament buildings, the Canadian Pacific Railway (CPR) steamship terminal (now housing the Bateman Gallery), and Crystal Garden. It's worthwhile walking through the hotel lobby to gaze—head back, mouth agape—at the interior razzle-dazzle, and to watch people partake in traditional afternoon tea hosted in the Lobby Lounge. Browse through the conservatory and gift shops, and drool over the menus of the various restaurants.

★ Maritime Museum of British Columbia

Behind the Fairmont Empress, the **Maritime Museum of British Columbia** (744 Douglas St., 250/385-4222, 10am-5pm Tues.-Sat., adults $10, seniors $8, youth $5, under age 13 free) traces the history of seafaring exploration of local waters, adventure, commercial ventures, and passenger travel through changing exhibits. Children especially will love the rotating displays of model ships. The museum is anchored by the Tilikum, a dugout canoe that was launched from Vancouver Island in the early 1900s by John Voss and Norman Luxton seeking to become the first to circumnavigate the world in a canoe (miraculously, they made it as far as Australia). Another staple are displays focusing on Indigenous people and the ways they navigated local waterways. The museum also has a nautically oriented gift shop.

Crystal Garden

One of the architectural highlights of Victoria is **Crystal Garden** (Douglas St. and Belleville St.), directly behind the Fairmont Empress. Inspired by London's famed Crystal Palace, Francis Rattenbury designed the glass and redbrick building to be the social epicenter of the city. When it opened in 1925, it boasted an Olympic-length swimming pool, Turkish baths, a ballroom, an arboretum, and a tearoom.

Crystal Garden was operated by the Canadian Pacific Railway until 1965 and was closed in 1971. In 1980, it reopened as a conservatory filled with tropical plants. After closing again in 2004, the historical building underwent extensive restoration and now operates as the **Victoria Convention Centre.** Its former grandeur is visible from the outside, but you can also wander through the lobby, a bright, beautiful space filled with totem poles.

South of the Fairmont Empress

Across from the Empress lies **Thunderbird Park** (Belleville St. and Douglas St.), a small green spot chockablock with authentic totem poles intricately carved by northwest coast First Nations people. Best of all, it's absolutely free.

Beside Thunderbird Park is **Helmcken House** (10 Elliot St.), the oldest house in the province still standing on its original site. It was built by J. S. Helmcken, pioneer surgeon and legislator, who arrived in Victoria in 1850 and aided in negotiating the union of British Columbia with Canada in 1870.

TOP EXPERIENCE

Parliament Buildings

Satisfy your lust for governmental, historical, and architectural knowledge by taking a free tour of the harborside **Provincial Legislative Buildings,** a.k.a. the parliament buildings. These prominent structures were designed by Francis Rattenbury and

1: the Inner Harbour 2: a peacock in Beacon Hill Park 3: Bateman Gallery

completed in 1897. The exterior is British Columbia Haddington Island stone, and if you walk around the buildings, you'll no doubt spot many a stern or gruesome face staring down from the stonework.

On either side of the main entrance stand statues of Sir James Douglas, who chose the location of Victoria, and Sir Matthew Baillie Begbie, who was in charge of law and order during the gold rush period. Atop the copper-covered dome stands a gilded statue of Captain George Vancouver, the first mariner to circumnavigate Vancouver Island. Walk through the main entrance and into the memorial rotunda, look skyward for a dramatic view of the central dome, and then continue upstairs to peer into the legislative chamber, the home of the government of British Columbia. Free guided tours (every 20 minutes 9am-4pm daily summer, 9am-noon and 1pm-5pm Mon.-Fri. winter) are offered. Tour times differ according to the goings-on inside; for current times, call the **tour office** (250/387-3046). Visitors can also eat in the parliamentary dining room (8:30am-3pm Mon.-Fri.), which is relatively inexpensive.

TOP EXPERIENCE

★ Bateman Gallery

Along the waterfront on Belleville Street, across the road from the parliament buildings, is the grandly ornate former Canadian Pacific Railway steamship terminal, now the **Bateman Gallery** (470 Belleville St., 250/940-3630, http://batemancentre.org, 10am-6pm Sun.-Wed., 10am-9pm Thurs.-Fri. summer, 10am-4pm Tues.-Sat. fall-spring, adults $10, seniors $8.50, children $6). Bateman resides on nearby Salt Spring Island and is renowned as one of the world's greatest wildlife artists. Each themed gallery is dedicated to a different subject—British Columbia and Africa are the highlights. Another gallery is dedicated to children and includes a hands-on nature learning area.

Laurel Point

For an enjoyable short walk from downtown, continue along Belleville Street from the parliament buildings, passing a conglomeration of modern hotels, ferry terminals, and some intriguing architecture dating to the late 19th century. A path leads down through a shady park to Laurel Point, hugging the waterfront and providing good views of the Inner Harbour en route. If you're feeling really energetic, continue to **Fisherman's Wharf,** where an eclectic array of floating homes are tied to floating wharves.

OLD TOWN

The oldest section of Victoria lies immediately north of the Inner Harbour between Wharf and Government Streets. Start by walking north from the Inner Harbour along historical Wharf Street, where Hudson's Bay Company furs were loaded onto ships bound for England, gold seekers arrived in search of fortune, and shopkeepers first established businesses. Cross the road to cobblestoned **Bastion Square,** lined with old gas lamps and decorative architecture dating from the 1860s to the 1890s. This was the original site chosen by James Douglas in 1843 for Fort Victoria, the Hudson's Bay Company trading post. At one time the square held a courthouse, a jail, and gallows. Today, restored buildings house touristy restaurants, cafés, nightclubs, and fashionable offices.

Centennial Square

Centennial Square, bounded by Government Street, Douglas Street, Pandora Avenue, and Fisgard Street, is lined with many buildings dating from the 1880s and 1890s, refurbished in recent times for all to appreciate. Don't miss the 1878 **City Hall** (fronting Douglas St.) and the imposing Greek-style building of the Hudson's Bay Company. In the heart of Centennial Square is **Spirit Square,** which is dedicated to First Nations people. Here you'll find two totem poles and a garden with native plants.

Chinatown

Continue down Fisgard Street into colorful **Chinatown,** Canada's oldest Chinese enclave (and second-oldest in North America behind San Francisco). Chinese prospectors and laborers first brought exotic spices, plants, and a love of intricate architecture and bright colors to Victoria in the late 1850s, and the exotic vibe continues to this day. The original Chinatown was much larger than today's and was home to more than 3,000 residents at its peak in the early 1900s. After being revitalized in the 1980s and being declared a National Historic Site of Canada in 1995, the precinct is now a popular visitor attraction. Its epicenter is Fisgard Street between Government and Store Streets, with the intricate **Gate of Harmonious Interest** providing the official entrance.

Today, Chinatown is a delicious place to breathe in the aroma of authentic Asian food wafting from the many restaurants. Poke through the dark little shops along Fisgard Street—where you can find everything from fragile paper lanterns and embroidered silks to gingerroot and exotic fruits and veggies—then cruise Fan Tan Alley, the center of the opium trade in the 1800s.

SOUTH OF THE INNER HARBOUR

Carr House

In 1871, artist Emily Carr was born in this typical upper-class 1864 Victorian-era home, which now hosts visitors as the **Carr House** (207 Government St., 250/383-5843, 11am-4pm Tues.-Sat. May-Sept., adults $8, seniors and students $6, children $4.50). Carr moved to the mainland at an early age, escaping the confines of the capital to draw and write about the First Nations people of the West Coast and the wilderness in which she lived. She is best remembered today for her painting, a medium she took up in later years.

Beacon Hill Park

Known to Coast Salish people as Meeacan (a First Nations word for "belly"), for its resemblance to a man lying on his back, this large tract of land immediately south of downtown was protected as parkland in 1882. Today, the 25-hectare (62-acre) park is an oasis of green that extends just south of Thunderbird Park along Douglas Street out to cliffs that offer spectacular views of Juan de Fuca Strait and, on a clear day, the distant Olympic Mountains.

Old Town is filled with historic brick buildings.

The park is geographically divided in two by Dallas Road. On the downtown side of the road are landscaped gardens protected by grand Garry oak trees, tennis courts, bowling greens, playgrounds, mini golf, bird-filled ponds, and even a cricket pitch.

Beacon Hill Children's Farm (Circle Dr., 250/381-2532, 10am-4pm daily Apr.-Oct., adults $4, children $3) is home to chickens, pigs, donkeys, and goats. The farm was originally part of a much larger zoo complex that operated between 1883 and 1990. Although zoo animals have long since been removed, peacocks that were let loose upon its closure run free through the surrounding greenery.

South of Dallas Road, natural beauty takes precedence over landscaped gardens. Here, you can catch a sea breeze and gaze at all the strolling, cycling, dog-walking, and stroller-pushing Victorians passing by. For a tidbit of history, explore rocky Finlayson Point, once the site of a fortified First Nations village. Between 1878 and 1892, two enormous guns mounted on the point protected Victoria against an expected but unrealized Russian invasion.

ROCKLAND

This historical part of downtown lies behind the Inner Harbour, east of Douglas Street, and is easily accessible on foot.

Christ Church Cathedral

Along Quadra Street, three blocks uphill from the Inner Harbour, **Christ Church Cathedral** (930 Burdett Ave., 250/383-2714) is the seat of the Bishop of the Anglican Diocese of British Columbia. Built in 1896 in 13th-century Gothic style, it's one of Canada's largest churches. Self-guided tours are possible (8:30am-5pm Mon.-Fri. and 7:30am-8:30pm Sun., free). Visit www.christchurchcathedral.bc.ca for a listing of musical performances hosted by the cathedral. The park next to the cathedral is a shady haven to rest weary feet, and the gravestones make fascinating reading.

TOP EXPERIENCE

Art Gallery of Greater Victoria

From Christ Church Cathedral, walk up Rockland Avenue for four blocks through the historical Rockland district, passing stately mansions and colorful gardens on tree-lined streets. Turn left on Moss Street and you'll come to the 1889 Spencer Mansion and its modern wing, which together make up the **Art Gallery of Greater Victoria** (1040 Moss St., 250/384-4101, 10am-5pm Mon.-Wed. and Fri.-Sat., 10am-9pm Thurs., noon-5pm Sun., adults $13, seniors $11, children $2.50). The gallery contains Canada's finest collection of Japanese art, a range of contemporary art, an Emily Carr gallery, and traveling exhibits, as well as a Japanese garden with a Shinto shrine. The Gallery Shop sells art books, reproductions, and handcrafted jewelry, pottery, and glass.

Government House

Continue up Rockland Avenue from the art gallery to reach **Government House,** the official residence of the lieutenant governor, the queen's representative in British Columbia. Open to the public throughout the year, the surrounding gardens include an English-style garden, a rose garden, and a rhododendron garden, along with green velvety lawns and picture-perfect flower beds. On the front side of the property, vegetation has been left in a more natural state, with gravel paths leading to benches that invite one to pause and take in the city panorama.

TOP EXPERIENCE

★ Craigdarroch Castle

A short walk up (east) from the art gallery along Rockland Avenue and left on Joan Crescent brings you to the baronial four-story mansion known as **Craigdarroch Castle** (1050 Joan Cres., 250/592-5323, http://thecastle.ca, 9am-7pm daily summer,

10am-4:30pm daily fall-spring, adults $19, seniors $18, children $8). From downtown take bus 11 (Uplands) or 14 (University) to Joan Crescent, then walk 100 meters (110 yards) up the hill. The architectural masterpiece was built in 1890 for Robert Dunsmuir, a wealthy industrialist and politician who died just before the building was completed. For all the nitty-gritties, tour the mansion with volunteer guides who really know their Dunsmuir, and then admire at your leisure all the polished wood, stained-glass windows, Victorian-era furnishings, and the great city views from upstairs.

★ SCENIC ROUTE TO OAK BAY

This driving starts south of the Inner Harbour and follows the coastline of Juan de Fuca Strait all the way to the University of Victoria. Allow around one hour to reach the university, but allow at least half a day if you plan multiple stops. If you don't have your own transportation, most city tours take in the sights along the route.

You can take Douglas Street south alongside Beacon Hill Park to access Juan de Fuca Strait, but it's best to continue east along the Inner Harbour to the mouth of Victoria Harbour proper, along Belleville then Kingston Streets to Ogden Point, which is the official starting point of the scenic drive (marked by small blue signs).

Ogden Point

Named for a Hudson's Bay Company trader, Ogden Point has been an important port facility since the early 1900s, when a grain-handling terminal was built on a pier. Today, it is home to a major Canadian Coast Guard Base and **Cruise Ogden Point,** which serves over 200 cruise ships and 500,000 passengers each summer season. Protecting the cruise ship terminal from ocean swells is **Ogden Point Breakwater,** which is only 3 meters (10 feet) wide, but it extends for 800 meters (0.5 mile) into Juan de Fuca Strait. This is a super-popular stroll, especially in the early morning.

At the foot of the breakwater, the **Breakwater Bistro and Bar** (199 Dallas Rd., 250/386-8080, 9am-10pm daily summer, 8am-8pm daily fall-spring) has ocean-facing outdoor seating and a wide selection of hot drinks and filling lunches.

Ogden Point toward Oak Bay

For the first few kilometers beyond the breakwater, the Olympic Mountains in Washington State are clearly visible across Juan de Fuca Strait, and a string of roadside lookouts allows you to stop and take in the panorama, including **Finlayson Point,** which is in Beacon Hill Park, and **Clover Point,** which has a much larger parking area. East beyond Clover Point, **Ross Bay Cemetery** (gates open daylight hours Mon.-Fri.) is the final resting place of many of early Victoria's most prominent residents. Volunteer hosts are on hand throughout the summer to point out the graves of Emily Carr; British Columbia's first governor, Sir James Douglas; members of the coal-baron Dunsmuir family; and Billy Barker, of gold rush fame.

Continuing east, Dallas Road takes you through quiet residential areas, past small pebble beaches covered in driftwood, and into the ritzy mansion district east of downtown, where the residents have grand houses, manicured gardens, and stunning water views. One plot of land that has escaped development is the **Chinese Cemetery** on Harling Point. Developed in 1903 on a rocky headland overlooking the water, it is the resting place of at least 400 Chinese settlers. It is on the east side of Gonzales Bay at the end of Crescent Road.

Oak Bay

As the coastal drive (this section is officially Beach Drive) descends from Harling Point to the protected waters of McNeill Bay and then passes through the well-manicured fairways of the Royal Victoria Golf Club on Gonzales Point, it enters the refined neighborhood of Oak Bay. Although the Hudson's Bay Company developed a farm on Cadboro Bay in the 1850s, it wasn't until the early 1900s that Oak Bay gained popularity with wealthy Victoria residents as a place to live. British influences can still be seen in much of the residential architecture, but the commercial district along Oak Bay Avenue is an inviting mix of new and old, both in building styles and shopping and dining experiences.

At the north end of Oak Bay, **Uplands Park** is a good place to see the neighborhood's namesake Garry oak trees, some of which are 400 years old. The park also protects Cattle Point, a rocky headland with sweeping ocean views.

University of Victoria

Home to around 22,000 students during the school year, this sprawling campus sits on a high point of land at the northern end of Oak Bay. Established in 1903 as Victoria College and affiliated with Montreal's famed McGill University for many years, the facility gained autonomy in 1963 and has grown in stature to now be ranked one of the world's top universities. Encompassing 163 hectares (400 acres), the campus is dominated by a perfectly circular ring road that completely surrounds the academic facilities. Outside the ring road are university-related buildings, such as residences and sporting facilities, as well as the forested diversion of Mystic Vale.

A good starting point for exploring the campus is the **Welcome Centre** (street level of the University Centre, Ring Rd., 250/721-7211, 8:30am-4:30pm Mon.-Fri., 11:30am-3:30pm Sat.). Campus walking tours are mostly attended by potential students, but anyone is welcome to join the groups. Tours (1pm-2:30pm Mon.-Sat.) depart from the Welcome Centre.

Onward from Oak Bay

From Oak Bay, head southwest along Cadboro Bay Road and then Yates Street to get back downtown (around 8 kilometers/5 miles), or continue north along Cadboro Bay Road and then Arbutus Road to eventually reach Highway 17, the main route north up the Saanich Peninsula toward famous Butchart Gardens. Along the latter route, the road passes through **Mount Douglas Park,** which extends from the summit of Mount Douglas to the calm water of Cordova Bay. Walking trails dominated by towering Douglas fir and cedar trees lead to the park's 260-meter (850-foot) summit and down to a sandy stretch of beach.

GORGE WATERWAY

This natural canal leads north from the Inner Harbour to Portage Inlet, a small saltwater lake beside Highway 1. At the far end of the waterway are **Craigflower Manor** and **Craigflower Schoolhouse,** two historically important buildings that are not open to the public but may be easily viewed from outside the grounds. They were built in the 1850s on what was the island's first farm. To reach Craigflower, take Gorge Road (Hwy. 1A) north from downtown to the Craigflower Bridge (around 4 kilometers/2.5 miles). The schoolhouse is on the left, and the manor is across the bridge on the right.

The best way to see the Gorge is from sea level, aboard a **Victoria Harbour Ferry** (250/708-0201). This company runs funky little 12-passenger vessels (round-trip tour adults $30, seniors $28, children $15) to a turnaround point at Gorge Park by the Tillicum Road Bridge.

Point Ellice House

Built in 1861, the restored **Point Ellice House** (2616 Pleasant St., 250/380-6506, 11am-5pm daily May to mid-Sept., adults $6, children $3) sits amid beautiful gardens along the Gorge on Point Ellice, less than 2 kilometers (1.2 miles) from the Inner Harbour. The house's second owner, Peter O'Reilly, a successful

1: Hatley Park National Historic Site 2: Craigdarroch Castle 3: Wander out onto the Ogden Point Breakwater for sweeping ocean views. 4: Fisgard Lighthouse at Fort Rodd Hill

entrepreneur and politician, bought it in 1868 and entertained many distinguished guests here. Original Victorian-era artifacts clutter every nook and cranny of the interior. To get here from the Inner Harbour, jump aboard a Victoria Harbour Ferry (10 minutes, $16 round-trip), or by road, take Government or Douglas Streets north from downtown, turn left on Bay Street, and turn left again on Pleasant Street.

Craigflower Manor

Completed in 1856 using local lumber, stately **Craigflower Manor** on the Gorge Waterway was built for Kenneth McKenzie, who employed colonists to farm the surrounding land. It was one of the island's first farms and helped in the transition of the area from a fur-trading camp to a permanent settlement. Surrounded by commercial and residential sprawl, the scene today is a far cry from the 1800s, when the grand home was a social hub for Victorian socialites and naval officers from nearby Esquimalt. Although currently closed for tours, you can appreciate the pioneer architecture from the street and admire the adjacent garden filled with the same vegetables and herbs that the original owners planted.

Directly across the Gorge Waterway is Craigflower Schoolhouse, dating from a similar era as the manor and built with lumber cut from a steam-powered sawmill operated by the McKenzie family. It served children from the adjacent farm, while the second floor provided living quarters for the teacher's family.

To reach Craigflower, take Gorge Road (Hwy. 1A) north from downtown to the Craigflower Bridge (around 4 kilometers/2.5 miles). The schoolhouse is on the left, and the manor is across the bridge on the right.

WEST OF DOWNTOWN

CFB Esquimalt Naval & Military Museum

The small **CFB Esquimalt Naval & Military Museum** (250/363-4312, 8am-4pm Mon.-Fri., adults $5, seniors and children $3) lies within the confines of Canadian Forces Base (CFB) Esquimalt, on Esquimalt Harbour west of downtown. A couple of buildings have been opened to the public, displaying naval, military, and general maritime memorabilia. To get here from downtown, take the Johnson Street Bridge and follow Esquimalt Road to Admirals Road; turn north, then take Naden Way, and you're on the base; follow the museum signs.

Hatley Park National Historic Site

Hatley Park National Historic Site (2005 Sooke Rd., 250/391-2666) protects a sprawling estate established over 100 years ago by James Dunsmuir, son of coal baron Robert Dunsmuir and then premier of British Columbia. The site has also been used as a military college and is currently part of Royal Roads University. Visitors are invited to walk through the classic Edwardian-style garden, a rose garden, and a Japanese garden, and to stroll through an old-growth forest that extends to Esquimalt Lagoon. Dunsmuir's imposing 40-room mansion is also open for guided tours (four times daily Mon.-Fri. summer, adults $18, seniors $15.50, students $10.50).

Fort Rodd Hill National Historic Site

Clinging to a headland across the harbor entrance from CFB Esquimalt, the picturesque **Fort Rodd Hill National Historic Site** (603 Fort Rodd Hill Rd., Colwood, 250/478-5849, 10am-5:30pm daily mid-Feb.-Oct., 9am-4:30pm daily Nov.-mid-Feb., adults $5, seniors $4, children $2.50) comprises **Fort Rodd,** built in 1898 to protect the fleets of ships in the harbor, and **Fisgard Lighthouse,** which dates to 1873. The expansive grounds are an interesting place to explore; audio stations bring the sounds of the past alive, much of the original fortifications are open for exploration, workrooms

The Salmon Life Cycle

Each fall, thousands of chum salmon return to spawning grounds along the Goldstream River, an event that is repeated along shallow streams and rivers all around Vancouver Island. Chum are one of five salmon species native to local waters. All are anadromous—that is, they are born in freshwater, live most of their lives in saltwater, and then return to freshwater to spawn. The life cycle of these creatures is truly amazing. Hatching from small red eggs upriver from the ocean, the fry find their way to the ocean, undergoing massive internal changes along the way that allow them to survive in saltwater. Depending on the species, they then spend two to six years in the open water, traveling as far as the Bering Sea.

After reaching maturity, they begin the epic journey back to their birthplace, to the exact patch of gravel on the same river from where they emerged. Their navigation system has evolved over a million years; it is believed that they rely on a sensory system that uses measurements of sunlight, the earth's magnetic field, and atmospheric pressure to find their home river. Once the salmon are in range of their home river, scent takes over, returning them to the exact spot where they were born. Once the salmon reach freshwater, they stop eating. Unlike other species of fish, including Atlantic salmon, Pacific salmon die immediately after spawning—hence the importance of returning to their birthplace, a spot the salmon instinctively know gives them the best opportunity for the chance to reproduce successfully.

are furnished as they were at the turn of the 20th century, and on a low rocky outcrop, the lighthouse has been fully restored and is open to visitors. To get here from downtown, take the Old Island Highway (Gorge Rd.), turn left on Belmont Road, and then left onto Ocean Boulevard. By bus, take bus 50 from downtown, then transfer to bus 52.

Esquimalt Lagoon

Easily recognized from the lookout point dotted across Fort Rodd Hill is Esquimalt Lagoon, immediately to the west. The lagoon's protected waters are a haven for a great variety of birdlife, including shorebirds such as gulls, terns, black oystercatchers, plovers, sandpipers, and killdeers. Waterfowl present throughout summer include mergansers, pinheads, grebes, Canada geese, swans, cormorants, and great blue herons, as well as buffleheads, which migrate through in late fall. The lagoon is separated from the open water by a narrow 1.5-kilometer (0.9-mile) causeway. An unpaved road leads along its length, providing access to a driftwood-strewn beach that is a popular swimming and sunbathing spot in summer. Access is along Ocean Boulevard,

down the forested road beyond the Fort Rodd Hill National Historic Site turnoff.

★ GOLDSTREAM PROVINCIAL PARK

Lying 20 kilometers (12 miles) from the heart of Victoria, this 390-hectare (960-acre) park straddles the Trans-Canada Highway northwest of downtown on its loop around the south end of Saanich Inlet.

The park's most distinctive natural feature is the Goldstream River, which flows north into the Finlayson Arm of Saanich Inlet. Forests of ancient Douglas fir and western red cedar flank the river; orchids flourish in forested glades; and at higher elevations, forests of lodgepole pine, western hemlock, and maple thrive.

Salmon Viewing

Although Goldstream is a great place to visit any time of year, the natural highlight occurs late October through December, when mostly chum salmon—and limited numbers of cohos and chinooks—fight their way upriver through the park to spawn themselves out on the same shallow gravel bars where they were born four years previously. Bald eagles begin arriving in December, feeding off the spawned-out salmon until February. From the picnic area parking lot, 2 kilometers (1.2 miles) north of the campground turnoff, a trail leads 400 meters (440 yards) along the Goldstream River to **Freeman King Visitor Centre** (250/478-9414, www. goldstreampark.com, 9am-4:30pm daily, free), where the life cycle of salmon is described.

Practicalities

The park's only **campground** (519/858-6161 or 800/689-9025, https://camping.bcparks. ca, Apr.-Oct., $35) is on the west side of the Trans-Canada Highway 19 kilometers (11 miles) from downtown. It offers 159 well-spaced campsites scattered through an old-growth forest—it's one of the most beautiful settings you could imagine close to a capital city. The campground offers free hot showers but no hookups. Many walking trails begin from the campground, including to the most scenic section of the Goldstream River, and back across the highway to the visitors center. The campground entrance is on the edge of the small town of Goldstream, where you can find a midsize grocery store.

To reach the excellent **Freeman King Visitor Centre** (250/478-9414, www.gold-streampark.com, 9am-4:30pm daily, free), look for the parking lot on the east side of the Trans-Canada Highway, 2 kilometers (1.2 miles) north of the campground turnoff. From the main parking area, the center is an easy 400-meter (440-yard) walk along a forested trail. In addition to displays, the center hosts interpretive programs throughout summer and the fall salmon- and eagle-viewing season; it also has a bookstore.

SAANICH PENINSULA

The Saanich Peninsula is the finger of land that extends north from downtown. It holds Victoria's most famous attraction, Butchart Gardens, as well as Victoria International Airport and the main arrival point for

ferries from Tsawwassen. If you've caught the ferry over to Vancouver Island from Tsawwassen, you'll have arrived at **Swartz Bay,** on the northern tip of the Saanich Peninsula; from here it's a clear run down Highway 17 to downtown Victoria and the waterfront town of Sidney. If you're coming from Goldstream Provincial Park, head north, or from Nanaimo on Highway 1, head south, to reach **Mill Bay,** where a ferry departs regularly for **Brentwood Bay** on the Saanich Peninsula. (Brentwood Bay is home to Butchart Gardens.) Ferries run in both directions nine times 7:30am-6pm daily. Peak one-way fares for the 25-minute crossing cost adults $7, children $3.50, and vehicles $17.50. For exact times, contact **BC Ferries** (250/386-3431, www.bcferries.com).

★ Butchart Gardens

Carved from an abandoned quarry, the delightful **Butchart Gardens** (800 Benvenuto Dr., Brentwood Bay, 250/652-4422, www. butchartgardens.com, 9am-10pm daily summer, 9am-4pm winter, varying closing time spring and fall, summer adults $38, ages 13-17 $21, ages 5-12 $4, less in winter) are Victoria's best-known attraction. They're approximately 20 kilometers (12 miles) north of downtown.

A Canadian cement pioneer, R. P. Butchart, built a mansion near his quarries. He and his wife, Jennie, traveled extensively, collecting rare and exotic shrubs, trees, and plants from around the world. By 1904, the quarries had been abandoned, and the couple began to beautify them by transplanting their collection into formal gardens interspersed with concrete footpaths, small bridges, waterfalls, ponds, and fountains. The gardens now contain more than 5,000 varieties of flowers, and the extensive nurseries test-grow some 35,000 new bulbs and more than 100 new roses every year. Go there in spring, summer,

1: Japanese maple in Butchart Gardens
2: Goldstream Provincial Park

or early autumn to treat your eyes and nose to a marvelous sensual experience (many gardeners would give their right hands to be able to work in these gardens). Highlights include the Sunken Garden (the original quarry site) with its water features and annuals; the formal Rose Garden, set around a central lawn; and the Japanese Garden, with views to Saanich Inlet. In winter, when little is blooming, the basic design of the gardens can best be appreciated. Summer visitors are in for a special treat on Saturday nights in July and August, when a spectacular fireworks display lights up the garden.

As you may imagine, the attraction is very busy throughout spring and summer. For this reason, try to arrive as early as possible, before the tour buses do. Once through the tollgate and in the sprawling parking lot, make a note of where you parked. On the grounds, pick up a flower guide and follow the suggested route. After you've done the rounds (allow at least two hours), you can choose from a variety of eateries. You'll also find a gift shop specializing in—you guessed it—floral items, as well as a store selling seeds.

Victoria Butterfly Gardens

In the same vicinity as Butchart Gardens, **Victoria Butterfly Gardens** (1461 Benvenuto Dr., 250/652-3822, www.butterflygardens.com, 10am-4pm daily summer, 10am-3pm daily fall-spring, adults $17, seniors and students $13, children $6.50) offers you the opportunity to view and photograph some of the world's most spectacular butterflies at close range. Thousands of these beautiful creatures—species from around the world—live here, flying freely around the enclosed gardens and feeding on the nectar provided by colorful tropical plants. You'll also be able to get up close and personal with exotic birds such as parrots and cockatoos.

The west side of the Saanich Peninsula facing Finlayson Arm is dotted with rocky beaches and tracts of forest. Much of this coastline in the central section of the peninsula is protected by Gowlland Tod Provincial Park, which extends from Finlayson Arm Road in the south to the Tod Inlet of Brentwood Bay in the north. The inland portion of the park, extending west to the Gowlland Range, includes towering Douglas fir, grassy meadows that fill with wildflowers in early summer, and rocky outcrops. In the north, a short trail leads down to Tod Inlet from Wallace Drive.

TOURS
Carriage Tours

The classic way to see Victoria is from the comfort of a horse-drawn carriage. Throughout the day and into the evening, **Victoria Carriage Tours** (250/383-2207 or 877/663-2207, www.victoriacarriage.com) has horse carriages lined up along Menzies Street at Belleville Street awaiting passengers. A 30-minute tour (seating up to 6, $115) goes around the downtown waterfront precinct; there's also a 45-minute tour ($165), or take the 60-minute Royal Tour ($215). Tours run 9am-midnight daily in summer, and bookings aren't necessary, though there's often a line.

Bus Tours

Big red double-decker buses are as much a part of the Victoria tour scene as horse-drawn carriages. These are operated by **Gray Line** (250/744-3566 or 800/663-8390, www.sightseeingvictoria.com) from beside the Inner Harbour. There are many tours to choose from, but to get oriented while also learning some city history, take the 90-minute Grand City Drive Tour (every 40 minutes, adults $40, students $30, children $15), departing from the harborfront. The most popular of Gray Line's other tours is the one to Butchart Gardens ($84, including garden admission).

Ferry Tours

Victoria Harbour Ferry (250/708-0201, www.victoriaharbourferry.com, late Feb.-late Oct.) offers boat tours of the harbor and

Gorge Waterway. The company's funny-looking boats each seat around 20 passengers and depart regularly 9am-dusk from below the Fairmont Empress. The 45-minute loop tour (adults $30, seniors $28, children $15) allows passengers the chance to get on and off where they want, or travel pieces of the entire loop for $5-15 per sector.

Sports and Recreation

All of Vancouver Island is a recreational paradise, but Victorians find plenty to do around their own city. Walking and biking are especially popular, and from the Inner Harbour, it's possible to travel on foot or by pedal power all the way along the waterfront to Oak Bay. Commercial activities are detailed here, but the best place to get information on a wide variety of operators is the **Victoria Visitor Centre** (812 Wharf St., 250/953-2033, www.tourismvictoria.com), overlooking the northeast corner of the Inner Harbour.

HIKING

If you're feeling energetic—or even if you're not—plan on walking or biking at least a small section of the Scenic Marine Drive, which follows the shoreline of Juan de Fuca Strait from Ogden Point all the way to Oak Bay. The section immediately south of downtown, between Holland Point Park and Ross Bay Cemetery, is extremely popular with early-rising locals, who start streaming onto the pedestrian pathway before the sun is up.

Out of town, **Goldstream Provincial Park,** beside Highway 1, offers the best hiking opportunities. Goldstream is worth visiting for its network of hiking trails. Starting from the visitors center, the 200-meter (220-yard) **Marsh Trail** will reward you with panoramic water views from the mouth of the Goldstream River. Another popular destination is **Goldstream Falls,** at the south end of the park. This trail leaves from the back of the park campground and descends to the picturesque falls in around 300 meters (330 yards). Noncampers should park at the campground entrance; from there it's 1.2 kilometers (0.7 mile) to the falls. One of the park's longer hikes is the **Goldmine Trail,** which begins from a parking lot on the west side of Highway 1 halfway between the campground and day-use area. This trail winds 2 kilometers (1.2 miles) one-way through a mixed forest of lodgepole pine, maple, and western hemlock, passing the site of a short-lived gold rush and coming to **Niagara Falls,** a poor relation of its eastern namesake but still a picturesque flow of water. Of a similar length, but more strenuous, is the trail to the summit of 419-meter (1,370-foot) **Mount Finlayson,** which takes about one hour each way and rewards successful summiteers with views back across the city and north along Saanich Inlet. The trail is accessed from Finlayson Arm Road.

The **Galloping Goose Regional Trail** follows a rail line that once linked Victoria and Sooke. For 55 kilometers (34 miles), it parallels residential back streets, follows waterways, and passes through forested parkland. The railbed has been graded the entire way, making it suitable for both walkers and cyclists. The official starting point is the disused railroad station at the top end of downtown where Wharf and Johnson Streets merge, and from the end of the trail in Sooke, bus 1 will bring you back to the city. Obviously, you can't walk the entire trail in a day, but even traversing a couple of short sections during your stay is worthwhile for the variety of landscapes en route.

BIKING

For those keen on getting around by bike, it doesn't get much better than the bike path

A Whale of a Time

Once nearly extinct, today an estimated 20,000 gray whales swim the length of the British Columbia coast twice annually between Baja, Mexico, and the Bering Sea. The spring migration (Mar.-Apr.) is close to the shore, with whales stopping to rest and feed in places such as Clayoquot Sound and Haida Gwaii. Orcas, also known as killer whales, are not actually whales but the largest member of the dolphin family. Adult males can reach 10 meters (33 feet) in length and up to 10 tons in weight, but their most distinctive feature is a dorsal fin that protrudes more than 1.5 meters (5 feet) from their back. Orcas are widespread in oceans around the world, but they are especially common in the waters between Vancouver Island and the mainland. Three distinct populations live in local waters: resident orcas feed primarily on salmon and travel in pods of up to 50; transients travel by themselves or in very small groups, feeding on marine mammals such as seals and whales; and offshore orcas live in the open ocean, traveling in pods and feeding only on fish.

following the coastline of the peninsula on which Victoria lies. From downtown, ride down Government Street to Dallas Road, where you'll pick up the separate bike path running east along the coast to the charming seaside suburb of Oak Bay. From there, Oak Bay Road will take you back into the heart of the city for a round-trip of 20 kilometers (12 miles).

You can rent bikes at Sports Rent (1950 Government St., 250/385-7368, www.sportsrentbc.com, 9am-5pm Mon.-Sat., 10am-5pm Sun.), just north of downtown, for $40-70 per 24 hours for a regular bike and $80 for a hybrid ebike. Despite not actually renting bikes, North Park Bicycle Shop (1833 Cook St., 250/386-2453, www.northparkbikeshop.com, 9am-5:30pm Mon.-Fri., 9am-5pm Sat., noon-4pm Sun.) has a range of bikes for sale at all price points, as well as a repair shop. Once you reach Oak Bay, stop by Oak Bay Bicycles (1990 Oak Bay Ave., 250/598-4111, www.oakbaybikes.com, 10am-6pm Wed.-Fri., 10am-5pm Sat.-Tues.) for an eye-popping selection of bikes for everyone, including kids, tandem, road, racing, and mountain. They also have a modern repair shop and rentals.

WHALE-WATCHING

Heading out from Victoria in search of whales is something that can be enjoyed by everyone. Both resident and transient whales are sighted during the local whale-watching season (mid-Apr.-Oct.), along with sea lions, porpoises, and seals. Trips last two to three hours, are generally made in sturdy inflatable boats with an onboard naturalist, and cost $110-130 pp. Recommended operators departing from the Inner Harbour include Orca Spirit Adventures (250/800-3747 or 877/815-7255) and Prince of Whales (250/383-4884 or 888/383-4884). Eagle Wing Tours (250/384-8008 or 800/708-9488) offers longer tours (up to four hours) in a fleet of larger boats.

KAYAKING AND PADDLEBOARDING

With a waterfront location within easy walking distance of downtown, Ocean River Sports (400 Swift St., 250/381-4233 or 800/909-4233, www.oceanriver.com, 9:30am-6pm daily) is the most convenient place to head for kayak and paddleboard rentals. Single kayaks, paddleboards, and canoes (2 hours $44, full-day $95) and double kayaks (2 hours $65, full-day $140) are available. Throughout summer, Ocean River offers a variety of guided paddles, including a relaxing 2.5-hour tour ($79 pp) and the more adventurous 3-hour SUP tour of the harbor ($79 pp).

SCUBA DIVING

Close to downtown Victoria lie several good dive sites, notably **Ogden Point Breakwater,** which since its construction in 1916 has become a haven for marinelife, including octopuses, eels, anemones, starfish, and schools of rockfish. At Fisherman's Wharf, near the breakwater, is **Rockfish Divers** (19 Dallas Rd., 250/516-3483, www. divevictoria.com, 10am-5pm Mon.-Fri., 9am-4pm Sat., 9am-1pm Sun.), which offers rentals ($90-100 for a full package with tank), instruction, and a free guided shore dive every Sunday.

To access the great diving in the Straits of Georgia and Juan de Fuca, you'll need to charter a boat. One particularly interesting site is **Race Rocks,** a 25-minute boat ride from Victoria. Because of strong tides, this site is for experienced divers only, but those who do venture out have the chance of seeing sea lions, abalones, giant sea urchins, king crabs, and an abundance of fish. Farther north, off the Saanich Peninsula's north end, the 110-meter (360-foot) **HMCS** *Mackenzie* destroyer escort was scuttled especially for divers.

SWIMMING

The best beaches and ocean swimming are east of downtown starting at Oak Bay and extending all the way up the Saanich Peninsula. Most of the summer crowds spend the day at these beaches sunbathing; although a few hardy individuals brave a swim, water temperature here tops out at around 17°C (63°F). **Willows Beach,** at Oak Bay, is popular with local residents, but doesn't have as much sand as points north.

At the south end of Arbutus Cove is **Hollydene Beach,** a short stretch of sand that is as soft as anything found in the Victoria region. Continuing north is **Cordova Bay Beach,** a wider stretch of sand with similar cool waters. Farther north still is **Island View Beach Regional Park,** where a long stretch of sand is backed by piles of driftwood and a forested area.

Warmer than the ocean are lakes dotted throughout the region. I've swum in most places and found **Eagle Beach** on **Elk Lake** to have the warmest water. It's a large shallow lake with a mostly sandy bottom that warms the water through the day—plus the beach is backed by a row of grand old willow trees. To get here, follow Highway 17 north toward the ferry terminal; you'll see the lake off to the left of the highway before reaching Sayward Road, where you exit. At forest-encircled **Thetis Lake,** west of downtown along the Trans-Canada Highway, the water is cooler than Elk Lake, but the small stretch of sand is a pleasant spot to relax in the sun.

If the ocean water surrounding Victoria is a little cold for your liking (as it is for most people), head downtown to **Crystal Pool** (2275 Quadra St., 250/361-0732, 5:30am-11pm Mon.-Thurs., 5:30am-10pm Fri., 6am-4pm Sat., 8:30am-4pm Sun., adults $5.75, seniors $4.50, children $4), which has an Olympic-size pool, a water slide, two kids' pools, a sauna, and a whirlpool.

Entertainment and Events

Victoria has a vibrant performing arts community, with unique events designed especially for the summer crowds. The city lacks the wild nightlife scene of neighboring Vancouver, but a large influx of summer workers keeps the bars crowded and a few nightclubs jumping during the busy season. The city does have more than its fair share of British-style pubs, and you can usually get a good meal along with a pint of lager. The magazine *Monday* (www.mondaymag.com) offers a comprehensive arts and entertainment section.

THE ARTS
Theater

Dating to 1914 and originally called the Pantages Theatre, the grand old **McPherson Playhouse** (known lovingly as the "Mac" by local theatergoers) went through hard times during the 1990s but has seen a recent revival of fortunes and now hosts a variety of performing arts. It's in Centennial Square, at the corner of Pandora Avenue and Government Street. The Mac's sister theater, the **Royal Theatre** (805 Broughton St.), across downtown, began life as a roadhouse and was used as a movie theater for many years. Today, it hosts stage productions and musical recitals. For schedule information and tickets at both theaters, contact the **Royal & McPherson Theatres Society** (250/361-0800, www.rmts.bc.ca).

Performing arts on a smaller scale can be appreciated at the **Belfry Theatre** (1291 Gladstone Ave., 250/385-6815, www.belfry.bc.ca, Oct.-Apr., $25-40), in a historical church that offers live theater.

Music and Dance

Pacific Opera Victoria (250/385-0222, www.pov.bc.ca) performs three productions each year (usually Oct.-Apr., $32-80) in the McPherson Playhouse. The **Victoria Operatic Society** (250/381-1021, www.vostheatre.ca) presents musical theater year-round at the McPherson Playhouse.

The highlight of **Symphony in the Summer** (250/385-6515, www.victoriasymphony.ca) on the first Sunday of August, the **Victoria Symphony** performs on a barge moored at the Inner Harbour. This kicks off the performing arts season, with regular performances through May at the Royal Theatre and other city venues.

NIGHTLIFE
Bars

To take full advantage of the harbor's beauty over drinks, plan on finding a place with water views. The following three choices are at "harbor level" on the north side of the Inner Harbor. **Flying Otter Grill** (950 Wharf St., 250/414-4220, 11am-9:30pm Mon.-Fri., 11am-10pm Sat.-Sun. summer only) is an over-sized patio right on the Inner Harbour. In the vicinity to the north (access is via stairs leading down from opposite Bastion Square), **Lido Waterfront Bar** (1234 Wharf St., 250/414-4220, 11am-10pm daily) is a little less touristy, with better prices to match. Both places also serve excellent food—head to the Flying Otter for seafood and Lido for pizza. Continue north over the Johnson Street Bridge and drop back down to the harbor to reach **Tug Eatery** (407 Swift St., 250/385-4616, 3pm-10pm Wed.-Fri., noon-10pm Sat.-Sun.), where, on a warm summer day, the waterfront tables are the perfect place to try local craft beers and BC wines, with live music in the evenings a free bonus.

Although it's not cheap, enjoying a drink at the **Lower Veranda** (721 Government St., 250/384-8111, 11am-10:30pm daily May-Sept.) is a memorable experience. With a prime harbor-front location from the covered veranda of the iconic Fairmont Empress, you can enjoy a wide variety of beers, wines, cocktails, and champagne.

Closer to the Inner Harbour and converted from an old grain warehouse is **Swans Brewery & Pub** (Swans Hotel, 506 Pandora St., 250/940-7513, 11am-1am Mon.-Sat., 11am-midnight Sun.), which brews its own beer. Unlike many other smaller brewing operations, this one uses traditional ingredients and methods, such as allowing the brew to settle naturally rather than filtering it. The beer is available at the hotel's bar, in its restaurants, and in the attached liquor store. The main bar is a popular hangout for local businesspeople and gets busy 5pm-8pm Monday to Friday.

The **Strathcona Hotel** (919 Douglas St., 250/383-7137) is Victoria's largest entertainment venue, featuring four bars, including one with a magnificent rooftop patio and the Sticky Wicket, a traditional British pub with lots of draught beer (but with a North American pub-style food menu).

On the north side of downtown, a couple of blocks from the Victoria Public Market, head to **Citrus & Cane** (1900 Douglas St., 778/265-1774, 5pm-1am Thurs.-Mon.), where it's easy to imagine you're transported south—and back—to a mid-century Palm Springs cocktail bar, with a drinks menu to match.

Having opened in 1984 as Canada's first brewpub, **Spinnakers Brewpub** (308 Catherine St., 250/386-2739, 9am-11pm daily), across the Inner Harbour from downtown, continues to produce its own European-style ales, including the popular Spinnakers Ale. The original downstairs brewpub is now a restaurant, while upstairs is now the bar. Most important, both levels have outdoor tables with water views. The classic Spinnakers combo is a pint of pale ale and beer-battered halibut and chips ($21).

Victoria's many English-style pubs usually feature a wide variety of beers, congenial atmosphere, and inexpensive meals. The closest of these to downtown is the **James Bay Inn** (270 Government St., 250/384-7151, 11am-11pm daily). Farther out, **Six Mile Pub** (494 Island Hwy., 250/478-3121, 11am-10pm daily) is a classic Tudor-style English pub that was established in 1885, making it the province's oldest pub. To get there, head west out of the city along Highway 1 and take the Colwood exit.

Clubs and Live Music

Most of Victoria's nightclubs double as live music venues attracting a great variety of acts. In the Strathcona Hotel, **Distrikt** (919 Douglas St., 250/383-7137) is a city hot spot. It comes alive with live rock-and-roll some nights and a DJ spinning the latest dance tunes on other nights. In the same hotel, **Big Bad John's** (919 Douglas St., 250/383-7137) is the city's main country music venue. At the bottom of Bastion Square, **Darcy's Pub** (1127 Wharf St., 250/380-1322, 11am-1am daily) is a great place for lunch or an afternoon drink, but Thurs.-Sat. nights it dishes up live rock to a working-class crowd.

Victoria boasts several good jazz venues. The best of these is **Hermann's Jazz Club** (753 View St., 250/388-9166, 5:30pm-midnight daily). Check the **Victoria Jazz Society website** (www.jazzvictoria.ca) for a schedule of local jazz performances.

FESTIVALS

Due to its mild climate, Victoria's outdoor festivals extend beyond the summer into spring and fall, with the first major event occurring in May. The website of **Tourism Victoria** (www.tourismvictoria.com) has an easy-to-navigate event schedule for the entire year.

Spring

Officially, of course, February is still winter, but Victorians love the fact that spring arrives early on the West Coast, which is the premise behind the **Greater Victoria Flower Count** (throughout the city, www.flowercount.com, last week in Feb.). For other Canadians, summer is a long way off, but locals count the number of blossoms in their own yards, in parks, and along the streets. Totals in the tens of millions are tabulated and gleefully reported across the country.

The birthday of Queen Victoria has been celebrated in Canada since 1834 and is especially relevant to those who call her namesake city home. The Inner Harbour is alive with weekend festivities that culminate in the **Victoria Day Parade** (downtown, Mon. preceding May 25). The parade takes two hours to pass a single spot. Although Queen Victoria's actual birthday was May 24, the event is celebrated with a public holiday on the Monday preceding May 25.

Hosted by the Royal Victoria Yacht Club and with more than 60 years of history behind it, **Swiftsure International Yacht Race** (finishes at Inner Harbour, 250/592-9098, www.swiftsure.org, last weekend of May) attracts thousands of spectators to the shoreline of the Inner Harbour to watch a wide variety of vessels cross the finish line in six different classes, including the popular pre-1970 Classics division.

Summer

At **Victoria International Jazzfest** (downtown, 250/388-4423, www.jazzvictoria.ca, last week of June), more than 300 musicians from around the world descend on the capital for this weeklong celebration at various city venues.

At **Symphony Splash** (Inner Harbour, 250/385-9771, www.victoriasymphony.ca, first Sun. in Aug.), the local symphony orchestra performs from a barge moored in the Inner Harbour to masses crowded around the shore. This unique musical event attracts upward of 40,000 spectators who line the shore or watch from kayaks.

The water comes alive during the **Victoria Dragon Boat Festival** (Inner Harbour, 250/704-2500, www.victoriadragonboatfestival.com, mid-Aug.), with up to 100 dragon boat teams competing along a short course stretching across the Inner Harbour. Onshore entertainment includes the Forbidden City Food Court, classic music performances, First Nations dancing, and lots of children's events.

Victoria Fringe (throughout the city, 250/383-2663, www.intrepidtheatre.com, last week of Aug., $10-20) is a celebration of alternative theater, with more than 350 acts performing at venues throughout the city, including outside along the harbor foreshore and inside at the Conservatory of Music on Pandora Street.

Shopping

Victoria is a shopper's delight. Although the city doesn't have defined shopping precincts, the following descriptions provide an overview of shopping destinations within the downtown core. In the Inner Harbour, **Government and Douglas Streets** are the main strip of tourist and gift shops. The bottom end of Douglas, behind the Fairmont Empress Hotel, is where you'll pick up all those souvenir T-shirts and such. The touristy shops are all open Sunday.

All summer, the historical precinct of **Bastion Square** is filled with local artisans selling their wares at the **Bastion** Square Public Market (11am-5pm Thurs.-Sat., 11am-4pm Sun.). Linking Broad and Government Streets (near View St.), the cobblestoned **Trounce Alley** is off most visitors' radar, but worth searching out for the spiritual gifts at **Instinct Art & Gifts** (622 View St., 250/388-5033, 10am-5:30pm Mon.-Sat., noon-5pm Sun.). Cross under the arch across Fisgard Street and enter Chinatown, with vendors selling produce and Asian curios, and then wander down **Fan Tan Alley,**

1: Eagle Beach on Elk Lake 2: Capital Iron is in the heart of Old Town. 3: Swiftsure International Yacht Race

1

2

3

Canada's narrowest street, and through an eclectic array of shops and boutiques.

Fort Street between Cook and Quadra Streets has been branded **Mosaic Village** in recognition of the wide variety of local merchants in the area—antiques shops, art galleries, clothing boutiques, and cooking supply stores.

Downtown

Up Government Street, away from the Inner Harbour, are stylish shops, such as First Nations-owned and operated **Eagle Feather Gallery** (633 Courtney St., 250/388-4330, 11am-5:30pm Mon.-Fri., 11am-4:30pm Sat., 12:30pm-4pm Sun.), selling a wide range of authentic arts and crafts including original prints, Inuit carvings, totem poles, and jewelry from the island's coastal communities.

Cowichan Trading (1328 Government St., 250/383-0321, 10am-5:30pm daily) specializes in Cowichan sweaters and other products hand-knitted by the Cowichan people of Vancouver Island. It also sells art and pewter.

Murchie's (1110 Government St., 250/381-5451, 9am-6pm daily) sells an incredibly diverse selection of teas from around the world, as well as tea paraphernalia such as teapots, gift sets, and collector tins. Traditions also continue at **Rogers Chocolates** (913 Government St., 250/881-8771, 10am-6pm Mon.-Sat., 11am-6pm Sun.), which is set up like a candy store of the early 1900s, when Charles Rogers first began selling his homemade chocolates to the local kids.

Old Town

In Old Town, the colorful, two-story **Market Square** courtyard complex was once the haunt of sailors, sealers, and whalers who came ashore looking for booze and brothels. It's been jazzed up, and today shops here specialize in everything from kayaks to condoms.

In the vicinity, a few blocks to the north, **Capital Iron** (1900 Store St., 250/385-9703, 10am-6pm daily) is the real thing. Housed in a three-story building that dates to 1863,

this business began in the 1930s by offering the public goods salvaged from ships. In the 80-plus years since, it has evolved into a department store stocking an eclectic variety of hardware and housewares, many of which are maritime-related.

Bookstores

Don't be put off by the touristy location of **Munro's Books** (1108 Government St., 250/382-2464 or 888/243-2464, 10am-6pm Sat.-Wed., 10am-7pm Thurs.-Fri.), in a magnificent neoclassical building that originally opened as the Royal Bank in 1909. It holds a comprehensive collection of fiction and nonfiction titles related to Victoria, the island, and Canada in general. In seaside Oak Bay, **Ivy's Bookshop** (2188 Oak Bay Ave., 250/598-2713, 10am-5pm Mon.-Sat., noon-5pm Sun.) is a friendly little spot with a wide-ranging selection, from local literature to current best-sellers.

Bibliophiles the world over are familiar with www.abebooks.com, a website devoted to helping book lovers find used and rare books. What they probably don't know is that the conglomerate had its humble roots in Victoria (the company was started by two local couples in 1996, one of whom owned a secondhand bookstore in the western suburb of Colwood). Ironically, the success of www. abebooks.com has led to the closure of many local used bookstores, as has happened the world over, but one that remains is **Russell Books** (747 Fort St., 250/361-4447, 9:30am-6pm daily), specializing in rare regional and nautical titles.

A suburban bookstore of note, this one specializing in general used books, is **James Bay Coffee and Books** (143 Menzies St., 250/386-4700, 8am-4pm Mon.-Fri., 8:30am-5pm Sat.-Sun.). A huge selection of used books is only part of the appeal, as you can order familiar breakfasts and lunches, and enjoy live music on Friday evenings. To get there from downtown, follow Menzies Street south from the Inner Harbour for five blocks.

Food

Although Victoria has traditionally been associated with quaint tearooms dotted around the suburbs, the dining scene today has evolved greatly. Like the rest of Vancouver Island, chefs are big on produce organically grown and sourced from island farms. Locally sourced seafood—halibut, shrimp, mussels, crab, and salmon—also feature prominently on most restaurant menus.

DOWNTOWN

Although locals are often disdainful of the touristy restaurants clustered around the Inner Harbour and complain that both the quality of food and service don't justify the prices, these restaurants do have a couple of redeeming features—many have water views and all are handy to downtown accommodations. Additionally, because of the thriving tourist trade centered on the Inner Harbour, chances are you will find something to suit your tastes and budget close at hand—pub fare, seafood, Canadian, Asian, Italian, Mexican, and even Himalayan. Unlike many cities, and aside from the small Chinatown, international restaurants are not confined to particular streets. On the other hand, Fort Street east of Douglas has a proliferation of restaurants that are as trendy as it gets on Vancouver Island.

You will still find great interest in traditional English fare, including afternoon tea, which is served everywhere from motherly corner cafés to the grand Fairmont Empress. English cooking in general is much maligned but worth trying. For the full experience, choose kippers and poached eggs for breakfast, a ploughman's lunch (crusty bread, a chunk of cheese, pickled onions), and then roast beef with Yorkshire pudding (a crispy pastry made with drippings and doused with gravy) in the evening.

Coffeehouses

While Victoria is generally associated with afternoon tea, there are some serious coffee lovers in the capital. The focus at minimalist **Habit Coffee** (552 Pandora St., 250/294-1127, 7am-6pm Mon.-Fri., 8am-6pm Sat.-Sun.) is most definitely the coffee, though it offers an eclectic collection of magazines to browse through. The wooden benches out front are a great people-watching spot. Walk through Market Square from Habit to ★ **Hey Happy** (560 Johnson St., 250/590-9680, 8am-4pm Mon.-Fri., 9am-5pm Sat.-Sun.), a small brightly lit place with a few outdoor tables. Ordering coffee at Hey Happy is part of the experience—beans are ground individually for each order, and the baristas make a show of each serving. Expect specialty drinks, such as coconut milk iced lattes. Also recommended by the caffeine crowd is **Serious Coffee** (1609 Blanshard St., 250/385-1100, 6am-4pm Mon.-Fri., 8am-3pm Sat.-Sun.), a local chain with cafes throughout the island.

Shatterbox (Victoria Public Market, 1701 Douglas St., 778/432-2121, 7:30am-6pm Mon.-Sat., 8:30am-5pm Sun.) is a casual European-style café popular for its wide range of highly regarded coffee drinks and a friendly atmosphere. Similarly, a good percentage of locals consider **Moka House** (345 Cook St., 250/388-7377, 7am-8pm daily), on the east side of Beacon Hill Park, as pouring the best coffee in the city. As a bonus, bagels are excellent and there is a shaded patio.

Bakeries

A few blocks back from the harbor, ★ **Crust Bakery** (730 Fort St., 250/978-2253, 8am-4:30pm daily) is a bright, modern space with a huge variety of artisan breads and pastries, all baked daily on-site. Sandwiches, quiches, sausage rolls, and traditional Australian meat pies—you can't go wrong. A few doors

Afternoon Tea

afternoon tea in the Fairmont Empress

Afternoon tea, that terribly English tradition that started in the 1840s as a between-meal snack, is one ritual you should definitely partake in while visiting Victoria. Many North Americans don't realize that there is a difference between afternoon tea and high tea, and even in Victoria the names are sometimes used in place of one another. Afternoon tea is the lighter version, featuring fine teas (no tea bags) accompanied by delicate crustless sandwiches, scones with clotted cream and preserves, and a selection of other small treats. High tea (traditionally taken later in the day, around 6pm) is more substantial—more like dinner in North America.

You can immerse yourself in the ritual at one of many tearooms throughout the city, with prices ranging greatly. To enjoy the experience at a smaller tearoom on the outskirts of downtown, make reservations at the **White Heather Tea Room** (1885 Oak Bay Ave., 250/595-8020, 10am-3pm Tues.-Sat., $38-58). With sittings at 11:30am and 1:30pm, it's a small, homey setting, with a great deal of attention given to all aspects of afternoon tea—right down to the handmade tea cozies.

Within walking distance of downtown, the **Pendray Tea House** (309 Belleville St., 250/388-3892, 11am-2pm Wed.-Fri., 11am-3pm Sat.-Sun., $64) is in a restored waterfront mansion, complete with stained-glass windows, antique furnishings, and immaculately set tables. The **Fairmont Empress** (721 Government St., 250/389-2727, $89) offers the grandest of grand afternoon teas in their Lobby Lounge, but you'll pay for it. Still, it's so popular in midsummer that you must book at least a week in advance through summer and reserve a table at sitting times between 11am and 4pm.

As you'd expect, it's a touristy affair at **Butchart Gardens** (800 Benvenuto Dr., Brentwood Bay, 250/652-4422, noon-4pm daily, $45), with Cornish pasties, tasty sandwiches, trifle, and more. It is less expensive than other places, and the setting, in the original owner's residence, is rather charming.

Finally, **Murchie's** (1110 Government St., 250/381-5451, 9am-6pm daily), in the heart of the downtown tourist precinct, sells teas from around the world as well as tea paraphernalia such as teapots, gift sets, and collector tins. The adjacent café pours teas from all over the globe in a North American-style coffeehouse.

back toward the harbor, ignore the dated furnishings at the **Dutch Bakery** (718 Fort St., 250/383-9725, 8am-4pm Tues.-Sat.) and tuck into freshly baked goodies and handmade chocolates. Two blocks north from these two places is **Fol Epi** (732 Yates St., 778/265-6311, 7am-6pm Mon.-Fri., 8am-6pm Sat.-Sun.), also renowned for its delicious breads, all prepared from scratch (even the flour is ground by stone) and sold though this modern café. Similarly, and nearby, **Wildfire Bakery** (1517 Quadra St., 250/381-3473, 8:30am-5pm Mon.-Sat.) is best known for its hand-shaped, preservative-free breads that begin with in-house grinding of island-grown wheat.

Markets

Victoria Public Market (1701 Douglas St., 778/433-2787, 11am-6pm Mon.-Sat., 11am-5pm Sun.) is on the northeast corner of downtown in a grandly restored, century-old building that was built for the Hudson's Bay Company. In addition to island-grown produce and game, there are excellent dining options. For delicious made-from-scratch soup, search out **Big Spoon** (778/432-2121); **Shatterbox** (778/432-2121) pours Italian-style coffee; **Roast** (778/433-6639) piles sandwiches high with top-notch ingredients, and **Taco Stand** (778/778-432-4775), well, that one is self-explanatory. Seating is spread through the central area, under high ceilings and surrounded by the bustle of the market.

Mostly the haunt of locals, **Oaklands Sunset Market** (2827 Belmont Ave., 4:30pm-8:30pm every Wed. July-Aug.) brings together around 50 island farms and artists in a friendly setting east of downtown toward Cadboro Bay. A beer garden and live music add to the welcoming ambiance.

Casual Dining

The Veranda (Fairmont Empress, 721 Government St., 250/384-8111, 11am-10:30pm daily May-Sept., $14-40) enjoys a prime location at the front of Victoria's best-know hotel, with unobstructed views across landscaped gardens to the Inner Harbour. Food prices are not as high as you may expect, with seafood chowder ($16), single-serve pizza ($25), and halibut and chips ($36) for the refined setting and wonderful location.

Tractor Foods (805 Government St., 778/247-0354, 8am-8pm daily, lunches $10-20) draws in crowds like a magnet from its central location right across from the information center. But for its touristy location, the food is surprisingly good. The emphasis is on healthy eating, including salads, soups, sandwiches, and exotic stews. Outdoor dining is the best option in warmer weather, but the large, bright indoor dining area is also appealing.

Heading north from the Inner Harbour, at the foot of Bastion Square, **The Local** (1205 Wharf St., 250/385-1999, 11:30am-10pm Sun.-Thurs., 11:30am-midnight Fri.-Sat., $16-32) offers a menu of simple, globally inspired cooking, although the outdoor tables are reason enough to stop by. The halibut and chips, the tandoori chicken wrap, the coconut prawn tacos—it's all excellent.

A few blocks north of The Local, in Old Town, the small **Sour Pickle Café** (1623 Store St., 250/384-9390, 8am-3pm daily, lunch $10-16) is an excellent place for well-priced breakfasts, healthy sandwiches, and single-serve pizzas.

Well worth searching out, **Blue Fox** (919 Fort St., 250/380-1683, 8am-2pm Mon.-Fri., 8am-3pm Sat.-Sun., lunch $9-14) nearly always a line for tables. Breakfast includes Eggs Benedict Pacífico (with smoked salmon and avocado) and Apple Charlotte (French toast with apples and maple syrup). At lunch, try an oversize Waldorf salad or a curried chicken burger with sweet date chutney.

Downstairs in the James Bay Inn, south of downtown, **Art Deco Café Restaurant** (270 Government St., 250/388-9928, 7:30am-2:30pm and 4:30-9pm daily, $12-25) has an art deco theme, friendly staff, and a predictable wide-ranging menu that suits the tastes of in-house guests (who receive a 15 percent discount on their food) and hungry locals avoiding the waterfront area. In the vicinity of the James Bay Inn, **James Bay Coffee and Books** (143 Menzies St., 250/386-4700, 8am-6pm Mon.-Fri., 8:30am-6pm Sat.-Sun., lunch $9-14) is an old-fashioned used bookstore that also offers a simple yet varied menu that includes cooked breakfasts, BLTs, and gluten-free vegetarian chili.

Old-Style Diners

Much as visitors flock to the cafés and restaurants of the Inner Harbour and Government Street, the area away from the waterfront remains the haunt of lunching locals. Reminiscent of days gone by, **John's Place** (723 Pandora Ave., 250/389-0711, 8am-3pm daily, lunches $12-18), just off Douglas Street, serves excellent value for those in the know. The walls are decorated with movie posters, old advertisements, and photos of sports stars, but this place is a lot more than just another greasy-spoon restaurant. The food is good, the atmosphere casual, and the waiters actually seem to enjoy working here. It's breakfast, burgers, salads, and sandwiches throughout the week, but weekend brunch is busiest, when there's nearly always a line spilling onto the street.

Near the top (east) end of Chinatown is **QV Café and Bakery** (1701 Government St., 250/384-8831, 8:30am-9pm daily, $9-15), in a converted gas station and with a large patio out front. It offers inexpensive Western-style breakfasts ($11-14) in the morning and simple grilled cheese sandwiches, burgers, and hot dogs the rest of the day.

Opposite Beacon Hill Park and in business since 1958, **Beacon Drive-In** (126 Douglas St., 250/385-7521, 8am-9:30pm daily, $7-12) dishes up the usual collection of cooked breakfasts and loaded burgers, with so-so milkshakes to wash it all down.

Seafood

Fish-and-chips is a British tradition, sold as such at a number of places around town, ranging from touristy harborfront hangouts to suburban haunts known mostly only to locals. For the former, it's hard to beat ★ **Red Fish Blue Fish** (1006 Wharf St., 250/298-6877, 11:30am-7pm daily mid-Feb.-Oct., $14-26.50), down on the docks below downtown. This takeout-only place is ensconced in a brightly painted shipping container. Unusual for a fish-and-chip joint, the emphasis is on wild, sustainable fisheries. Prices (two pieces of halibut with chips for $26.50) are similar to other fish-and-chip shops scattered through the city, and the quality of fish is excellent. Other choices include fish chowder and seafood tacos. Expect a line in summer.

Occupying a prime downtown location on a floating dock amid whale-watching boats, seaplanes, and shiny white leisure craft just south of Red Fish Blue Fish, the ★ **Flying Otter Grill** (950 Wharf St., 250/414-4220, 11am-9:30pm Mon.-Fri., 11am-10pm Sat.-Sun. summer, $18-30) is just steps from the main tourist trail, but it's far enough removed to make it a popular haunt for a quiet, casual waterfront meal. The setting alone makes the Flying Otter a winner, but the menu is a knockout. Choose crab cakes or pan-fried oysters or sweet chili chicken wings to share, and then move on to mains like seafood paella. To get here, walk north along the harbor from the information center.

The location alone makes ★ **Barb's Fish & Chips** (Fisherman's Wharf, foot of St. Lawrence St., 250/384-6515, 11am-8:30am daily Mar.-Oct., $16-27), a sea-level eatery on a floating dock, a favorite with both tourists and locals. It's not a restaurant as such, but a shack surrounded by outdoor table settings, some protected from the elements by a canvas tent. The food is as fresh as it gets. Choose cod-and-chips, halibut-and-chips, or clam chowder, or splash out on a steamed crab. Adding to the charm are the surrounding floating houses and seals that hang out waiting for handouts. An enjoyable way to reach Barb's is by ferry from the Inner Harbour. Also on Fisherman's Wharf is **The Fish Store** (250/383-6462,

---

1: crispy fish and chips from Barb's Fish & Chips
2: Chinatown

11am-6pm daily, longer hours in summer), which sells a wide variety of local seafood, as well as fish-and-chips, steamed crab, fish tacos, and other light meals.

One of my favorite places for fish-and-chips away from the tourist-clogged streets of the Inner Harbour (but still within walking distance) is **Old Vic Fish & Chips** (1316 Broad St., 250/383-4536, noon-7pm daily, $14-26), which has been in business since 1930. The other is family-operated **Brady's Fish & Chips** (50 Burnside Rd., 250/382-3695, 11am-7pm Mon.-Sat., 3:30pm-7pm Sun., $15-25.50). Fish choices include halibut, haddock, and cod, which are served with perfectly cooked chips. Other options include a halibut burger and popcorn shrimp. It's located two kilometers north of town off Highway 1.

Back on the waterfront, touristy **Finn's** (1208 Wharf St., 250/360-1808, 11:30am-10pm daily, $17-40) is a bustling waterfront complex with a maritime theme and family atmosphere. Beyond the Wharf Street entrance is the main dining room and a two-story deck, where almost every table has a stunning water view. Seafood starters to share include prawn and pork dim sum and steamed mussels. Mains include everything from burgers to lobster tails, with lots of local seafood in between. Prices in this central location are higher than at other restaurants, but during happy hour (4pm-5:30pm daily), some drinks and food items are heavily discounted.

Canadian

Of course, there's seafood on the menu at one of Victoria's best restaurants, **Agrius** (732 Yates St., 778/265-6312, 9am-2pm Sat.-Sun. and 5pm-9pm daily, $25-38), a small 36-seat restaurant with a chic-industrial setting and open kitchen. But the main draw is the slow-food concept, with all dishes made from scratch using island and British Columbia suppliers—even the ketchup and sausages are prepared in the Agrius kitchen. Diners are offered a variety of breads to start, all made from scratch in-house, and can then choose between a strawberry salad or beef tartare,

before moving on to mains such as pork chop, dry aged on the premises, accompanied by seasonal island vegetables.

At **Hallway** (1724 Douglas St., 778/265-8988, 3pm-11pm Tues.-Sat., $20-38), the emphasis is on modern West Coast cooking using island ingredients and game. Local beers and wines dominate, with a 3pm-5pm happy hour providing good discounts on both food and drinks.

Spinnakers Brewpub (308 Catherine St., 250/386-2739, 8am-11pm daily, $13-29) was Canada's first in-house brewpub, and it's as popular today as when it opened in 1985. The crowds come for the beer but also for great food served up in a casual, modern atmosphere. You can order British-style pub fare (think ploughman's lunch) at the bar, but on a warm day, you'll want to be out on the patio enjoying West Coast and seafood dishes, such as seafood chowder and roast lingcod.

Chinese

Victoria's small Chinatown surrounds a short, colorful strip of Fisgard Street between Store and Government Streets. Generally, the menus are filled with familiar Westernized Chinese choices.

One of the least expensive places in the area is **Wah Lai Yuen** (560 Fisgard St., 250/381-5355, 11am-8pm Tues.-Sun., $8-15), a simply decorated, well-lit restaurant with fast and efficient service. The wonton soups are particularly good. Try the Szechwan prawns, or get adventurous and order salted squid. Out front is a bakery with offerings such as peanut-almond soft cake.

Down the hill a little and up a flight of stairs is **Don Mee Restaurant** (538 Fisgard St., 250/383-1032, 11am-9pm Mon.-Fri., 10am-9pm Sat.-Sun., $11-23) has been a Chinatown staple since the 1920s. This vast dining room specializes in the cuisine of Canton, and although there is an emphasis on seafood, the Peking duck, served over two courses, is a highlight. Four-course dinners (under $30 pp) for two or more are a good deal.

A few blocks from Chinatown and just off Douglas Street is **Lotus Pond** (617 Johnson St., 250/380-9293, 11am-2:30pm and 5pm-8:30pm Tues.-Sat., 2pm-8pm Sun., $13-21), a no-frills vegetarian Chinese restaurant with a combo meal for just $16.

Other Asian Restaurants

Noodle Box (818 Douglas St., 250/384-1314, 11am-9pm daily, $10-14) started out as a street stall and now has multiple locations, including uphill from the back entrance to the Fairmont Empress. The concept is simple—an inexpensive noodle bar, serving up fare made to order (including spice level) and similar to what you'd find on the streets of Southeast Asia.

One of the best Thai restaurants in the city is **Sookjai Thai** (893 Fort St., 250/383-9945, 11:30am-9:30pm Mon.-Thurs., 11:30am-10:30pm Fri.-Sat., $16-30). The tranquil setting is the perfect place to sample traditional delights such as *tom yum goong* (a prawn and mushroom soup with a hint of tangy citrus) and baked red snapper sprinkled with spices sourced from Thailand. The New Zealand mussels is the most expensive main, and there are several inspiring vegetarian choices.

The Mint (1414 Douglas St., 250/386-6468, 5pm-2am daily, $16-25) is a dark, richly decorated room downstairs on the main thoroughfare through downtown, so it's easy to miss. The menu blends Nepalese cooking styles with seafood and Western produce to create tasty and innovative dishes at reasonable prices, such as butter chicken poutine and a three-curry combo plate. The kitchen is open until 2am, making it a popular late-night haunt.

European

One of the most popular restaurants in downtown Victoria is **Pagliacci's** (1011 Broad St., 250/386-1662, 11:30am-10pm Mon.-Sat., 10am-10pm Sun., $18-42), known for hearty Italian food, homemade bread, great desserts, and loads of atmosphere. Small and always busy, the restaurant attracts a lively local crowd, many with children; you'll inevitably have to wait for a table during the busiest times (reservations are not taken). Main attractions include the option to pick your own meat or seafood and the way it is prepared, along with the sauce and the sides. Pasta options include a prawn fettuccine topped with tomato mint sauce.

The setting of **Il Terrazzo** (Waddington Alley, 250/361-0028, 4pm-10pm daily, $18-50), in a redbrick building in the historical Old Town precinct, is perfect for this traditional northern Italian dining room. The pasta is made in-house, and when combined with local seafood (think halibut baked with a peppercorn and blackberry demi-glace on a bed of three-cheese fusilli pasta), the combination is divine.

The energetic atmosphere at ★ **Café Brio** (944 Fort St., 250/383-0009, 5pm-9pm Wed.-Sat., $26-39) is contagious, and the food is as good as anywhere in Victoria. The Mediterranean-inspired dining room is adorned with lively artwork and built around a U-shaped bar, while out front are a handful of tables on an alfresco terrace. A creative menu combines local, seasonal produce with expertise and flair. The charcuterie, prepared in-house, is always a good choice to begin with, followed by wild salmon prepared however your server suggests. Order the sticky date toffee pudding, even if you're full.

Vegetarian

★ **Rebar** (50 Bastion Square, 250/361-9223, 11:30am-8pm Mon.-Fri., 10am-8pm Sat.-Sun., $15-19) is a cheerful, always-busy 1970s-style primarily vegetarian restaurant with a loyal local following. Dishes such as the almond burger at lunch and blackened rockfish burger at dinner are full of flavor and made with only the freshest ingredients. Still hungry? Try the nutty carrot cake. Children are catered to with fun choices such as banana and peanut butter on sunflower-seed bread. It's worth stopping by just for juice: vegetable and fruit juices, power tonics, and wheatgrass infusions are made to order.

OAK BAY

Oak Bay, east of downtown, is a picturesque seaside suburb with many grand homes and bustling shopping strip dotted with cafés. It's also the end of the scenic coastal drive from downtown. One of the most popular cafés in Oak Bay is **Discovery Coffee** (1964 Oak Bay Ave., 250/590-7717, 7am-5pm daily), which roasts its own beans and has local artwork on its walls. A few blocks south, **Demitasse** (2164 McNeill Ave., 250/598-6668, 8am-6pm Mon.-Sat., lunches $10-16) is a friendly little place that is part café, part deli, and part garden center. Thin crust pizza and creative salads are menu highlights.

Ottavio Italian Bakery (2272 Oak Bay Ave., 250/592-4080, 8am-6pm Tues.-Sat., lunch $10-16) has been operated by three generations of the same Italian family. The hand-rolled breads are baked daily, the very best imported oils and spices are reasonably priced, and the gelato is as good as anywhere in the city. At lunch, enjoy grilled gruyère cheese on sourdough or a traditional Italian salad topped with cured meats.

Although the **Oak Bay Beach Hotel** (1175 Beach Dr., 250/598-4556) is a modern replacement for the historical hotel that once stood on this waterfront site, dining options remain similar to those enjoyed by generations of locals and visitors alike. **Snug Pub** (11am-midnight daily, $14-24) was a busy social hangout as early as the 1950s, and in the reinvented hotel it continues this role, with dishes such as fish-and-chips, and steak and kidney pie, all best enjoyed with a pint of beer on the waterfront patio. Modern **Faro** (7am-9pm daily, $20-38) is renowned for woodfired pizza, best enjoyed on the patio if the weather is warm. The classic cooking offered in the upscale 34-seat **Dining Room** (7am-11am and 6pm-9pm daily, $26-48) has been impressing the genteel residents of Oak Bay for generations.

WEST OF DOWNTOWN

If you are staying on Bear Mountain, head to **Bear Mountain Market** (1325 Bear Mountain Pkwy., 778/265-7108, 6am-9pm daily) for the best coffee on the mountain, as well as sandwiches and other light lunches made in-house. For a resort-like setting, head over to the nearby Westin Bear Mountain, where the **Pool Side Bar & Grill** (1999 Country Club Way, 250/391-7160, 11am-7pm daily July-Aug., lunch $14-17) is the perfect place to dine and dip on a warm afternoon. The sandwiches, wraps, and salads are all reasonably priced, and the setting can't be beat. The resort's main restaurant is **Bella** (1999 Country Club Way, 250/391-7160, 6:30am-11:30am and 5pm-10pm daily, $20-39), where the emphasis is on healthy breakfasts such as blueberry and orange pancakes, and refined evening dining.

Heading north from Victoria toward Nanaimo, **Malahat Chalet** (Moon Water Lodge, 265 Trans-Canada Hwy., 778/432-4606, 9am-8pm daily, $15-32) offers sweeping views across Saanich Inlet from a lofty location high above the water. Outdoor tables are the place to be on warm days, but inside is also cozy and inviting. You can stop by and enjoy the panorama over a coffee, but the food is good, much of it created using local seafood and produce. The seafood chowder (halibut, salmon, prawns, and clams) is filling enough to suffice as a main, but if you're still hungry, the beer-battered halibut or braised short rib are both good choices.

SAANICH PENINSULA

Seahorses Cafe (799 Verdier Ave., Brentwood Bay, 250/544-1565, 10:30am-4pm Mon. and Wed.-Fri., 9:30am-4pm Sat.-Sun., lunch $11-18) has a prime waterfront location beside the ferry dock in Brentwood Bay, with lots of outdoor tables taking full advantage of the setting. In addition to the usual array of coffee drinks, the breakfast bun is a great way to start the day. Crab cakes, sockeye salmon burgers, and pulled pork sandwiches anchor the lunch menu. As a bonus, Seahorses has the least expensive kayak rentals ($20 for 2 hours) I have found on Vancouver Island.

Across the ferry dock from Seahorses Cafe

is **Brentwood Bay Pub** (849 Verdier Ave., Brentwood Bay, 250/544-5102, 11:30am-10pm Sun.-Thurs., 11:30am11pm Fri.-Sat., $17-35), part of Brentwood Bay Resort, where the waterfront patio is extremely busy on weekends, but you can usually talk your way to a table with a view midweek. The menu is a step or two above typical pub fare, with a charcuterie board, oversized salads, and mains such as blackened chicken and ribs.

★ **Café Zanzibar** (1164 Stelly's Cross Rd., 250/652-1228, 9:30am-3pm Sun.-Tues., 9:30am-8pm Wed.-Sat., $19-36) is in a delightful rural setting inland from Brentwood Bay (off West Saanich Rd.), with a patio draped in greenery, providing the best seating on warmer days. Full English breakfasts using free-range local eggs and quality bacon draw morning diners, but it is the global-inspired lunch and dinner menus that are the real star, with prices much lower than you'd pay in downtown Victoria. Tandoori chicken and mango salad, wild salmon and arugula fettuccine, or North African lamb shanks—it's hard to go wrong with anything on the Zanzibar menu.

Accommodations

Victoria accommodations come in all shapes and sizes. A couple of downtown hostels cater to travelers on a budget, but there are also a surprising number of convenient roadside motels with rooms for under $100, including one right off the Inner Harbour. Bed-and-breakfasts are where Victoria really shines, with more than 300 at last count. You'll be able to find bed-and-breakfast rooms for under $150, but to fully immerse yourself in the historical charm of the city, expect to pay more. In the same price range are boutique hotels such as the Bedford Regency— that is, older hotels that have been restored and come with top-notch amenities and full service. Most of the upscale hotel chains are not represented downtown; a harborfront Marriott is the exception. The city has no Four Seasons, Hilton, Hotel Inter-Continental, Hyatt, Radisson, or Regent. Finally, if you have wads of cash to spare or are looking for a splurge, the surrounding area is blessed with two lodges (Sooke Harbour House in Sooke and Brentwood Bay Resort) that regularly garner top rankings in the glossy travel magazine polls.

In the off-season (Oct.-May), the nightly rates quoted here are discounted up to 50 percent, but occupancy rates are high as Canadians flock to the country's winter hot spot. No matter what time of year you plan to visit, arriving in Victoria without a reservation is unwise, but especially in the summer months, when crowds of visitors compete for a relative paucity of rooms. As a last resort, staff at the **Victoria Visitor Centre** (Wharf St., 250/953-2022 or 800/663-3883, www.tourismvictoria.com) can offer help finding a room. Regardless of your budget, you can't go wrong staying at one of the following specially selected places.

DOWNTOWN

All but a couple of the venues in this section are within easy walking distance of the Inner Harbour. If you're traveling to Victoria outside summer, don't be put off by the quoted rates, because the downtown hotels offer the biggest off-season discounts. If you're simply looking for a motel room and don't want to pay for the location, check any online travel site for options along the routes leading into downtown from the north, including Wyndham Hotels (www.wyndhamhotels.com), which has multiple properties in this area.

Under $100

Budget travelers are well catered to in Victoria, although no particular backpacker lodge stands out above the rest.

In the heart of the oldest section of downtown Victoria is **HI-Victoria** (516 Yates St., 250/385-4511 or 866/762-4122, www.hihostels.ca, dorm $35, nonmembers $38.50, private room $85-120 s or d). The 108-bed hostel enjoys a great location only a stone's throw from the harbor. Separate dorms and bath facilities for men and women are complemented by two fully equipped kitchens, a large meeting room, a lounge, a library, a game room, travel services, and an informative bulletin board. There are a limited number of private rooms and a women's-only dorm.

Housed in the upper stories of an old commercial building, **Ocean Island Backpackers Inn** (791 Pandora Ave., 250/385-1789 or 888/888-4180, www.oceanisland.com, dorm from $35, private room $56-120 d) is just a couple of blocks from downtown. This a party place—exactly what some young travelers are looking for, but annoying enough for some to generate letters to harried travel writers. On the plus side, the lodging is clean, modern, and welcoming throughout. Guests have use of kitchen facilities and a laundry room. There's also plenty of space to relax, such as a reading room, a music room (guitars supplied), a television room, and a street-level bar open until midnight. In addition to regular dorms, there are "pod dorms" with privacy curtains, micro private rooms, and a family room that sleeps four.

$100-150

In the summer high season, no downtown hotels fall into this price category. Outside of summer, many offer deeply discounted rates that fall below $150. Check hotel websites for details.

$150-200

Dating to 1911 and once home to artist Emily Carr, **James Bay Inn** (270 Government St., 250/384-7151 or 800/836-2649, www.jamesbayinn.com, $164-244 s or d) is five blocks from the harbor and within easy walking distance of all city sights and Beacon Hill Park. From the outside, the hotel has a clunky, uninspiring look, and many of the rooms are older, but those in the adjacent Heritage House have a bright and breezy decor and newer beds, making them a pleasant place to rest your head.

In a quiet residential area immediately east of downtown, **The Craigmyle** (1037 Craigdarroch Rd., Rockland, 250/595-5411 or 888/595-5411, www.victoriahomestay.ca, from $179-249 s, $199-249 d) has been converted from part of the original Craigdarroch Estate—it stands directly in front of the famous castle. This rambling 1913 home is full of character, comfortable furnishings, and lots of original stained-glass windows. The 15 guest rooms include singles, doubles, and family suites; some share baths, while others are en suite. An inviting living room with a TV, a bright sunny dining area, and friendly longtime owners make this a real home away from home. Check-in is 2pm-6pm.

In the oldest section of downtown, surrounded by the city's best dining and shopping opportunities, is the **Bedford Regency** (1140 Government St., 250/384-6835 or 800/665-6500, www.bedfordregency.com, $189-229 s or d), featuring 40 guest rooms of varying configurations. Stylish, uncluttered art deco furnishings and high ceilings make the standard rooms seem larger than they really are. A better deal are the deluxe rooms and suites, which provide more space and better amenities for only slightly more money.

In the heart of the city center, the six-story 1913 **Strathcona Hotel** (919 Douglas St., 250/383-7137 or 800/663-7476, www.strathconahotel.com, $199-264 s or d) holds a variety of bars, including a couple of the city's most popular, as well as 86 guest rooms. They are sparsely furnished but clean, comfortable, and regularly revamped. It's worth upgrading to the much larger deluxe rooms.

1: Parkside Hotel & Spa 2: HI-Victoria 3: Dashwood Manor

$200-300

Just four blocks from the Inner Harbour, the 1905 ★ **Beaconsfield Inn** (988 Humboldt St., 250/384-4044 or 888/884-4044, www.beaconsfieldinn.com, $209-279 s or d) is exactly what a Victorian bed-and-breakfast should be. Original mahogany floors, high ceilings, classical moldings, imported antiques, and fresh flowers from the garden create an upscale historical charm throughout. Each of the nine guest rooms is individually decorated in Edwardian style. I stayed in the Emily Carr Suite, named for the renowned artist who spent her early years in the city, with a rich burgundy and green color scheme, Carr prints on the walls, a regal mahogany bed topped by a goose-down comforter, an oversize bath and jetted tub, and a separate sitting area with a fireplace. After checking in, you'll be invited to join other guests for high tea in the library and then encouraged to return for a glass of sherry before heading out for dinner. Breakfast, served in a formal dining room or a more casual conservatory, is a grand affair, with multiple courses of hearty fare delivered to your table by your impeccably presented host.

Every time I visit Victoria, I expect to see that the old **Surf Motel** (290 Dallas Rd. 250/386-3305, www.surfmotel.net, Mar.-Oct., $215-245 s or d) has been demolished, but it's still here, offering priceless ocean and mountain views from its old-fashioned but spacious rooms. It's south of the Inner Harbour; take Oswego Road from Belleville Street.

If you're looking for a modern feel, centrally located ★ **Swans Suite Hotel** (506 Pandora Ave., 250/361-3310 or 800/668-7926, www.swanshotel.com, $220-400 s or d) is an excellent choice. Located above a restaurant-pub complex that was built in the 1880s as a grain storehouse, each of the 30 split-level suites holds a loft, a full kitchen, and a dining area, and some have separate bedrooms. The furnishings are casual yet elegantly rustic, with West Coast artwork adorning the walls and fresh flowers in every room. In the off-season, all rooms are discounted up to 40 percent.

Yes, it's a chain hotel, but **Days Inn Victoria on the Harbour** (427 Belleville St., 250/386-3451 or 800/665-3024, www.daysinnvictoria.com, from $290 s or d) has a prime waterfront location that will make you feel like you're paying more than you really are. Befitting the location, rooms have a subtle nautical feel and, like all Days Inns, practical yet comfortable furnishings. In winter, you'll pay from just $180 for a suite with a view, with a light breakfast included. Year-round bonuses include free parking, in-room coffeemakers, and bottled water.

$300-400

Right on the Inner Harbour, **Pendray Inn** (309 Belleville St., 250/388-3892, www.pendrayinnandteahouse.com, from $300-330 s or d) has a central position across from the water. Dating to 1897, this magnificent property has been elegantly restored, with stained-glass windows, a magnificent fireplace, lots of exposed wood, crystal chandeliers under a gabled roof, and antiques decorating every corner. Afternoon tea is served in a comfortable lounge area off the lobby, and the restaurant has a nice veranda. Packages make staying at the Gatsbyesque mansion more reasonable, or visit in winter for as little as $180 s or d.

Enjoying an absolute waterfront location right downtown is the **Victoria Regent** (1234 Wharf St., 250/386-2211 or 800/663-7472, www.victoriaregent.com, $310-700 s or d). The exterior of this building is nothing special, but inside, the rooms are spacious and comfortable. The best-value rooms at the Regent are the harbor-facing suites, which include a full kitchen and a balcony.

Separated from downtown by Beacon Hill Park, **Dashwood Manor** (1 Cook St., 250/385-5517 or 800/667-5517, www.dashwoodmanor.com, $329-379 s or d), a 1912 Tudor-style heritage house on a bluff overlooking Juan de Fuca Strait, enjoys a panoramic view of the entire Olympic Mountain range. The 12 guest rooms are elegantly furnished, and the hosts will happily recount the historical details of each room. The Oxford

Grand room ($339) holds a chandelier, a stone fireplace, and antiques.

Very different from Victoria's traditional accommodations is the contemporary **Parkside Hotel & Spa** (810 Humboldt St., 250/940-1200 or 855/616-3557, www.parksidevictoria.com, $360-410 s or d). Within walking distance of the Inner Harbour, the guest rooms have a contemporary ambience, and each has one or two bedrooms, a full kitchen with stainless-steel appliances, and large wall-mounted TVs. Rooms on the upper floors have city views, and some have balconies. Other highlights include a fitness room, an indoor pool, a theater, day spa services, a rooftop patio, a street-level café, and underground parking.

Similar in style and amenities is **Oswego** (500 Oswego St., 250/294-7500 or 877/767-9346, www.oswegohotelvictoria.com, from $350-600 s or d). Rooms on the upper floors have water views, including the two three-bedroom penthouse suites. Amenities include a fitness room, underground parking, and a contemporary bistro, all within walking distance of downtown.

Coast Victoria Hotel (146 Kingston St., 250/360-1211 or 800/716-6199, www.coasthotels.com, $369-479 s or d) is the last of the string of accommodations along the south side of the harbor but is still within easy walking distance of downtown. Rates here fluctuate greatly. The rack rate for a harbor-view room with a very small balcony is $449 s or d, but book online and you could get the same room in the off-season, with breakfast included, for under $300. The in-house Blue Crab Seafood House is notable for its extensive seafood menu.

In the same vicinity and sitting on a point of land jutting into the Inner Harbour, the **Inn at Laurel Point** (680 Montreal St., 250/386-8721 or 800/663-7667, www.laurelpoint.com, $359-600 s or d) offers a distinct resort atmosphere within walking distance of downtown. Two wings hold around 200 rooms; most have water views and a private balcony. Amenities include an indoor pool, beautifully landscaped Japanese-style gardens, a sauna, a small fitness facility, Aura Restaurant, and a lounge.

The ★ **Magnolia Hotel & Spa** (623 Courtney St., 250/381-0999 or 877/624-6654, www.magnoliahotel.com, $379-529 s or d, off-season from $239) is a European-style boutique hotel just up the hill from the harbor. It features an elegant interior with mahogany-paneled walls, Persian rugs, chandeliers, a gold-leaf ceiling, and fresh flowers throughout public areas. The rooms are each elegantly furnished and feature floor-to-ceiling windows, heritage-style furniture in a contemporary room layout, richly colored fabrics, down duvets, a work desk with cordless phone, and coffee-making facilities. Many also feature a gas fireplace. The baths are huge, each having marble trim, a soaker tub, and a separate shower stall. The hotel is also home to the Magnolia Spa and a stylish West Coast-themed restaurant.

In a prime waterfront position next to the parliament buildings is the **Hotel Grand Pacific** (463 Belleville St., 250/386-0450 or 800/663-7550, www.hotelgrandpacific.com, from $379 s or d). Aside from more than 300 rooms, this modern property is also home to Spa at the Grand, a health club, a large pool, and restaurants and lounges. All rooms are well appointed, spacious, and have small private balconies.

Over $400

Across the Inner Harbour from downtown, offering stunning city views, is the modern, upscale **Delta Hotels Victoria Ocean Pointe Resort** (100 Harbour Rd., 250/360-2999 or 888/236-2427, www.marriott.com, from $410 s or d). This hotel offers all of the services of a European-style spa resort, with the convenience of downtown just a short ferry trip away. The rooms are simple yet stylishly furnished, with huge windows taking advantage of the views. Each comes with a work desk, luxurious bathroom, and plush robes. Facilities include a large health club, an indoor glass-enclosed pool, spa and massage services, tennis, a lounge, a seasonal outdoor terrace, and two restaurants.

The grand old **Fairmont Empress** (721 Government St., 250/384-8111 or 800/257-7544, www.fairmont.com, from $529 s or d) is Victoria's best-loved accommodation. With only magnificent gardens separating it from the Inner Harbour, it's also in the city's best location. Designed by Francis Rattenbury in 1908, the Empress is one of the original Canadian Pacific Railway hotels. The 464 guest rooms are offered in 90 different configurations, but as in other hotels of the era, most are small. Each is filled with Victorian-period furnishings and antiques. The least expensive Fairmont rooms start at $529 in summer, but if you really want to stay in this Canadian landmark, consider upgrading to a Fairmont Gold room. Although not necessarily larger, these rooms have harbor views, private check-in, nightly turndown service, and a private lounge with a patio where hors d'oeuvres are served in the evening; from $659, rates include a light breakfast. If you don't stay at the Empress, plan on at least visiting one of the restaurants or having a drink at the Veranda, which overlooks the harbor.

WEST OF DOWNTOWN

The small community of Malahat is strung out along the main route up the island 25 kilometers (16 miles) from downtown Victoria, making it a good place to spend the night for those who want to get an early start on northward travel. Along the way to Malahat, you'll pass by Bear Mountain.

$100-150

If you just need somewhere to spend the night, it's hard to go past the cozy cabins at **Malahat Bungalows Motel** (300 Trans-Canada Hwy., 250/478-3011, $120-130 s or d). No surprises here; expect fairly basic motel-style units spread around well-maintained grounds. There is no air-conditioning, but each room has wireless Internet and a flat-screen TV.

$200-300

Moon Water Lodge (265 Trans-Canada Hwy., Malahat, www.moonwaterlodge.com, 778/432-3123, $265-350 s or d) may be right beside the island's main highway, but you'd never know it once inside the building, where views extend across the coastal forest to the protected waters of Saanich Inlet. Almost all rooms have water views and private balconies, while the in-house Malahat Chalet Restaurant, across the parking lot, also has a great outlook. The rooms are all well decorated and come with gas fireplaces, bathrobes, comfortable beds, and free calls within North America.

Over $300

The Westin Bear Mountain (1999 Country Club Way, 250/391-7160 or 888/533-2327, www.bearmountain.ca, $370-500 s or d) is a small part of an ambitious real estate and recreational development that sprawls over the namesake mountain summit about 30 minutes' drive from downtown. Access is from Highway 1's exit 14, off Millstream Road. More than 150 rooms are spread throughout two buildings, and all have luxurious touches such as slate floors, deep soaker tubs, and super-comfortable beds. The main lodge holds a spa facility and multiple dining options, while a separate building is home to a health club, an outdoor heated pool, and more dining options. Rooms have balconies, and many have full kitchens. Check online for golf packages (from $200 pp).

SAANICH PENINSULA

With the exception of the waterfront Brentwood Bay Resort, these accommodations are along Highway 17, the main route between downtown Victoria and the BC Ferries terminal at Swartz Bay. These properties are best suited to travelers arriving at or departing from the airport or ferry terminal, but are also handy to Butchart Gardens.

$100-200

Right beside the highway, **Motel 6** (2401

Mt. Newton Cross Rd., 250/652-4464, www. motel6.com, $100-140 s or d) has a large variety of affordable rooms, English-style gardens, and complimentary coffee in the lobby each morning. Traveling families will want to upgrade to the ample family rooms ($140), which sleep up to six people.

At the same intersection as the Motel 6 is **Quality Inn Waddling Dog** (2476 Mt. Newton Cross Rd., 250/652-1146 or 800/567-8466, www.qualityinnvictoria.com, $183-203 s or d), styled as an old English guesthouse complete with an English pub. The Waddling Dog offers several well-priced packages that include meals and admission to Butchart Gardens.

Over $400

You'll feel like you're a million miles from the city at ★ **Brentwood Bay Resort** (849 Verdier Ave., Brentwood Bay, 250/544-2079 or 888/544-2079, www.brentwoodbayresort. com, $419-589 s or d), an upscale retreat overlooking Saanich Inlet. It's one of only three Canadian properties with a Small Luxury Hotels of the World designation, and you will want for nothing. You can learn to scuba dive, take a water taxi to Butchart Gardens, enjoy the latest spa treatments, or join a kayak tour.

The guest rooms take understated elegance to new heights. Filled with natural light, they feature contemporary West Coast styling (lots of polished wood and natural colors), the finest Italian sheets on king beds, and private balconies. Dining options include a beautiful restaurant specializing in Vancouver Island produce and local seafood, and an upscale pub with a waterfront patio.

CAMPING
West of Downtown
Fort Victoria RV Park (340 Island Hwy., 250/479-8112, www.fortvictoria.ca, $65) is six kilometers (four miles) northwest of the city center on Highway 1A. This campground provides full hookups (including cable TV), free showers, laundry facilities, and wireless Internet.

North Along Highway 1
Continuing west from the campgrounds west of downtown, Highway 1 curves north through **Goldstream Provincial Park** (19 kilometers/11 miles from downtown, $35) and begins its up-island journey north. The southern end of the park holds 161 well-spaced campsites scattered through an old-growth forest—it's one of the most beautiful

Brentwood Bay Resort

settings you could imagine close to a capital city. The campground rates include hot showers, but there are no hookups. The park's interpretive center is farther north along the highway, and many trails lead off from the campground, including a 10-minute walk to photogenic Goldstream Falls. The campground is also within walking distance of a grocery store. Make reservations through **BC Parks** (519/858-6161 or 800/689-9025, https://camping.bcparks.ca).

In Malahat, seven kilometers (four miles) farther north along Highway 1, is **Cedar Springs Ranch** (230 Trans-Canada Hwy., 250/478-3332, www.cedarspringsranch.com,

mid-May-mid-Sept., tents $43, hookups $54-59), which has basic cabins ($92-125 s or d) that sleep four to six in bunk beds (bring your own bedding). Facilities include showers, an outdoor pool, a laundry room, a store, and a game room.

Saanich Peninsula

Halfway between downtown Victoria and Sidney is **Island View Beach Regional Park** (Homathko Dr., 250/652-0548, late May-early Sept., $15-20), right on the beach three kilometers (two miles) east of Highway 17. Online reservations at www.crd.bc.ca are essential.

Information and Services

TOURISM OFFICES

Tourism Victoria runs the bright, modern **Victoria Visitor Centre** (812 Wharf St., 250/953-2033 or 800/663-3883, www.tourismvictoria.com, 8:30am-8:30pm daily May-Sept., 9am-5pm daily Oct.-Apr.), which overlooks the Inner Harbour. The friendly staff can answer most of your questions. They also book accommodations, tours and charters, restaurants, entertainment, and transportation, all at no extra cost; sell local bus passes and map books with detailed area-by-area maps; and stock an enormous selection of brochures. Also get the free *Accommodations* publication and the free local news and entertainment papers—the best way to find out what's happening while you're in town.

Coming off the ferry from Vancouver, stop in at **Sidney Visitor Centre** (2281 Beacon Ave., 250/665-7362, www.sidney.ca, 9am-5pm daily summer, closed weekends the rest of the year), which is just off the highway along the road leading into Sooke.

EMERGENCY SERVICES

In a medical emergency, call 911 or contact **Victoria General Hospital** (1 Hospital Way, 250/727-4212), northwest of downtown

just off the Trans-Canada Highway. For cases that aren't urgent, a handy facility is **James Bay Medical Treatment Centre** (230 Menzies St., 250/388-9934, 11am-5:30pm Mon.-Fri., 10am-3:30pm Sat.). For dental care, try the **Cresta Dental Centre** (3170 Tillicum Rd., at Burnside St., 250/384-7711, 8am-8:30pm Mon.-Fri., 9am-5pm Sat.-Sun.). You can fill prescriptions at **Shoppers Drug Mart** (1222 Douglas St., 250/381-4321, 6am-10pm daily).

COMMUNICATIONS

The main **post office** is on the corner of Yates and Douglas Streets (9am-5pm Mon.-Fri.). The main **area code** for Victoria is **250** (the same as all of British Columbia, except Vancouver and the Lower Mainland), although additional area codes that have been established in recent years include 778, 236, and 672.

Telus provides free public wireless Internet hotspots throughout the city (non-Telus customers will need to download the app to take advantage of this service). To find a hotspot near you, go to https://wififinder.telus.com. All of Victoria's accommodations have wireless Internet access. As a general rule, the least expensive lodgings offer wireless access for free, but upscale properties like the Fairmont Empress charge a fee. Most cafés offer access for the price of a coffee.

Books

The central branch of the **Greater Victoria Public Library** (735 Broughton St., at Courtney St., 250/382-7241, www.gvpl.ca, 9am-6pm Mon. and Fri.-Sat., 9am-9pm Tues.-Thurs. summer, 9am-6pm Mon. and Fri.-Sat., 9am-9pm Tues.-Thurs., 1pm-5pm Sun. fall-spring) has a special collection

focusing on the history and peoples of Vancouver Island.

PHOTOGRAPHY

North of downtown along Hwy. 17 to Sidney, **Kerrisdale Cameras** (3531 Ravine Way, 250/475-2066, 9:30am-6pm Mon.-Sat., 11am-5pm Sun.) is the city's best camera shop, with a wide selection of cameras and accessories as well as a quick and reliable print service. A reliable centrally located repair shop is **Victoria Camera Service** (864 Pembroke St., 250/383-4311, 9:30am-4pm Mon.-Fri.).

Getting There and Around

AIR

Air Canada (604/688-5515 or 888/247-2262, www.aircanada.ca), **Pacific Coastal** (604/273-8666 or 800/663-2872, www.pacific-coastal.com), and **WestJet** (604/606-5525 or 800/538-5696, www.westjet.com) have scheduled flights between Vancouver and Victoria, but the flight is so short that the attendants don't even have time to throw a bag of peanuts in your lap. These flights are really only practical if you have an onward destination—flying out of Victoria, for example, with Los Angeles as a final destination.

Several companies operate seaplanes between downtown Vancouver and downtown Victoria. From Coal Harbour, on Burrard Inlet, **Harbour Air** (250/384-2215 or 800/665-0212, www.harbourair.com) has scheduled floatplane flights to Victoria's Inner Harbour. Expect to pay around $130 pp one-way for any of these flights.

Victoria International Airport

Victoria International Airport (YYJ, www.victoriaairport.com), the island's main airport, is on the Saanich Peninsula, 20 kilometers (12 miles) north of Victoria's city center. Once you've collected your baggage from the carousels, it's impossible to miss the car-rental outlets (Avis, Budget, Hertz, and National)

across the room, where you'll also find a currency exchange and an information booth. Outside is a taxi stand and the ticket booth for the shuttle bus. The modern terminal also houses a lounge, various eateries, and a profusion of greenery.

YYJ Airport Shuttle (778/351-4995 or 855/351-4995, www.yyjairportshuttle.com, adults $25, children $15 one-way) operates buses between the airport and major downtown hotels as well as **Capital City Station** (721 Douglas St.) every 30 minutes. The first departure from downtown to the airport is 5am. A **taxi** costs approximately $65 from the airport to downtown.

FERRY

From Vancouver

BC Ferries (250/386-3431 or 888/223-3779, www.bcferries.com) links Vancouver and Victoria with a fleet of ferries that operate year-round. Ferries depart Vancouver from **Tsawwassen,** south of Vancouver International Airport (allow one hour by road from downtown Vancouver) and **Horseshoe Bay,** on Vancouver's North Shore. They terminate on Vancouver Island at **Swartz Bay,** 32 kilometers (20 miles) north of Victoria. On weekends and holidays, the one-way fare on either route costs adults $17.60, children

$8.80, and vehicles $59.50. Limited vehicle reservations ($15 per booking) are accepted online at www.bcferries.com.

In high season (late June-mid-Sept.), the ferries run about once an hour 7am-10pm daily. September to June, they run a little less frequently. Both crossings take around 90 minutes. Expect a wait in summer, particularly if you have an oversize vehicle: each ferry can accommodate far fewer large vehicles than standard-size cars and trucks.

Try to plan your travel outside peak times, which include summer weekends, especially Friday afternoon sailings from Tsawwassen and Sunday afternoon sailings from Swartz Bay. Most travelers don't make reservations but simply arrive and prepare themselves to wait for the next ferry if the first one fills. Both terminals have shops with food and magazines, as well as summertime booths selling everything from crafts to mini doughnuts.

From Washington State

From downtown Seattle's Pier 69, **Clipper Navigation** (800/888-2535, www.clippervacations.com, adults US$200-260, children US$100-130 round-trip) runs passenger-only ferries to Victoria's Inner Harbour. In summer, sailings are made five times daily, with the service running fall-spring on a reduced schedule. Travel is discounted with seven days advance purchase, and in the off-season.

North of Seattle, Anacortes is the departure point for **Washington State Ferries** (206/464-6400, www.wsdot.wa.gov/ferries, adults US$21, seniors and children US$10.50, vehicles with driver US$65) to Sidney, 32 kilometers (20 miles) north of Victoria on Vancouver Island, with a stop en route in the San Juan Islands. Make reservations at least 24 hours in advance.

The final option is to travel from Port Angeles to Victoria. The **MV *Coho*** (250/386-2202 or 360/457-4491, www.cohoferry.com, adults US$21, children US$10.50, vehicles with driver US$70) runs year-round, with up to four crossings daily in summer. Reservations cost $11-16 per booking and are essential in summer.

BUS

Capital City Station (721 Douglas St.) is behind the Fairmont Empress. **BC Ferries Connector** (866/986-3466, www.bcfconnector.com) operates bus service between Vancouver International Airport and downtown Victoria ($60.50 one-way, includes ferry fare); the trip from the airport to Victoria, via

MV *Coho* fills the Inner Harbour.

the ferry, takes 3.5 hours. This service also operates from downtown Vancouver. Capital City Station is also the southern terminus for **VI Connector** buses (866/986-3466, www.vi-connector.com), which serve island communities as far north as Campbell River.

Most central attractions can be reached on foot, but the **Victoria Regional Transit System** (250/385-2551, www.transitbc.com, $2.50 per ride, day pass $5) is excellent and easy to jump on and off to get everywhere you want to go. The website has details on the buses needed to reach all the major sights, parks, beaches, and shopping areas.

BIKE

Victoria has some excellent designated bike paths, including one that follows the coastline from the Inner Harbour to Oak Bay. For rentals ($40-70 per 24 hours for a regular bike, from $80 for an ebike.), **Sports Rent** (1950 Government St., 250/385-7368, www.sportsrentbc.com, 9am-5pm Mon.-Sat., 10am-5pm Sun.) has a handy downtown location, and their website has links to all the best riding options. Or try **Oak Bay Bicycles** (1990 Oak Bay Ave., 250/598-4111, www.oakbay-bikes.com, 10am-6pm Tues.-Thurs., 10am-5pm Wed.-Mon.).

TAXI

Taxis operate on a meter system, charging $3.30 at the initial flag drop, plus around $2 per kilometer. Call **Blue Bird Cabs** (250/382-2222), **Victoria Taxi** (250/383-7111), or **Yellow Cab** (250/381-2222).

Southern Vancouver Island

While the charms of Victoria may be hard to
leave behind, there are many reasons to explore the region within the
immediate vicinity of the capital—including an archipelago of accessible islands, long coastal hikes, historic towns, and untouched old-growth forests.

The Southern Gulf Islands range from rocky outcrops to sprawling rural oases. They're easily accessible from the busy ferry terminal north of Sidney at Swartz Bay, roughly 40 minutes' drive from downtown Victoria. The most popular islands offer a wide variety of lodging, camping, restaurants, and even vineyards. Other pockets of

Highlights

Look for ★ to find recommended sights, activities, dining, and lodging.

© MOON.COM

★ **Sidney Spit:** This sliver of white sand is only accessible by boat, but the solitude and beauty make the journey worthwhile (page 77).

★ **Galiano Island:** Each of the Southern Gulf Islands has its own personality, but Galiano Island is a favorite for **kayaking** (page 87).

★ **Saturna Island:** Hiking trails to remote headlands and an award-winning winery exemplify the charms of this little-known island (page 90).

★ **Sandcut Beach:** This beach is worth visiting for an oceanfront **waterfall** that has the Olympic Mountains as a backdrop (page 94).

★ **Juan de Fuca Provincial Park:** Soak up the sights and smells of the Pacific Ocean along driftwood-strewn beaches (page 94).

★ **West Coast Trail:** Winding through 77 kilometers (48 miles) of old-growth forest, with the Pacific Ocean close at hand, this ambitious trail is one of the world's great long-distance hikes (page 97).

★ **Tubing:** No, it's not just for kids. Floating down the Cowichan River is a delightful way to relax on a summer's day (page 102).

Southern Vancouver Island

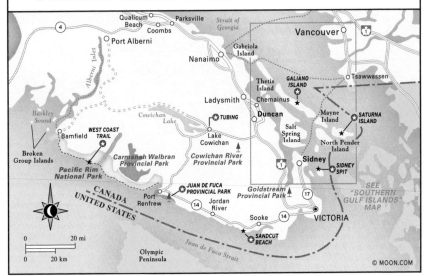

the archipelago are protected by Gulf Islands National Park, including some accessible by vehicle and others only by boat.

Two main highways lead out of Victoria: The Trans-Canada Highway (Hwy. 1, also known as the Island Highway) heads north, while Highway 14 heads west. This ocean-hugging stretch of road passes provincial parks, delightful oceanfront lodgings, and a panorama that extends across Juan de Fuca Strait to the snowcapped peaks of the Olympic Mountains in Washington State. It ends at Port Renfrew, best known as the starting point for the rugged and remote West Coast Trail, which beckons long-distance hikers from all over the world.

The Trans-Canada Highway (Hwy. 1) is the main route north, or up-island. It passes many other destinations worthy of your time, including the towns of Duncan, Chemainus, and Ladysmith, each with its own particular charms. West of Duncan are massive Cowichan Lake, an inland paradise for

anglers and boaters, and Carmanah Walbran Provincial Park, protecting a remote watershed full of ancient Sitka spruce that miraculously escaped logging.

PLANNING YOUR TIME

Exploring Vancouver Island beyond Victoria requires some advance planning and an idea of where you want to end up. If you have just a day to spare, you could visit the boat-accessible beaches of **Sidney Spit** or one or two of the Southern Gulf Islands (for their beautiful beaches and laid-back vibe, my favorites are **Galiano Island** and **Saturna Island**), but to explore the archipelago properly, you should schedule at least two days and preferably more.

The **West Coast Trail** is a multiple-night trek (most folks spend five to seven days on the trail) requiring advance planning to organize permits and transportation. Most importantly, it requires a high level of backcountry experience. You'll need to carry your

Previous: hiking Juan de Fuca Marine Trail; Juan de Fuca Provincial Park; orca surfacing in the waters off Galiano Island.

own food and camping equipment. Juan de Fuca Marine Trail through **Juan de Fuca Provincial Park** is a good alternative for those not as experienced in backcountry travel. The Juan de Fuca Marine Trail can be hiked as a multiple-night excursion, or as a day trip from Victoria.

Many sights and activities don't require anything more than a desire to get outdoors and go beyond the ordinary, such as visiting the hidden waterfall at **Sandcut Beach** and **tubing** down the Cowichan River.

Sidney

The bustling seaside town of Sidney (pop. 12,000) lies on the east side of the Saanich Peninsula, just east of Victoria International Airport and south of the ferry terminal at Swartz Bay. It can be reached in around 40 minutes from downtown Victoria, but its relaxed atmosphere is a world away from the capital. Visitors head out to the beaches of Sidney Spit by ferry, or simply soak up the sights and smells of the ocean along seawall trails and in waterfront parks. While Sidney is perhaps best known as the departure point for ferries to the Southern Gulf Islands and San Juan Islands in Washington, it also has a charming waterfront precinct anchored by the impressive Sidney Pier Hotel & Spa. It's a pleasant spot to explore on foot—enjoy the many outdoor cafés, walk the piers, and soak up the nautical ambience.

SIGHTS AND RECREATION
Shaw Centre for the Salish Sea

Beside the Sidney Pier Hotel & Spa, at the **Shaw Centre for the Salish Sea** (9811 Seaport Place, 250/665-7511, 10am-4:30pm daily, adults $18, seniors $14.50, children $12.50), the underwater world of the local waterways reveals itself through aquariums, interpretive panels, and a marine education center. The Salish Sea—a term used to describe the Strait of Georgia, the Strait of Juan de Fuca, and Puget Sound—is filled with marinelife, of which 160 species are displayed here in over 30 aquariums, including a

touch-tank stocked with sea cucumbers, starfish, and sea urchins. Many of the displays are designed for children, but the center gives an insight into marinelife for all ages.

Sidney Museum

Back along the main street, **Sidney Museum** (2423 Beacon Ave., 250/655-6355, 10am-4pm daily, donation) provides an interesting insight into the peninsula's earliest settlers, early industry, and the importance of shipping to the local economy.

Shoal Harbour Bird Sanctuary

North of Sidney along Resthaven Drive is Shoal Harbour Bird Sanctuary. Established in 1931, it is now surrounded by marinas and land-based developments but still provides an important stop for a wide variety of birds. Best known are the smartly colored black-and-white buffleheads, famous for arriving at the sanctuary with uncanny regularity on October 15 each year to spend the winter. Other species include great blue herons, bald eagles, Canada geese, loons, cormorants, and black oystercatchers. Access is signposted off Resthaven Drive 2 kilometers (1.2 miles) north of downtown Sidney.

★ Sidney Spit

A wonderful escape from mainland Vancouver Island, this long sandy spit at the north end of Sidney Island is protected as part of Gulf Islands National Park. Facilities are limited to restrooms, but the lack of development makes the destination even more charming. Most visitors come over for just the day to stroll the beaches, search out hidden treasures amid the driftwood, or simply relax and have a picnic.

The island has a small national park campground (www.reservation.pc.gc.ca, $18.75), but you'll need to be totally self-sufficient with your own tent, food, and drinking water. Unless you have your own boat, the island is only accessible by scheduled 20-minute ferry transfers between late May and September, when the **Sidney Spit Ferry** (888/656-7599, www.sidneyspitferry.com, adults $20, seniors and children $16 round-trip) operates. The departure point is the silver dock on the south side of the Sidney Pier Hotel & Spa. To be assured of a seat, reserve online well in advance. You can visit the island outside of this ferry's operating season with **Eco Cruising** (250/655-5211).

Whale-watching

Three-hour whale-watching cruises ($135 pp) by **Sidney Whale-Watching** (2537 Beacon Ave., 250/656-7599 or 888/656-7599, Mar.-Nov.) also departs from Sidney Pier three times daily. For most people, orcas (killer whales) are the highlight and can be seen throughout the summer months. Other whale species sighted throughout the season include grays, minkes, and humpbacks. The waters here are calmer than trips departing Victoria's Inner Harbour.

FOOD

The main dining precinct is Beacon Avenue, between 5th Street and the waterfront. Here you'll find **Third Street Café** (2466 Beacon Ave., 250/656-3035, 8am-3pm daily, lunch $10-16), a bustling café with large well-priced portions at both breakfast and lunch.

If you've arrived by ferry and this is your first trip to Vancouver Island, Sidney may be your introduction to **Serious Coffee** (2417 Beacon Ave., 250/655-7255, 7:30am-5pm daily, lunch $9-13), a chain of local coffeehouses all over the island. The menu is similar at all locations—baked goods, breakfast burritos, paninis, and of course, excellent coffee. With a similarly modern setting, **10 Acres** (Sidney Pier Hotel & Spa, 9805 Seaport Place, 250/220-8008, 7am-5pm daily, lunch $12-16), is a café-restaurant-bar combo at street level in Sidney's premier hotel, with many oceanfront tables. As many ingredients as possible are sourced from the nearby namesake farm, including fruit, vegetables, pork, and even honey from their beehives.

Sidney

The lunch menu includes sandwiches, salads, pizza, and gelato.

Fish O Chips (10153 Resthaven Dr., 250/656-4435, 3pm-8pm Tues., 11:30am-8pm Wed.-Sat., noon-7pm Sun., $13-29) isn't the healthiest place to dine, but lovers of traditional deep-fried fish-and-chips will love the number of options, including cod or halibut, with the latter well worth the extra dollars. Fish O Chips is a few blocks north of the main shopping strip.

My favorite spot for lunch is **Sea Glass Waterfront Grill** (2320 Harbour Rd., 778/351-3663, 11am-8pm daily, $18-29). Lunch and dinner choices are fresh and creative, with lots of island ingredients (think crab and romano cheese dip with homemade potato chips as a starter, and espresso-braised short ribs for a main). The setting is also notable; the restaurant is built right over the water at Van Isle Marina, a large marina north of town off Resthaven Road.

ACCOMMODATIONS

Hotels and Motels

Linked to town by an oceanfront walking path, **The Cedarwood** (9522 Lochside Dr., 250/656-5551 or 877/656-5551, www.thecedarwood.ca, from $155 s or d) lies a short distance south of downtown Sidney. Highlighted by an expansive landscaped garden filled with outdoor seating overlooking the Strait of Georgia, the regular motel rooms are clean and comfortable, but better deals are the multiple-room suites and individually furnished cottages, some with full kitchens.

Dominating the downtown waterfront is ★ **Sidney Pier Hotel & Spa** (9805 Seaport Place, 250/655-9445 or 866/659-9445, www.sidneypier.com, $249-469 s or d), a sparkling complex dominated by floor-to-ceiling windows on all seven floors. Standard rooms don't have water views but do come with king beds. The most expensive rooms are the Pier Suites, all of which are on the higher floors and have gorgeous ocean views and full kitchens. All rooms are decorated in slick, contemporary color schemes and have very comfortable beds. Amenities include a gift store, a café, a restaurant, a fitness center, spa services, and free airport shuttle.

Camping

If you're driving up from Victoria, continue north through town to the Wain Road exit and turn right onto Macdonald Park Road (which leads back south into Sidney) to access **Smonecten Campground** (10740 Macdonald Park Rd., mid-May-Sept., $18.75), a forested oasis right beside the highway. The facility, part of Gulf Islands National Park, has 49 campsites, each with a picnic table and a fire pit, but no hookups or showers. Reservations can be made through the National Reservation Service (877/737-3783, www.reservation.pc.gc.ca) for a small fee.

Information

Sidney Visitor Centre (2281 Beacon Ave., 250/665-7362, www.sidney.ca, 9am-5pm daily summer, Mon.-Fri. only the rest of the year) is well signed on the east side of Highway 17 as it passes through Sidney.

Getting There

Officially, Sidney is just 26 kilometers (16 miles) north of downtown Victoria along Highway 17 (also known as Patricia Bay Hwy.), but allow at least 30 minutes to drive, or 40 minutes during busier times of day.

The town makes a wonderful introduction to Vancouver Island when arriving by BC Ferries (250/386-3431 or 888/223-3779, www.bcferries.com, adults $17.60, children $8.80, and vehicles $59.50) from the mainland, with ferries docking seven kilometers (four miles) north of Sidney at Swartz Bay. **Washington State Ferries** (206/464-6400, 250/381-1551, or 888/808-7977, www.wsdot.wa.gov/ferries) dock in Sidney, with regular service to the San Juan Islands and on to Seattle (US$19.45, seniors and children US$9.70, vehicles with driver US$53.65).

Southern Gulf Islands

Spread throughout the Strait of Georgia between mainland British Columbia and Vancouver Island, this group of islands is Canadian territory but linked geologically to the San Juan Islands, immediately south. Five of the islands—Salt Spring, the Penders, Galiano, Mayne, and Saturna—are populated, and each is linked to the outside world by scheduled ferry service.

The mild, almost Mediterranean climate, beautiful scenery, driftwood-strewn beaches, quaint towns, and wide-ranging choice of accommodations combine to make the islands popular in summer, when laid-back locals share their home with flocks of visitors. Still, there's plenty of room to get away from the hustle, with pockets of the archipelago protected by **Gulf Islands National Park,** mile after mile of remote coastline, and easily reached peaks beckoning to be explored. After kayaking, biking, or hiking, the best way to end the day is at one of the many island restaurants, feasting on salmon and crab brought ashore that morning.

The islands have been partly cleared for agriculture, but where old-growth forests survive, you'll find stands of magnificent Douglas fir and western red cedar, with gnarled arbutus (Pacific madrone) dominating the shoreline. Closer to ground level, you'll see lots of daisies, as well as native roses, bluebells, and orchids flowering through summer. In late summer, gooseberries, huckleberries, and blackberries are ripe for the picking. The surrounding waterways host an incredibly diverse number of marine mammals, including sea lions, seals, sea otters, and orcas. If you spent a full year on the islands counting bird species, you'd come up with more than 300, including bald eagles, blue herons, cormorants, hummingbirds, robins, wrens, finches, and swallows. Fall is the best time to watch for migrating shorebirds, which stop to rest and feed throughout the archipelago. Children will love exploring tidal pools, where colorful anemones and starfish are among the many critters that make a home.

PLANNING YOUR TRIP

Before you head for the islands, get the latest rundown from the **Tourism Vancouver Island** website (www.vancouverisland. travel). Once on Vancouver Island, stop by the **Victoria Visitor Centre** (812 Wharf St., 250/953-2033 or 800/663-3883, www.tourismvictoria.com, 8:30am-8:30pm daily May-Sept., 9am-5pm daily Oct.-Apr.) in downtown Victoria, or the **Sidney Visitor Centre** (2281 Beacon Ave., 250/665-7362, www.sidney.ca, 9am-5pm daily summer, Mon.-Fri. only the rest of the year), along Highway 17 near the Swartz Bay Ferry Terminal. *Island Tides* (www.islandtides.com) and the website www.gulfislandstourism.com are good online resources.

Many visitors own island getaways or rent cottages by the week, but there are still plenty of options for shorter stays. Choices range from primitive tent sites to world-class lodges, with bed-and-breakfasts—there are hundreds—falling somewhere in the middle price-wise. Whatever your preference, make reservations for summer as far in advance as possible, especially for weekends. Be aware that many bed-and-breakfasts close through winter, and some don't take credit or debit cards. You will find cafés and restaurants on each island, but not a single McDonald's or similar fast-food chain. Groceries and gas are available in most villages; banks and ATMs are less common.

Ferry Service

The main transportation provider is **BC Ferries** (250/386-3431 or 888/223-3779, www.bcferries.com), which operates scheduled

Southern Gulf Islands

To Nanaimo

Vancouver

VANCOUVER
INTERNATIONAL
AIRPORT

99

0   5 mi

0   5 km

Valdes
Island

Strait of Georgia

Tsawwassen

17

Thetis
Island

Penelakut
Island

GALIANO
ISLAND

UNITED STATES
CANADA

Chemainus

To
Nanaimo

St Mary
Lake

Montague
Harbour
Provincial
Park

Montague
Harbour

Vesuvius Bay

Crofton

Sturdies Bay

Long
Harbour

Miners
Bay

Ganges

Prevost
Island

Village Bay

Mayne Island

Mt Maxwell
Provincial
Park

Otter
Bay

Browning
Harbour

Lyall Harbour

Tumbo
Island

Duncan

Fulford
Harbour

Ruckle
Provincial
Park

North
Pender
Island

SATURNA
ISLAND

SEE
"DUNCAN"
MAP

Bruce
Peak

Salt Spring
Island

Portland
Island

Gulf Islands
National Park

South Pender
Island

Piers
Island

Moresby
Island

1

Coal
Island

Swartz Bay

Vancouver

Island

Saanich Inlet

Mill Bay

SIDNEY
SPIT

Sidney

San Juan

Islands

Brentwood
Bay

Saanich
Peninsula

Sidney
Island

17

To Victoria

© MOON.COM

year-round services to the Southern Gulf Islands from both Vancouver Island and Vancouver. The main departure points are Swartz Bay, 32 kilometers (20 miles) north of Victoria, and Tsawwassen, on the south side of Vancouver. All ferries take vehicles (including RVs), motorcycles, bicycles, canoes, and kayaks. It's important to check the timetables (online or posted at each terminal) because some ferries are nonstop and others make up to three stops before reaching the more remote islands. Also try to avoid peak periods, such as Friday and Sunday afternoons. Aside from that, simply roll up and pay your fare.

Regardless of the final destination, the round-trip fare from Swartz Bay (Victoria) to any of the Southern Gulf Islands is a reasonable (adults $11.65, children $5.85, vehicles $36.40). Interisland travel is charged on a one-way basis (adults $5.85, children $2.90, vehicles $12.50). The fare system is designed to be flexible; for example, if you plan to travel to Galiano Island from Swartz Bay, with a stop on Salt Spring Island on the way out, you would pay the interisland fare departing Salt Spring and then use the return portion of the main ticket from Galiano.

From the mainland Tsawwassen terminal (south of downtown Vancouver), the fare is the same regardless of which island you travel to: one-way adults $18, children $9.05, vehicles $68.40. Operating a couple of times daily, this service stops at all but Saturna Island, with Salt Spring the final stop, two hours after departure from Tsawwassen.

SALT SPRING ISLAND

Largest of the Southern Gulf Islands, 180-square-kilometer (70-square-mile) Salt Spring (pop. 10,500) lies close to Vancouver Island, immediately north of Saanich Inlet. Ferries link the south and north ends of the island to Vancouver Island, and myriad roads converge on the service town of **Ganges.** The island is home to many artisans, along with hobby farmers, retirees, and wealthy Vancouverites who spend their summers at private getaways.

Ganges

Ask any longtime local and they'll tell you the island's main town, Ganges, is overly commercialized. But it's still quaint, and well worth visiting—at the very least to stock up with supplies. Set around a protected bay, the original waterfront buildings have undergone a colorful transformation, and where once you would have found boat-builders, you can now browse through art galleries, shop for antiques, or dine on innovative cuisine. Across from the harbor, one of the most eye-catching shops is the **Jill Louise Campbell Art Gallery** (110 Purvis Ln., 250/537-1589, 11am-5pm Mon.-Sat.), featuring the whimsical painting of its namesake. In a converted cottage one block to the west, **Twang & Pearl** (112 Hereford Ave., 250/537-0028, 10am-4pm Sun.-Tues., 10am-5pm Wed.-Sat.) combines boutique clothing with home decor. Outdoor enthusiasts should head to **Axe and Reel Outdoor Emporium** (111 Rainbow Rd., 250/537-9666, 10am-5pm Mon.-Sat.) for their adventure needs. On the north side of the village, **Mahon Hall** (166 Lower Ganges Rd., 250/537-0899, www.ssartscouncil.com) is filled with arty booths during regular art shows, while the Saturday market in Centennial Park also showcases the work of local artists.

Within walking distance of the waterfront is **Mouat Park,** a quiet reprieve from the bustle. From the west end of Seaview Avenue, trails lead into and around the forested park, which also has a fern-filled area set aside for disc golf (free; bring your own Frisbee).

Recreation

Even if you've never kayaked or paddleboarded, plan on joining a tour with **Beachside** (163 Fulford-Ganges Rd., 250/537-2553, www.ssbeachside.com). Explore a white-sand beach on a deserted island ($85), enjoy the calm evening water on the Sunset Paddle ($85), or spend five hours ($170) exploring the coastline, with a break for a picnic lunch on a remote beach.

Landlubbers have plenty to see on Salt Spring. From the Fulford Harbour ferry terminal, take Beaver Point Road east to 486-hectare (1,200-acre) Ruckle Provincial Park. The access road ends at the rocky headland of Beaver Point, from where trails lead north along the coastline, providing great views across to North Pender Island. The land that's now protected as a park was donated to the province by the Ruckle family, whose 1876 farmhouse still stands.

Along the road north to Ganges, small Mount Maxwell Provincial Park protects the slopes of its namesake mountain. A rough unsealed road off Musgrave Road leads to the 588-meter (1,930-foot) summit, from where views extend south across the island to Vancouver Island and east to the other Gulf Islands. South of Mount Maxwell is 704-meter (2,300-foot) Mount Bruce, the island's highest peak.

Food

Head to Ganges and wander around the waterfront for the island's widest choice of dining options. T. J. Beans Coffee Shop (110 Lower Ganges Rd., 250/537-1216, 8am-5pm daily, lunch $6-9) is away from the waterfront, but popular with locals for excellent coffee and well-priced soup and sandwich lunch specials.

Just around the corner, Barb's Bakery and Bistro (121 McPhillips Ave., 250/537-4491, 7am-5pm Mon.-Sat., lunch $11-15) is another locally loved business, this one with an extensive breakfast and lunch menu that includes a delicious clam and salmon chowder—or just stop by for a smoothie or made-daily sweet pastry.

In the same vicinity is another café that I just can't help but recommend. Within a historic telegraph building, Switchboard (122 Hereford St., 250/931-7070, 8am-3pm Tues.-Sat., $7-11) is a small café with an interesting range of hot drinks (beetroot latte, anyone?) and pastries to match. The outdoor tables are spread across a shaded patio.

Right along the busy waterfront area of Ganges is ★ Tree House Café (106 Purvis Lane, 250/537-5379, 8am-8pm daily, $12-27).

The "tree" is a plum tree and the "house" is the kitchen. Most people dine outside in the shade of the tree, choosing freshly made dishes with mostly local ingredients, such as roasted yam quesadilla or vegan chili. Live music most summer evenings adds to the charm.

Accommodations

Short-term accommodations are limited on Salt Spring Island, so reservations should be made before arriving, especially in July and August. St. Mary Lake, a largish body of fresh water north of Ganges, is home to a few of old-fashioned cabin accommodations suitable for families or those looking for a simple relaxing stay. All three recommended here have lake access and small stretches of sandy beach, while the lake itself holds a hungry population of bass and trout that can be caught right from the shoreline. Least expensive is Lakeside Gardens (1450 North End Rd., 250/537-5773, www.lakesidegardensresort.com, June-Sept., $110-180 s or d), with rustic waterfront cabanas that share baths, and self-contained cottages in a forested lakefront setting.

Along the same stretch of lakeshore, Cedar Beach Resort (1136 North End Rd., 250/537-2205 or 888/537-4366, www.saltspring-accommodations.com, $165-225) has larger cabins, each with a full kitchen and up to two bedrooms. For me, the allure of the lodging at Maple Ridge Cottages (301 Tripp Rd., 250/537-5977, www.mapleridgecottages.com, $150-250 s or d) is the location on St. Mary Lake, but the rustic charm of the wooden cottages brings families back year after year. Relax on the deck while your catch of the day cooks on the barbecue for the full effect. Free use of canoes and kayaks is a popular bonus.

My pick for lodging on the island is ★ Spindrift Oceanfront Cottages (255 Welbury Point Rd., southeast of Ganges, 250/537-5311, www.spindriftsaltspringisland.com, Apr.-Oct., $175-295 s or d). The six cottages are spread around a private peninsula lightly forested with arbutus and fir trees. Trails lead to two sandy beaches and to a grassed area at the very tip of the peninsula.

The cottages themselves each have a kitchen, a wood-burning fireplace, and a deck with water views.

Mineral Springs Resort (1460 North Beach Rd., 250/537-4111 or 800/665-0039, www.mineralspringsresort.ca, $220-270 s or d) commands lots of attention for its spa services, but the accommodations are also noteworthy. Each spacious unit features lots of polished wood topping out in a vaulted ceiling, a modern kitchen, a fireplace, and a two-person spa tub filled with mineral water. Guests have use of rowboats, mountain bikes, a game room, and a barbecue area. During summer, there may be a five-night booking minimum.

Camping

The campground in Ruckle Provincial Park (mid-March-Oct., $20) conceals 78 sites in a forest of Douglas firs overlooking Swanson Channel. The camping area is a short walk from the parking lot, making this place unsuitable for RVs. Ensure a site by making reservations through BC Parks (519/858-6161 or 800/689-9025, https://camping.bcparks.ca). With more facilities and within walking distance of downtown Ganges is Garden Faire Campground (305 Rainbow Rd., 250/537-4346, www.gardenfaire.ca, tents $30, hookups $40), set in an old-growth forest. Facilities are limited, but it's 10 minutes of easy walking through Mouat Park to town.

Information and Services

Salt Spring Island Visitor Centre (121 Lower Ganges Rd., 250/537-5252, www.saltspringtourism.com, 9am-5pm daily summer, 11am-2pm daily fall-spring) is in downtown Ganges, on the main road above the marina. Head to Salt Spring Books (104 McPhillips Ave., 250/537-2812, 10am-4pm Mon.-Sat.) to pick up some holiday reading, puzzles, games, maps or nautical charts.

Getting There

Salt Spring has two ferry terminals with year-round service to two points on Vancouver Island operated by BC Ferries (250/386-3431, www.bcferries.com). If you're traveling up from Victoria, the Swartz Bay terminal is the most convenient departure point, with 10 to 12 departures daily for Fulford Harbour, a 20-minute drive south of Ganges. Sailings are even more frequent on the 20-minute run between Crofton, near the Vancouver Island town of Duncan, and Vesuvius Bay, at the island's north end. The round-trip fare on either of these routes is adults $11.65, children $5.85, vehicles $36.40, and you can depart from a different terminal than your arrival at no extra cost. Interisland ferries (adults $5.85, children $2.90, vehicles $12.50 one-way) depart from a third terminal, at Long Harbour, east of Ganges. From the mainland, daily sailings depart the Tsawwassen terminal (south of downtown Vancouver) bound for Long Harbour (adults $18.10, children $9.05, vehicles $68.55 one-way).

THE PENDERS

It's just a short hop by ferry from Salt Spring Island to Otter Bay on North Pender Island. Originally, North and South Pender Islands were joined, but in 1903, a canal was dredged between the two as a shipping channel. Today, a rickety wooden bridge forms the link. Between them, the two islands are home to around 2,000 people, most of whom live on North Pender.

Sights and Recreation

The island has dozens of little beaches to explore, with public roads providing ocean access at more than 20 points. One of the nicest spots is Hamilton Beach on Browning Harbour, south of the ferry terminal.

One of the Southern Gulf Islands' historic homes open to the public is the 1908 Roe House (2408 South Otter Bay Rd., 250/629-6935, 10am-4pm Sat.-Sun., donation), which operates as Pender Island Museum. Originally a simple farmhouse, the property operated as a farm-stay resort for many years, but was integrated with Gulf Islands National Park upon the park's creation in 2003. The local historical society has done an admirable job of restoring the home, which is now filled with artifacts collected from around the island. To get there from the ferry terminal, follow Otter Bay Road around Roe Inlet.

Cross the bridge to South Pender Island and look for the trailhead to **Mount Norman** along Canal Road. For hikers, this is the island's most strenuous outing. The trail leads to a 244-meter (800-foot) summit along a 1.6-kilometer (1-mile) trail. From the summit viewpoint, the panorama extends south to the Saanich Peninsula.

Food

The commercial hub of the Penders is the **Driftwood Centre,** a city-like shopping mall overlooking cleared pastureland south of the ferry terminal. In addition to gas, groceries, booze, and a bank, there are several eateries, including a super-busy **Vanilla Leaf Bakery Cafe** (4605 Bedwell Harbour Rd., 250/629-6453, 7:30am-4:30pm daily, lunch $7-10), which has excellent coffee and oversize cinnamon buns.

Northwest of Hope Bay, **Southridge Country Store** (3327 Port Washington Rd., 250/629-2051, 10am-3pm Mon.-Sat.) is stocked with seasonal produce, perfect for taking back to your island lodging. Eggs, fruit and vegetables, and organic beef are all sourced from island farms. Within the store is a small café pouring great coffee and offering a range of simple bakery items.

Accommodations and Camping

The least expensive way to enjoy an overnight stay on North Pender Island is to camp at **Prior Centennial Campground** (mid-May-mid-Oct., $18), a unit of Gulf Islands National Park. The 17 campsites have no showers or hookups, but the location among ferns and towering cedar trees is excellent. To be assured of a site, make reservations through the National Reservation Service (877/737-3783, www.reservation.pc.gc.ca) for a small additional fee. The campground is 6

kilometers (3.7 miles) south of the ferry terminal off Canal Road.

South Pender Island's most unique lodging is **Woods on Pender** (4709 Canal Rd., 250/629-3353, www.woodsonpender.com, $110-355 s or d). The regular motel rooms ($110-145 s or d) and cabins ($260) are good value, but the drawcard is the converted Airstream trailers. Each of the 10 units has been completely revamped, sleeping up to six people, and some even having their own hot tub and barbeque. Also on site is a coffee bar and restaurant, both offering local fare in a relaxing setting.

Also on the south island, **Poet's Cove Resort** (9801 Spalding Rd., 250/629-2100 or 888/512-7638, www.poetscove.com, $330-650 s or d) is one of the largest resort complexes in the Southern Gulf Islands. Overlooking a protected cove, it boasts a large freeform outdoor pool, a marina, canoe and kayak rentals, bike rentals, and spa services. Guest rooms come in three configurations—lodge rooms, cottages, and villas—with all units featuring comfortable furnishings and an abundance of natural materials throughout. Dining options include two restaurants and a waterfront café.

Information

Pender Island Visitor Centre (4605 Bedwell Harbour Dr., 250/629-3665, www.penderislandchamber.com, 9am-6pm daily summer) is in the Driftwood Centre.

Getting There

BC Ferries (250/386-3431, www.bcferries.com) has up to eight sailings 6:30am-9:30pm daily between Swartz Bay and Pender Island (nonstop, 40 minutes, adults $11.65, children $5.85, vehicles $36.40 round-trip). Interisland sailings (adults $5.85, children $2.90, vehicles $12.50 per sector) are equally regular. From Tsawwassen, there is just a single direct sailing (adults $18.10, children $9.05, vehicles $68.55 one-way) each week, on Friday evening, with all other trips making at least one stop.

MAYNE ISLAND

Separated from North Pender and Galiano Islands by narrow channels, Mayne Island is just 21 square kilometers (8 square miles) in area. Its year-round population of around 1,000 triples in summer, but the island never really seems crowded. Ferries dock at village-less Village Bay. All commercial facilities are at nearby Miners Bay, which got its name during the Cariboo gold rush, when miners used the island as a stopping point. From the ferry terminal, narrow roads meander to all corners of the island, including to Georgina Point Lighthouse, which was staffed between 1885 and 1997. Island beaches are limited to those at Oyster Bay, but visitors can enjoy interesting shoreline walks or take the winding road to the low summit of Mount Park for panoramic views. For something a little different, wander through Dinner Bay Park, where a small Japanese garden takes pride of place.

The best island kayaking originates from the sandy beach in Bennett Bay, which is within Gulf Islands National Park. This is the main departure point for tours led by Kayaking Gulf Islands (250/539-0864, www.kayakinggulfislands.com), with a three-hour paddling tour ($66) of this unit of Gulf Islands National Park. This same company has kayak and paddleboard rentals.

Food

Head to the Sunny Mayne Bakery Café (472 Village Bay Rd., 250/539-2323, 7am-3pm daily, lunch $8-12), less than one kilometer (0.6 mile) east of the ferry terminal, for freshly baked breads, homemade soups, picnic hampers, sumptuous cakes and pastries, healthy sandwiches, ice cream, and the island's best coffee concoctions.

For something a little more substantial, continue across the island to Bennett Bay Bistro (494 Arbutus Dr., 250/539-3122, noon-8pm daily, $12-19), with lots of outdoor seating on a tiled patio overlooking Bennett Bay. The menu is dominated by fresh, simple choices, none better than the $18 wild sockeye salmon burger. If you're staying at Blue Vista Resort, you're within easy walking distance of this restaurant. No-frills short-order grills are the draw at the old Springwater Lodge (400 Fern Hill Rd., 8am-8pm daily in summer, $9-18).

Accommodations

On the east side of the island, across the road from protected Bennett Bay, the emphasis at Blue Vista Resort (563 Arbutus Dr., 250/539-2463 or 877/535-2424, https://bluevistaresort.com, $175-215 s or d) is on outdoor recreation, with hosts eager to share their love of the island with you by filling your day with activity ideas. Rooms and cabins are furnished practically, with separate bedrooms, cooking facilities, and decks surrounded by native forest.

Camping at Mayne Island Eco Camping (359 Maple Dr., Miners Bay, 250/539-2667, www.mayneislandcamping.com, adults $25, children $15) is in a beautiful waterfront setting, designed for tents only. Spread around the back of a short beach, some walk-in sites are right on the water, whereas others are dotted throughout the forest. Facilities include outhouses, a hot water-fed "tree" shower, and kayak rentals. Part of the same property is the two-bedroom Seal Beach Cottage ($350).

Information

The Mayne Island website (www.mayneisland.com) is loaded with useful information, including links to current weather conditions, accommodations, services, and, for those who fall in love with island living, real estate agents.

Getting There

BC Ferries (250/386-3431, www.bcferries.com) has four nonstop 50-minute sailings daily between Swartz Bay and Mayne Island's Village Bay terminal (adults $11.65, children $5.85, vehicles $36.40 round-trip). Other sailings go via Pender Island, while the longest (two hours) detour out to Saturna Island. Two or three ferries each day link Tsawwassen with Mayne (adults $18.10, children $9.05, vehicles $68.55, round-trip), although most stop at Galiano Island en route. A regular stream of ferries arrive and depart from the other Southern Gulf Islands (adults $5.85, children $2.90, vehicles $12.50 per sector).

★ GALIANO ISLAND

Named for a Spanish explorer who sailed through the Strait of Georgia more than 200 years ago, this long, narrow island—27 kilometers (17 miles) from north to south but only a few kilometers wide—has some delightful beaches and good kayaking. Most of the 1,000 residents live in the south, within a five-minute drive of the ferry terminal at **Sturdies Bay.** While Montague Harbour Provincial Park gets most of the attention from visitors, the island is dotted with many less obvious ocean access points, several of which aren't even signposted. The beach below Active Pass Road is typical; look for the utility pole numbered 1038 and make your way down the steep trail to a protected cove. Ask at the information center or at your lodging for a full listing of similar spots.

Also worth visiting is **Bodega Ridge Provincial Park,** on the road to the island's northern tip. This park protects a high ridge that is home to rare peregrine falcons (a walking trail traverses the ridge top) and a string of intriguing sandstone cliffs accessible only by those kayaking or boating.

Montague Harbour Provincial Park

Climbing out of Sturdies Bay, roads tempt exploration in all directions. Take Porlier Pass Road to reach Montague Harbour Provincial Park, which protects an 89-hectare (210-acre) chunk of coastal forest and a beach of bleached-white broken seashells. You can walk out along the beach and return via a forested trail in around 20 minutes. At the end of the beach are middens, piles of empty shells that accumulated over centuries of indigenous people's feasts.

Kayaking

The best way to explore local waterways is with **Gulf Island Kayaking** (250/539-2442, seakayak.ca), based at the marina in Montague Harbour. Three-hour guided tours ($55) leave either early in the morning or at sunset. Another tour takes in the local marinelife on a five-hour paddle ($85). Those with previous experience can rent a kayak ($58 single, $90 double per day). The expert tour guides offer dockside instruction, in addition to information about the local wildlife and ecosystem. Keep an eye out for eagles, herons, seals, and river otters, as well as sea creatures—maybe even whales! A family-friendly company, Gulf Island Kayaking offers 50% off for kids ages 5-12.

Golfing

Galiano Golf Course (24 St. Andrews Cres., 250/539-5533) is typical of the many courses on the Southern Gulf Islands, with nine holes open year-round, inexpensive greens fees ($25), a relaxed atmosphere, and a summer-only clubhouse offering rentals and basic meals.

Food

To immerse yourself in the beauty of the island over a meal, plan on dining at **Crane and Robin** (3451 Montague Rd., 250/539-3334, noon-9pm daily mid-May-mid-Sept., $12-18). Housed in a waterfront building beside Montague Harbour, the most sought-after tables are out on the west-facing deck—the perfect place to enjoy a summer sunset. The menu takes full advantage of island produce and local seafood, and includes simple dishes such as smoked salmon chowder, a curried cauliflower sandwich, and salmon tacos.

While you're waiting for a ferry—or even if you're not—line up at the **Max & Moritz** food wagon (250/539-5888, Apr.-Oct., $8-16), in front of the parking lot at the ferry terminal, for a combination of German and Indonesian dishes, such as *nasi goreng* and bratwurst, and

gelato. Hours vary depending on ferry arrivals and departures, so call ahead if you're making the trip specially.

The stellar food is reason enough to dine at the **Galiano Oceanfront Inn** (134 Madrona Dr., 250/539-3388, 8:30am-10am, noon-3pm, and 6pm-8:30pm daily June-Sept., 6pm-9pm Wed.-Sun. Oct.-May, $25-42), but the unobstructed water views cost no extra. Although the upscale dining room has a touch of Old World elegance, the cooking is healthy and modern, with a seasonal menu that uses fresh island produce and local seafood. Professional service and an impressive wine list round out what many regard as the finest restaurant on the Southern Gulf Islands. In summer, a sunken patio buzzes with activity as locals and visitors from outlying islands enjoy lunchtime treats, such as pizza cooked in an outdoor wood-fired oven in a cultured garden setting.

Accommodations and Camping

Many of the travelers you'll meet on the ferry to Galiano will be staying for a week or more in an island cottage. If this style of vacation sounds ideal to you, check www.galianoisland.com for a choice of rentals, but do so well before planning your visit, because the best ones fill fast. **Paradise Rock Oceanfront Cottage** (310 Ganner Dr., 250/539-3404, www.paradiserockoceanfront.com, $200 s or d) is typical in all respects—water views from a private setting, self-contained, and with a deck holding a propane barbecue—except that it can be rented for as few as two nights in the off-season (four-night minimum in summer).

You'll see the magnificent gardens of the ★ **Galiano Oceanfront Inn** (134 Madrona Dr., 250/539-3388 or 877/530-3939, www.galianoinn.com, $300-420 s or d), at the head of Sturdies Bay, before the ferry docks. The elegant guest rooms infused with European charm come in three configurations, and all have views extending down the bay to Mayne

Island. Other highlights include private balconies, very comfortable beds, plush robes, and luxury baths with soaker tubs. The inn is also home to the **Madrona del Mar Spa,** the place to get pampered with a soothing hot stone massage or to kick back in the seaside hot tub.

The campground in **Montague Harbour Provincial Park** (reservations 519/858-6161 or 800/689-9025, https://camping.bcparks.ca, mid-Mar.-Oct., $25), 10 kilometers (6 miles) from the ferry, is one of the best in the Southern Gulf Islands. Sites are set below a towering forest of old-growth cedar and fir trees and open to a white shingle beach that aligns perfectly to watch the setting sun. As with most provincial park campgrounds, facilities are limited to picnic tables, pit toilets, and drinking water.

Information

Up the hill from the ferry terminal is the **Galiano Island Tourist Booth** (250/539-2233, www.galianoisland.com, 9am-5pm daily July-Aug.). The Southern Gulf Islands have a surprising number of bookstores, and none are better than **Galiano Island Books** (76 Madrona Dr., 250/539-3340, 10am-4:30pm daily), down the first left after exiting the dock area. Stop by for works by island writers, as well as Canadiana, children's titles, and some great cookbooks that use local ingredients.

Getting There

Read the schedule carefully before planning your trip between Galiano Island and Swartz Bay, as many sailings make two stops en route, and some require a transfer at Mayne Island. Regardless of the number of stops, the fare between Swartz Bay and Galiano is adults $11.65, children $5.85, vehicles $36.40 round-trip. Ferries arrive and depart from the other Southern Gulf Islands throughout the day, with services to Mayne Island (adults $5.85, children $2.90, vehicles $12.50, per sector) all nonstop. Two or three ferries each day link Tsawwassen with Galiano, two of which are nonstop (adults $18.10, children $9.05,

1: Tree House Café **2:** Montague Harbour Provincial Park **3:** Saturna Island sunset

vehicles $68.55 one-way). As with service to the other Southern Gulf Islands, all ferries are operated by **BC Ferries** (250/386-3431, www.bcferries.com).

If there's one island where you don't take your vehicle, make it Galiano. The ferry docks in the south at Sturdies Bay, which is within walking distance of most accommodations, the island's premier dining spot, and the local bookstore. Or you can rent an ebike, a moped, or small boat from **Galiano Adventures** (3451 Montague Park Rd., 250/539-3443, www.galianoadventures.com).

TOP EXPERIENCE

★ SATURNA ISLAND

Most remote of the ferry-accessible Southern Gulf Islands, 31-square-kilometer (12-square-mile) Saturna protrudes into the heart of the Strait of Georgia and features a long rugged northern coastline and around half its land area within **Gulf Islands National Park.** Although First Nations people visited the island seasonally, the first permanent settlers didn't arrive until the 1850s, and it was as recently as the 1970s that the island was linked to the outside world by a scheduled ferry service. The island's name comes from the *Saturnina,* a Spanish ship that passed by the island in the 1790s. Today, Saturna, with a year-round population of just 350, offers a couple of lodging and dining choices, but there are no banks, doctors, or pharmacies, and ferries only stop by a few times a day.

Sights

From the ferry dock at **Lyall Harbour,** two roads head southeast for around 14 kilometers (9 miles). East Point Road hugs the northern coastline, offering views across to Tumbo Island before ending at **East Point.** Here you can go swimming or simply admire the sweeping views across the border to the San Juans. Narvaez Bay Road parallels East Point Road, ending at its namesake **Narvaez Bay,** which is protected by Gulf Islands National Park.

Hiking

From Naravez Bay, a 1.7-kilometer (1-mile) trail heads west to an exposed headland surrounded by the calm blue waters of the Strait of Georgia. An alternate trail from this parking lot climbs along an old logging road to a viewpoint where the San Juan Islands are clearly visible across Boundary Pass; allow 40 minutes for this 2.5-kilometer (1.6-mile) loop.

The northern end of the island around peaceful **Winter Cove** is protected by another small unit of **Gulf Islands National Park.** Here, a 1.6-kilometer (1-mile) walking trail winds through a forest of Douglas fir before looping back beside a coastal salt marsh and along the shoreline.

Food

On the right as you arrive on the island and leave the ferry dock, **Vibrational Café** (100 East Point Rd., 604/725-8897, 10am-5pm daily May-Oct., lunch $7.50-12) offers locally roasted coffee, island-grown loose-leaf teas, and the smoothies blended to order. Food includes a delightful choice of soups, sandwiches, and pastries.

Below the café, **Saturna Lighthouse Pub** (100 East Point Rd., 250/539-5725, noon-10pm daily in summer, closed Mon.-Tues. the rest of the year, $19-24) has a fantastic deck with sweeping water views. The food, well-priced and delicious, includes choices such as a cod burger and halibut-and-chips, as well as shepherd's pie made with lamb, which, traditionally, it should be (but rarely is in North America). Live music is offered most summer Saturday nights.

Off East Point Road, at **Saturna Café** (101 Narvaez Bay Rd., 250/539-5177, 9am-6pm Sun.-Thurs., 9am-9pm Fri.-Sat., lunch $8-13.50), you can expect simple home-style cooking, casual ambience, and friendly service. In the same building, **Saturna General Store** (101 Narvaez Bay Rd., 250/539-2936, 9am-5pm daily) has a good supply of fresh groceries, including lots of island produce.

Accommodations and Camping

Overlooking Boot Cove and also within walking distance of the dock is **Saturna Lodge** (130 Payne Rd., 250/539-2254 or 866/539-2254, www.saturna.ca, May.-Oct., $159-199 s or d, includes breakfast). Right on the water, this modern lodging offers six guest rooms, a hot tub, a lounge with a fireplace, and extensive gardens.

Saturna has no vehicle-accessible campgrounds. **Arbutus Point Campground** (100 East Point Rd., 250/539-5725, www.saturna-pub.com, $40) has a few tent-only sites within walking distance of the ferry dock. With bike and kayak rentals available nearby, staying at this campground means you can leave your vehicle on the mainland. The only other campsites are accessible along the 1.7-kilometer (1-mile) walking trail out to **Narvaez Bay.** Here, within Gulf Islands National Park, is a small campground (877/737-3783, www.reservation.pc.gc.ca, mid-May.-Sept., $6 pp) beside Little Bay.

Information and Services

The best source of pre-trip planning information is the website www.saturnatourism.com, and although there is no official visitors center on the island, any of the 300 full-time residents should be able to help you out.

Getting There

BC Ferries (250/386-3431, www.bcferries.com) has a direct evening sailing between Saturna Island and Swartz Bay ($11.65, children $5.85, vehicles $36.40 round-trip), but the three or four other daily sailings are routed through Mayne Island. The 40-minute trip between Mayne Island and Saturna is a nonstop service running three times daily. Regardless of whether Mayne or one of the other Southern Gulf Islands (connect through Mayne) is your final destination, the fare (adults $5.85, children $2.90, vehicles $12.50 one-way) is the same.

Highway 14 to the West Coast

From the western outskirts of Victoria, Highway 14 passes through a mix of rural and forested landscapes before emerging at the town of Sooke, renowned as home to one of Canada's finest lodges and restaurants. This is where the spectacular scenery really begins: for 72 kilometers (45 miles), Highway 14 parallels Juan De Fuca Strait all the way to Port Renfrew, starting point of the famous West Coast Trail. The total distance between downtown Victoria and Port Renfrew is 104 kilometers (65 miles), but you should allow at least 90 minutes, as the road is winding and narrow.

SOOKE

About 34 kilometers (21 miles) from Victoria, Sooke (with a silent "e") is a forestry, fishing, and farming center serving a surrounding population of 13,000. The town is best known for a lodge that combines luxurious accommodations with one of Canada's most renowned restaurants, but a couple of other diversions are worth investigating as well.

Sights and Recreation

The town spreads along the shore of Canada's southernmost Pacific harbor. The safe haven for boats is created by **Whiffen Spit,** a naturally occurring sandbar that extends for over one kilometer (0.6 mile). Take Whiffen Spit Road (through town to the west) to reach the spit. It's a 20-minute walk to the end, and along the way you may spot seals and sea otters on the shoreline.

Another natural attraction is the **Sooke potholes,** a series of intriguing geological features found alongside the Sooke River.

To get here, turn north off Sooke Road onto Sooke River Road on the east (Victoria) side of the Sooke River.

Sooke Region Museum (2070 Phillips Rd., 250/642-6351, 9:30am-5pm Tues.-Sat., donation) is on the west side of Sooke River Bridge. When you've finished admiring the historical artifacts, relax on the grassy area in front or wander around the back to count all 478 growth rings on the cross-section of a giant spruce tree. The museum is also home to **Sooke Visitor Centre.**

Across the harbor is **East Sooke Regional Park,** protecting 1,422 hectares (3,512 acres) of coastal forest and rocky shoreline. It holds around 50 kilometers (30 miles) of trails leading along sea cliffs to the open meadows of an abandoned apple orchard and to lofty lookouts. Pick up a map from the visitors center to help find your way around the park. The main access is Gillespie Road, which branches south off Highway 14 on the east side of Sooke. One kilometer (0.6 mile) down Gillespie Road is a pullout on the left. Park here to access the Galloping Goose Trail. Linking downtown Victoria and Sooke, this stretch is a pleasant walk or bike through old-growth forest, with a spur to the left leading to a lookout above Roche Cove.

Food

The best place for a coffee in Sooke is **Stick in the Mud** (6715 Eustace Rd., 250/642-5635, 7:30am-3:30pm Mon.-Sat., $7.50-11), a bright and welcoming space where the coffee beans are roasted in-house and all the baked goods and sandwiches are prepared daily. For a simple, old-fashioned diner-style meal, head to **Mom's Café** (2036 Shields Rd., 250/642-3314, 8am-7pm daily, $12-16), where breakfasts are all hearty, and the rest of the day, halibut-and-fries is $19. Turn right onto Shields Road one block west of the Petro Canada gas station.

17 Mile House Pub (5126 Sooke Rd., 250/642-5942, 11am-9pm daily, $16-25) is a charming relic from the past. It dates from an era when travelers heading to Sooke would stop for a meal 17 miles from Victoria's City Hall. The walls of this 1894 building are decorated in a century's worth of memorabilia, and there's still a hitching post out back. The menu is typical pub fare, although one thing that definitely wasn't on the menu 100 years ago is a delicious chicken curry.

Accommodations

★ **Sooke Harbour House** (1528 Whiffen Spit Rd., 250/642-3421 or 800/889-9688, www.sookeharbourhouse.com, $329-559 s or d) combines the elegance of an upscale country-style inn with the atmosphere of an exclusive oceanfront resort. The restaurant attracts discerning diners from around the world, but the accommodations offered are equally impressive. The sprawling waterfront property sits on a bluff, with 28 guest rooms spread throughout immaculately manicured gardens. Each of the rooms reflects a different aspect of life on the West Coast, and all have stunning views, a wood-burning fireplace, and a deck or patio. Off-season, rates are reduced up to 40 percent.

SOOKE TO PORT RENFREW

The road west from Sooke takes you past gray pebbly beaches scattered with shells and driftwood, past **Gordon's Beach** to **French Beach,** about 20 kilometers (12 miles) from Sooke. Here you can wander down through a lush forest of Douglas fir and Sitka spruce to watch Pacific breakers crashing up on the beach—and keep an eye open for whales and eagles. It's a great place for a windswept walk, a picnic, or camping (with pit toilets, $18). An information board at the park entrance posts detailed maps and articles on area beaches, points of interest, plants, and wildlife.

Continuing west, the highway winds up and down forested hills for another 12 kilometers (7.5 miles) or so, passing evidence of regular logging as well as signposted forest trails to sandy beaches. Along this stretch of coast are

1: East Sooke Regional Park **2:** hiking path to Sandcut Beach **3:** Sooke Region Museum **4:** Sombrio Beach

two great accommodations. The first, located three kilometers (two miles) beyond French Beach, is **Point No Point Resort** (10829 West Coast Rd., 250/646-2020, www.point-nopointresort.com, $305-400 s or d), which features 28 cabins, each with ocean views, a full kitchen, and a fireplace. Explore the shore out front, relax on the nearby beach, or scan the horizon for migrating whales, with the Olympic Mountains as a backdrop. The in-house restaurant serves lunch daily and dinner (mains $29-42) Wednesday-Sunday.

Two kilometers (1.2 miles) farther west, high upon oceanfront cliffs, **Fossil Bay Resort** (11033 West Coast Rd., 250/646-2073, www.fossilbay.com, 2-night minimum weekends, $279 s or d) offers modern cottages, each with a hot tub, a private balcony with ocean views, a wood-burning fireplace, a king bed, a full kitchen, and Wi-Fi.

★ Sandcut Beach

Officially within Jordan River Regional Park, this scenic highlight was little known except to local residents until the creation of a park in 2010 (there was no signage along the highway, nor an official access trail). Today, a 10-minute walk through an old-growth forest leads to the beach. The highlight is an oceanfront **waterfall,** which is to the east (left) as you emerge at the beach. In any other location, the cascade would be of little consequence, but tumbling over a sandstone cliff with the ocean and Olympic Mountains as a backdrop makes this spot a photographer's dream (late afternoon has the best light).

Jordan River

When you emerge at the small settlement of Jordan River, take time to take in the smells of the ocean and the surrounding windswept landscape. The town comprises only a few houses, a logging operation, and **Jordan River Regional Park.** The park lies on a point at the mouth of the Jordan River. It's not the best campground ($15, cash only) you'll come across, but some sites are right on the ocean, while others are scattered along the river mouth and in the open forest for more protection from the elements; surfers often spend the night here, waiting for the swells to rise and the long right-hand waves known as Jordans to crank up.

★ Juan de Fuca Provincial Park

Established in 1996, this 1,528-hectare (3,776-acre) park protects a narrow swath of Pacific coastline between China Beach, three kilometers (two miles) west of Jordan River in the east, and Botanical Beach near Port Renfrew in the west. From Highway 14, there are four main access points, as well as the Juan de Fuca Marine Trail, which parallels the coast for the entire length of the park.

At the east side of the park, a 700-meter (0.4-mile) one-way trail leads down through towering Sitka spruce to **China Beach,** which is strewn with driftwood and backed by a couple of protected picnic sites. Between the driftwood and the ocean is a long stretch of sand that at low tide is also very wide. Vehicle-accessible camping ($20) is available back up by the highway. A few sites are first-come, first-served, but to ensure a spot, make reservations through **BC Parks** (519/858-6161 or 800/689-9025, https://camping.bcparks.ca).

Continuing west, parking areas at Sombrio Beach and Parkinson Creek are trailheads for beach access, with the former a popular surfing spot and also home to an interesting moss-filled canyon. The fourth and westernmost access point is Botanical Beach.

HIKING

While the West Coast Trail gets most of attention from serious hikers, the 47-kilometer (29-mile) **Juan de Fuca Marine Trail** is more accessible for the average hiker, easier, and does not have the high cost associated with its more famous neighbor. The forest and ocean scenery is arguably equal to the West Coast Trail, although there are fewer long stretches of sand, and due to the accessibility, there is not the same solitude.

Stretching from China Beach (just west of Jordan River) in the east to Port Renfrew in the west, the trail can be completed in three days, but with two additional access points (Sombrio Beach and Parkinson Beach), it's possible to enjoy sections of the trail as a day hike. One of the busiest sections of the trail is at the Port Renfrew end, where you can hike from Botanical Beach for a short distance to get a feeling for the coastal wilderness.

Along the trail are six wilderness campgrounds (no reservations, $10 pp), four of which are simply designated areas along the back of driftwood-strewn beaches. **West Coast Trail Express** (250/477-8700, www.trailbus.com) picks up and drops off along the route, so, for example, you could park at China Beach, hike to Port Renfrew, and then jump aboard the daily service to return to your vehicle ($30 pp).

PORT RENFREW

This small seaside community clings to the rugged shoreline of Port San Juan, 104 kilometers (65 miles) west of Victoria along Highway 14. Best known as the starting point of the West Coast Trail, the town attracts both anglers and hikers, with tourist facilities for both.

Botanical Beach

Follow the signs through town to Botanical Beach, the town's main "official" sight. At this fascinating intertidal pool area, low tide exposes hundreds of species of marine creatures at the foot of scoured-out sandstone cliffs. The 2.7-kilometer (1.8-mile) loop trail from the end of the road passes the beach, as well as Botany Bay, which is more of a rocky outlook than a beach. This is also the official end of the Juan de Fuca Marine Trail, a wilderness hiking trail extending back along the coast to China Beach.

Food

Always busy, and in a delightful treed setting near the entrance to town, is **Coastal Kitchen Café** (17245 Parkinson Rd., 250/647-5541, 8am-5pm daily, lunch $12-26). Coffee, boutique teas, and baked goods are all delicious, with lunches such as steamed clams and halibut-and-chips showcasing local seafood. A casual island ambience and lots of outdoor seating adds to the appeal.

Accommodations and Camping

Accommodations are available at the **Trailhead Resort** (17268 Parkinson Rd., 250/647-5468, www.trailhead-resort.com). Its suite rooms are relatively new, and basic but practical, with a kitchen ($199 s or d), or choose to stay in the Hiker's Huts that share baths ($95 s or d), or fully self-contained two-bedroom cabins ($329).

Drive down to the waterfront to reach the local dock, which is where you'll find a variety of lodging options operated by **Wild Renfrew** (17310 Parkinson Rd., 250/647-5541, www.wildrenfrew.com). Options include large motel rooms, some with kitchenettes, in the West Coast Trail Lodge ($139-159 s or d); out on the dock itself are Wharfside Studios, each with a king bed and kitchenette (from $229 s or d), while nearby are the 11 oceanfront Seaside Cottages, some with private fire pits ($329-399). My pick, though, is the spacious Seaside Luxury Tent ($399), which comes with a private cedar sauna, a funky outdoor shower fashioned from an aluminum rowboat, and ocean views.

Beyond town and within walking distance of the West Coast Trail office and ferry to the trailhead is **Pacheedaht Campground** (305 Pachidah Rd., 250/647-0090, May.-Oct., $30), which has limited facilities but does have access to a sandy beach. Also at the mouth of the San Juan River, **Port Renfrew Marina and RV Park** (250/483-1878, www.portrenfrewmarina.com, no reservations, May.-Oct., $25-35, cash only) has unserviced campsites and no showers. This place is primarily a marina complex, with boat charters and fishing gear for sale.

SAN JUAN VALLEY

If you don't want to return to Victoria along Highway 14, and you're eventually heading north up the island, consider traveling across the San Juan Valley 53 kilometers (33 miles) to Lake Junction and Lake Cowichan. The valley is forested with massive Douglas firs up to 800 years old. Be aware that this is an active logging area—logging trucks don't give way, *you* do. Make sure you have enough gas, and drive with your headlights on so the trucks see you from a good distance. You'll find rustic campgrounds (no hookups) at **Fairy Lake**, six kilometers (four miles) from Port Renfrew, and **Lizard Lake,** 12 kilometers (7.5 miles) farther along the road. Lizard Lake is best suited for small tents, and both have excellent fishing.

TOP EXPERIENCE

★ WEST COAST TRAIL

The magnificent West Coast Trail meanders 75 kilometers (47 miles) along Vancouver Island's untamed western shoreline, through the West Coast Trail unit of **Pacific Rim National Park.** It's one of the world's great hikes, exhilaratingly challenging, incredibly beautiful, and very satisfying—many hikers come back to do it again. The quickest hikers can complete the trail in four days, but by allowing six or seven days, you'll have time to fully enjoy the adventure. The trail extends from the mouth of the Gordon River, five kilometers (three miles) north of Port Renfrew to Pachena Bay, near the remote fishing village of Bamfield on Barkley Sound. Along the way you'll wander along beaches, steep cliff tops, and slippery banks; ford rivers by rope, suspension bridge, or ferry; climb down sandstone cliffs by ladder; cross slippery boardwalks, muddy slopes, bogs, and deep gullies; and balance on fallen logs. But for all your efforts, you're rewarded with panoramic views of sand and sea, dense lush rainforest of hemlock and cedar, waterfalls cascading into deep pools, all kinds of wildlife—gray whales, eagles, sea lions, seals, and seabirds—and the constant roar and hiss of the Pacific surf pummeling the sand.

Planning Your Hike

The first step in planning to hike the West Coast Trail is to do some research at the Parks Canada website (www.pc.gc.ca/pacificrim). The invaluable information covers everything you need to know, including an overview of what to expect, instructions on paying trail-user fees, a list of equipment you should take, a list of relevant literature, tide tables, and advertisements for companies offering trailhead transportation.

Permits

The West Coast Trail is open May through September, and it cannot be hiked without a reservation. Check online with the Parks Canada National Reservation Service (519/826-5391 or 877/737-3783, www.reservation.pc.gc.ca) to find out the exact date that reservations open (varies between January and April each year). On the day that reservations open, be prepared with information such as your proposed starting point, alternate dates, and information about members of your party. The trail-use permit is $136 pp, and the nonrefundable reservation fee is $25.75 pp. Once at Port Renfrew or Bamfield, all hikers must head for the registration office to pick up their trail-use permit, pay for the two ferry crossings (each $22 pp, cash only), and attend a 90-minute orientation session (10am and 2pm daily). The 2pm session is for those who want to head out on the trail early the following morning.

Hiking Conditions

The trail can be hiked in either direction. The first two days out from Port Renfrew traverse the most difficult terrain, meaning more enjoyable hiking for the remaining days. The first two days out from Pachena Bay are relatively easy, meaning a lighter pack for the more difficult section.

1: Juan de Fuca Provincial Park 2: Port Renfrew Marina

Hikers must be totally self-sufficient, because no facilities exist along the route. Go with at least one other person, and travel as light as possible. Wear comfortable hiking boots, and take a stove, at least 15 meters (50 feet) of strong light rope, head-to-toe waterproof gear (keep your spare clothes and sleeping bag in a plastic bag), a small amount of fire starter for an emergency, sunscreen, insect repellent, a first-aid kit (for cuts, burns, sprains, and blisters), and waterproof matches. Rainfall is least likely in the summer; July is generally the driest month, but be prepared for rain, strong winds, thick fog, and muddy trail conditions even then.

River Crossings

Along the trail are two river crossings that are made via ferry. One is at Gordon River outside Port Renfrew. The other, midway along the trail, crosses Nitinat Narrows, the treacherous mouth of tidal Nitinat Lake. Ferries run 9am-5pm daily through the hiking season. The ferry fees (each $22) are collected on behalf of private operators in conjunction with the trail permit. When there is no ferry service (Oct.-Apr.), the West Coast Trail is closed.

Information

West Coast Trail Information Centres are beside the Gordon River, five kilometers (three miles) north of Port Renfrew (Pachidah Rd., 250/647-5434, 9am-4pm daily May-Sept.) and Pachena Bay (250/728-3234, 9am-4pm daily May-Sept.). The cost of a trail-use permit includes a waterproof trail map, or purchase one at the information centers at each end of the trail.

Getting There

Unless you plan on turning around and returning to the beginning of the trail on foot, you'll want to make some transportation arrangements. Getting to and from either end of the trail is made easier by **West Coast Trail Express** (250/477-8700 or 888/999-2288, www. trailbus.com), which departs Victoria daily in the morning to both ends of the trail. The fare between Victoria and Port Renfrew is $66 one-way, while between Victoria and Pachena Bay it's $110. Pickups are made along the way, including from Nanaimo and Port Alberni. Travel between the trailheads costs $90.

Tip: If you leave your vehicle at the Port Renfrew end of the trail and return by bus, you won't have to shuttle a vehicle out to remote Bamfield.

Highway 1 North

From downtown Victoria, the Trans-Canada Highway, also known as Highway 1 or the Island Highway, jogs west and then north around Saanich Inlet, passing through the towns of Duncan, Chemainus, and Ladysmith before reaching the island's second-largest city, Nanaimo. Allow at least 90 minutes for the 112-kilometer (69-mile) trip between Victoria and Nanaimo. If you've been island-hopping through the Southern Gulf Islands, there is no need to backtrack to Victoria. Instead, make your way to Vesuvius Bay on Salt Spring Island and catch the ferry across Stuart Channel to Crofton, a short drive south of Chemainus.

DUNCAN

Duncan, self-proclaimed "City of Totems," lies along the Trans-Canada Highway about 60 kilometers (37 miles) north of Victoria. The small city of 5,000 serves the surrounding farming and forestry communities of the Cowichan Valley. In addition to the regular tourist services, it's worth planning a stop in Duncan to view the many totem poles dotted around downtown. Hockey fans may want to

Duncan

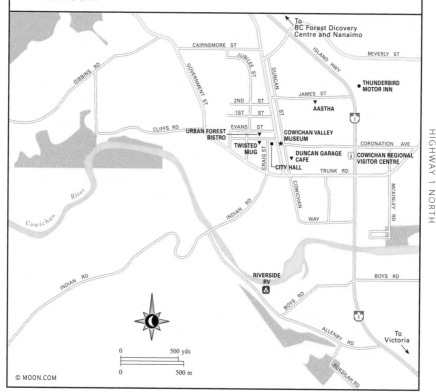

head to the local skating rink (Island Savings Centre, 2687 James St.), between the highway and downtown, home to the world's largest hockey stick and puck.

The historic downtown core lies west of the Trans-Canada Highway, beyond the sprawling malls. Here you'll find the majority of Duncan's 80 totem poles, including 42 that are part of a self-guided walking tour. Two distinctly different carvings stand side by side behind City Hall—a First Nations carving and a New Zealand Maori carving donated by Duncan's sister city in New Zealand, Kaikohe.

Cowichan Valley Museum

The best place to learn about the history of the town, beginning from the days when it was nothing more than a whistle-stop on William Duncan's farm, is the downtown railway station, which now operates as **Cowichan Valley Museum** (130 Canada Ave., 250/746-6612, 10am-4pm daily June-Sept., 11am-4pm Wed.-Fri. and 1pm-4pm Sat. Oct.-May, donation). The railway station is surrounded by pleasing older architecture, such as City Hall on the corner of Kenneth and Craig Streets.

BC Forest Discovery Centre

Another local attraction is the 40-hectare (100-acre) **BC Forest Discovery Centre** (2892 Drinkwater Rd., 250/715-1113, 10am-4pm daily July-Aug., 10am-4pm Thurs.-Mon. Apr.-June and Sept., adults $16, seniors $14, children $11), one kilometer (0.6 mile) north of town. You can catch a ride on an old steam train and puff back in time, through the forest and past a farmstead, a logging camp, and Somenos Lake. Then check out the working sawmill, restored planer mill, blacksmith's shop, and forestry and lumber displays. The main museum building holds modern displays pertaining to the industry, including hands-on and interactive computer displays and an interesting audiovisual exhibit. The grounds are a pleasant place to wander through shady glades of trees (most identified) or over to the pond, where you'll find a gaggle of friendly geese awaiting a tasty morsel.

Food

Always crowded with locals, **Duncan Garage Café & Bakery** (330 Duncan St., 250/748-6223, 7:30am-5pm Mon.-Sat., lunch $8-13) is well worth searching out across from the museum in the historic heart of downtown. Within the same complex is a store specializing in local organic produce, and a used bookstore. In the vicinity, **Twisted Mug** (80 Station St., 250/737-1200, 7:30am-5pm Mon.-Fri., 8:30am-4pm Sat., lunch $8-12) is a spacious café with all the usual hot drinks you'd expect at a big city café, but with a definite small-town vibe.

Thanks to a reader's tip, while researching this edition, our family had a wonderful meal at **Aastha Devotional Indian Restaurant** (2680 James St., 250/597-0995, 11am-9pm Mon.-Fri., noon-9pm Sat.-Sun., $12-19), north of downtown. Each style of curry is explained in simple terms, with the option to "build your own" with different meats and seafood. The kid's menu delves into mild Indian spices, with butter chicken poutine, while dishes from the traditional tandoor oven dominate the main menu.

Accommodations and Camping

Along the highway north of downtown, **Thunderbird Motor Inn** (5849 York Rd., 250/748-8192, www.thunderbirdholiday.com, $121-150 s or d) is a basic roadside motel with older but clean rooms, each with air-conditioning and wireless Internet. A step up in room quality is the **Best Western Cowichan Valley Inn** (6457 Norcross Rd., 250/748-2722, www.bestwestern.com, $194-234 s or d), a modern three-story hotel within walking distance of the Forest Discovery Centre north of downtown. Amenities include an outdoor pool, a fitness room, and a restaurant.

On the south side of the river, continue along Boys Road to **Riverside RV & Camping** (3065 Allenby Rd., 250/746-4352, www.riversidecampingduncan.com, $22-30), which has a mix of 50 shaded and sunny serviced sites and 25 riverside tent sites.

Information

Stop at **Cowichan Regional Visitor Centre** (2896 Drinkwater Rd., 250/746-4636 or 888/303-3337, www.duncancc.bc.ca, 10am-4pm Mon.-Fri.), at Coronation Avenue, for the complete rundown on the area. The staff provides information on local hiking and fishing and on traveling the logging roads beyond Lake Cowichan. They also offer a free map showing the location of all of Duncan's totem poles.

LAKE COWICHAN

Lake Cowichan (population 3,300) is the name of a sprawling town at the east end of Cowichan Lake. (The etymological reason for the reversal in the order of the town's name has been lost to time.) Vancouver Island's second largest lake, Cowichan is a 32-kilometer-long (20-mile) inland waterway known as Kaatza ("Land Warmed by Sun") to local Coast Salish people. Logging roads—mostly unpaved—encircle the lake for 75 kilometers (47 miles) round-trip and provide hikers access to the adjacent wilderness, which includes the legendary **Carmanah Valley** in Carmanah Walbran Provincial Park.

1: Duncan is famous for its totem poles. 2: tubing on the Cowichan River 3: Gordon Bay Provincial Park 4: Duncan Garage Café & Bakery

DUNCAN GARAGE

& BAKERY   ORGANIC MARKETS   BO

★ Tubing

Cowichan Lake is popular for a variety of water sports, but you really need a boat to take full advantage of its extensive waters. Instead, plan on tubing down the Cowichan River—it's a fun, inexpensive activity that everyone can enjoy. The starting point is waterfront Saywell Park beside the visitor center, from where the Cowichan River flows slowly eastward for around one hour of easy float time, passing riverfront homes and stretches of wilderness; things then speed up slightly before reaching the recommended pullout point at Little Beach, 2.5 hours from the starting point. The water is warm throughout summer, although the experience is most enjoyable on hot, sunny days, when all you need is a swimsuit, refreshments, and sunscreen.

Making the experience easy for everyone to enjoy is **The Tube Shack** (250/510-7433, www.cowichanriver.com, 10am-5pm daily summer), right at the put-in point. They charge $20 pp for tube rental and shuttle back from Little Beach to town. Families have the option of renting a larger tube for $60, which includes the shuttle.

Fishing

A major draw for serious anglers, salmon-filled **Cowichan River** has its source at Cowichan Lake, draining into the Strait of Georgia near Duncan. Much of its length is protected by **Cowichan River Provincial Park,** which extends over 750 hectares (1,850 acres) and 20 kilometers (12 miles). There are three access points to the park, including Skutz Falls (second access road), where salmon spawn each fall. Trails are well signposted and link into the Trans-Canada Trail, which follows the river west to Cowichan Lake.

Kaatza Station Museum

If tubing is not your thing, wander through Saywell Park to **Kaatza Station Museum** (125 South Shore Rd., 250/749-6142,

10am-4pm daily summer, 10am-4pm Mon.-Fri. the rest of the year, donation), at the end of a rail line that once linked the lake to the main line along Vancouver Island's east coast. In addition to the railway station, two school rooms are filled with artifacts, while outside, railway rolling stock includes a 1916 caboose.

Food

Jake's at the Lake (109 South Shore Rd., 250/932-2221, 11:30am-8pm Sun.-Thurs., 11:30am-9pm Fri.-Sat., $18-25) is the obvious place for lunch or dinner. Overlooking the Cowichan River right downtown, it has an enticing deck and a menu ranging from mango coconut curry to a salmon burger. Across the river from downtown is **Cow Café** (51 North Shore Rd., 250/749-4933, 11am-8pm Sun.-Thurs., 11am-9pm Fri.-Sat., $16-40), owned and operated by two local couples who have created an interesting menu that includes Millionaire's Meatloaf (with Wagyu beef and prawns) as well as Asian-inspired noodle bowls. The desserts are worth saving space for.

Accommodations and Camping

A few blocks back from the lakefront is **Lake Cowichan Lodge** (201 Cowichan Lake Rd., 250/749-6717, www.lakecowichanlodge.com, $125-200 s or d), a two-story motel with 30 simple but clean and comfortable rooms, some with kitchenettes.

Campers have the choice of staying at the local municipal campground, **Lakeview Park** (8815 Lakeview Park Rd., 250/749-3350, $33-42), three kilometers (two miles) west of Lake Cowichan, or **Gordon Bay Provincial Park** ($35), on the south side of the lake 23 kilometers (14.3 miles) farther west. Both campgrounds have hot showers, with reservations required for the latter (**BC Parks,** 519/858-6161 or 800/689-9025, https://camping.bcparks.ca).

Information

In a log cabin on the waterfront is **Cowichan Lake Visitor Centre** (125 South Shore

Rd., 250/932-1108, www.cowichanlake.ca, 9am-5pm daily summer, 10am-4pm daily fall-spring). The center is a good source of information on conditions along the logging roads lacing the valley.

CARMANAH WALBRAN PROVINCIAL PARK

If you're looking for a day trip to escape the tourist-clogged streets of Victoria, you can't get any more remote than the Carmanah Valley. Eyed by logging companies for many years, the Carmanah and adjacent Walbran Valley were designated a provincial park in 1995, providing complete protection for the 16,450-hectare (40,650-acre) watershed. For environmentalists, creation of the park was a major victory because this mist-shrouded valley extending all the way to the rugged west coast holds an old-growth forest of absolute wonder. Many 800-year-old Sitka spruce and 1,000-year-old cedar trees—some of the world's oldest—rise up to 95 meters (300 feet) off the damp valley floor. Others lie where they've fallen, their slowly decaying moss- and fern-cloaked hulks providing homes for thousands of small mammals and insects.

The only way to reach the park is via Lake Cowichan, following the south shore of Cowichan Lake to Nitinat Main, a logging road that leads south to Nitinat Junction (no services). There, the road is joined by a logging road from Port Alberni. From this point, Nitinat Main continues south to a bridge across the Caycuse River. Take the first right after crossing the river. This is Rosander Main, a rough road that dead-ends at the park boundary. The park is signposted from Nitinat Junction, but the signs are small and easy to miss.

From the road's-end parking lot, a rough 1.3-kilometer (0.8-mile) hiking trail (30 minutes one-way) descends to the valley floor and Carmanah Creek. From the creek, trails lead upstream to the Three Sisters (2.5 kilometers/1.5 miles, 40 minutes), through Grunt's Grove to August Creek (7.5 kilometers/4.6 miles, 2 hours), and downstream through a grove of Sitka spruce (2.4 kilometers/1.5 miles, 40 minutes) named for Randy Stoltmann, a legendary environmentalist who first brought the valley's giants to the world's attention.

CHEMAINUS

For four decades, Chemainus (pop. 3,000) has been billing itself as "The Little Town That Did." Did what, you ask? Well, Chemainus has always been a sleepy little mill town; its first sawmill dates back to 1862. Not wanting their town to slip into oblivion, residents hired local artists to cover the walls of downtown commercial buildings with larger-than-life murals depicting the town's history and culture. The result was outstanding, and in 1983, the artsy project won a prestigious downtown revitalization competition against towns and cities from around the world. Ironically, by 1985, the old mill had been modernized and reopened, and today, the thriving town is also home to one of the island's major theater companies.

Sights

Follow the signs to downtown Chemainus from Highway 1 and park at Waterwheel Park, central to local activities and eateries, and a pleasant downhill walk to the waterfront. Once the site of a grand home built for the sawmill manager, the tree-shaded park has a historical-themed playground, lots of flower beds, and a working replica of the waterwheel that powered the original 1862 sawmill. Pick up a walking tour map of the murals at Chemainus Visitor Centre, located at the park, where you'll see the first enormous mural—a street scene. From there you can explore the rest of Chemainus on foot, following the yellow footprints into town.

From beside the park, Chemainus Tours (250/246-5055, adults $20, children $10) operates horse-drawn carriage rides every 30 minutes through summer around town, passing all of the murals along the route.

Chemainus Theatre Festival

Chemainus Theatre Festival (9737 Chemainus Rd., 250/246-9820 or

800/565-7738, www.chemainustheatrefesti-val.ca) is a professional theater with produc-tions ranging from Canadian comedies to Broadway classics performed in a purpose-built 274-seat theater. Performances run Wednesday-Sunday with tickets ranging $30-70, or $60-100 with lunch or dinner. Purchase tickets online or at the on-site box office.

Food

The downtown streets of Chemainus are dot-ted with friendly little cafés and tearooms, but for a more substantial meal, most visitors dine as part of a theater package purchased from Chemainus Theatre Festival.

One of many inviting downtown cafés is **Owl's Nest Bakery Bistro** (9752 Willow St., 250/324-8286, 9am-4pm Tues.-Sun., lunch $8-15). Their breakfasts are healthy and delicious, the well-priced coffee is the best in town, and the wraps, salads, and grilled paninis are all tasty.

Willow Street Café (9749 Willow St., 250/246-2434, 8am-3pm daily, $10-15) is lo-cated in a historic downtown building that has served as a Masonic hall and post office. Today, renovations have created a cozy space, with lots of exposed wood and earthy colors throughout. The food is simple and inex-pensive—think homemade soup, thin-crust pizza, and wraps—and the patio is the per-fect place to enjoy the surrounding bustle of the town.

Accommodations

The theater company is popular enough that on show nights, the town's limited lodging is full, and often priced higher than you may imagine. Across the road from the theater is **Best Western Plus Chemainus Inn** (9573 Chemainus Rd., 250/246-4181, www.best-western.com, $200-240 s or d), a modern four-story hotel with a small indoor pool; a hot breakfast is included in the rates.

South of the theater and the downtown is **Country Maples RV Resort** (9010 Trans-Canada Hwy., 250/246-2078, www.holiday-trailsresorts.com, $40-86). Amenities include a swimming pool, mini golf, wireless Internet, and a small grocery store.

Information

Beside the large parking lot between down-town and Waterwheel Park is **Chemainus Visitor Centre** (9799 Waterwheel Cres., 250/737-3368, www.chemainus.bc.ca, 9am-4pm daily June-Sept., 9am-4pm Mon.-Fri. Oct.-May).

THETIS AND PENELAKUT ISLANDS

Jump aboard the small ferry from downtown Chemainus and cross Stuart Channel to reach Thetis Island, an idyllic rural retreat with around 350 residents. The island has no offi-cial sights, but its road system is popular with cyclists, and two marinas are busy throughout summer with yachties cruising through the Strait of Georgia.

Formerly known as Kuper Island, Penelakut is a reserve owned by the Penelakut First Nations, who are part of the much larger Hul'qumi'num people, a branch of the Coast Salish. Traditionally, the main village was located on a spit of land extending off the north end of the island. The island is home to around 300 Penelakut people, whose ancestors suffered a ferocious attack by British forces in the 1860s and the inhumanity of Canada's infamous residential schools in more recent times. Although BC Ferries makes a stop on the island on its run between Chemainus and Thetis Island, there are no services.

Food and Accommodations

Accommodations and services are very lim-ited on Thetis Island; most casual travel-ers come over for just the day. Less than 500 meters (0.3 mile) from the ferry termi-nal is **Thetis Island Marina** (46 Harbour Rd., 250/246-3464, www.thetisisland.com, $180 s or d), with three simple, ocean-facing rooms, a grocery store, and a pub-restaurant with waterfront seating. **Telegraph Harbour Marina** (Marina Dr., off Foster Point Rd., 250/246-9511, 9am-6pm daily

May-mid.-Sept.) has no accommodations but does offer a café and a general store, a laundry, and landscaped grounds sloping down to a protected bay.

Getting There

BC Ferries (250/386-3431) schedules up to 15 sailings daily between the terminal at the end of Oak Street in Chemainus and Thetis Island. The trip takes 20 minutes one-way. The peak round-trip fare is adults $9.50, children $4.70, vehicles $22.30.

LADYSMITH

The trim little village of Ladysmith, 88 kilometers (53 miles) north of Victoria, is set on a high point of land immediately west of the highway. The first of its two claims to fame is its location straddling the 49th parallel (a cairn is located in front of the post office on 1st Ave.), the invisible line separating Canada from the United States. After much bargaining for the 1846 Oregon Treaty, Canada got to keep all of Vancouver Island despite the 49th parallel bisecting the island. The second claim is a little less historically important—Ladysmith was the birthplace of actress Pamela Anderson, whose family operated a small cabin resort along the waterfront.

The town itself was laid out in 1904 by coal baron James Dunsmuir for his employees who worked in one of his mines north of the village. When the mine closed in 1936, logging took over as the most important local industry.

Sights

Ladysmith has done a wonderful job of preserving its heritage, both through saving historic buildings and developing walking and driving routes that are dotted with artifacts and interpretive panels. Along the historic main street (1st Ave.) are many century-old buildings, including Edwardian-era hotels, shops, the post office, and churches, that have changed little in appearance since the coal-mining era. Also look for items such as an anchor, a tractor, and the **Ladysmith Museum** (721 1st Ave., 250/245-0423, noon-4pm Tues.-Sat., free), which includes a small archive crammed with historical documents and photos.

From beside the visitors center, take Roberts Street downhill across the highway to reach the Waterfront and Railway districts. Here, at Transfer Beach Park, a whaling harpoon gun and a "boom boat," used to push log booms into place, are on display.

Ladysmith waterfront

The Dunsmuir Family

Dunsmuir is a name you'll hear often when touring Vancouver Island. The family's Victoria mansions, Craigdarroch Castle and Hatley Park, get most of the attention, but their influence spread well beyond the capital. Born in Scotland in 1825, Robert Dunsmuir's family connections in the coal-mining industry led him to Vancouver Island in 1851, after making the six-month journey from England with his wife and two young daughters. Originally landing at Fort Rupert at the north end of the island, they soon moved to Nanaimo, where Dunsmuir managed a mine owned by the Hudson's Bay Company (HBC). As HBC leases expired, he began staking his own claims, mostly around Nanaimo. By the mid-1870s, Dunsmuir was producing the vast majority of coal mined on the island, with his most important customer being the Canadian navy. Dunsmuir was elected to the British Columbia legislature in 1882, by which time he had 10 children. Dunsmuir was granted large tracts of land to build a rail line between Victoria and Nanaimo, completing the line in 1886, then adding spur lines to his own coal mines in later years. By the time of his death in 1899, Dunsmuir was the richest person in British Columbia and had built the grandly opulent Craigdarroch Castle in Victoria.

Best known of his offspring was James, heir to the family fortune. In 1898, James founded the town of Ladysmith for workers at his nearby coal mines; in 1900 he was elected the premier of British Columbia, and in 1905 he sold the family railway company to the Canadian Pacific Railway.

Readers familiar with California history may be also familiar with the Dunsmuir name. Another of Robert's sons, Alexander, moved to the San Francisco area to manage an arm of the family business and built Oakland's 37-room Dunsmuir House in 1899 for his new bride. The mansion is now protected as a National Historic Site, although Dunsmuir never got to live in it, as he died on his honeymoon.

Food and Accommodations

A number of cafés have great food and inviting ambiance. Right on the main street, **Wild Poppy Market** (541 1st Ave., 250/924-8696, 9am-5pm daily, lunch $8-13.50) has an array of gluten-free baked items, ranging from delicious breads to sweet treats. The oversized cobb salad stars on the lunch menu, while other choices include quiche, soups, and sandwiches. On the same block, but on the other side of the road, is **Old Time Bakery** (510 1st Ave., 250/245-2531, 8am-4pm Tues.-Sat.), where for over 90 years residents have gathered for made-from-scratch bakery items, including bread, pies, and pastries. But where this place really shines is with its mouthwatering cinnamon buns. **In the Beantime Café** (18 High St., 250/245-2305, 8am-3pm daily, lunch $8-16) is a popular local spot between 1st Avenue and the highway. It's a small friendly place, and as home to Gulf Island Roasting (you'll find their coffee throughout the island), you know the coffee is super-fresh. The menu is also more extensive than the above two recommendations, with full cooked breakfasts and beef dip.

Just north of Ladysmith, beside the main highway, is the **Microtel Inn & Suites** (12570 Trans-Canada Hwy., 250/912-9000, $200-240 s or d), a modern chain motel with comfortable rooms, an indoor pool and hot tub, a fitness room, and a daily breakfast buffet included.

Information

Ladysmith Visitor Centre (33 Roberts St., 250/245-2112, www.tourismladysmith.ca, 9:30am-4pm daily July-Aug., 9:30am-4pm Mon.-Fri. Sept.-June) is at the south end of the historic main street, within easy walking distances of the cafés recommended above.

Central Vancouver Island

Central Vancouver Island refers to the region

between Nanaimo and the Comox Valley, and west to Pacific Rim
National Park and Tofino. It's under a three hour's drive coast to coast,
but the region is incredibly diverse,
with family-friendly beaches and bustling holiday towns in the east,
and wild and rugged untamed stretches of beach in the west.

The gateway to the region is Nanaimo, Vancouver Island's second largest city. Perfectly blending historic attractions and big-city perks like stylish cafés, the city itself has an enviable reputation for its ideal climate, waterfront setting, and the nearby rural oasis of Gabriola Island.

Highlights

Look for ★ to find recommended sights, activities, dining, and lodging.

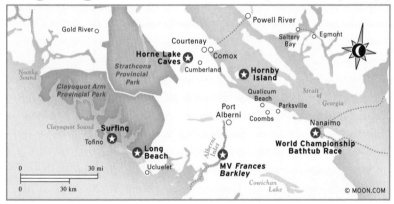

★ **World Championship Bathtub Race:** No, you're not imagining it—locals have been racing bathtubs around Nanaimo Harbour since 1967 (page 114).

★ **MV *Frances Barkley:*** Take to the calm waters of Alberni Inlet aboard this historic vessel that heads out as far as Barkley Sound (page 128).

★ **Long Beach:** Pacific Rim National Park protects this stretch of unspoiled sand, one of the country's most magnificent beaches in Canada (page 133).

★ **Surfing at Tofino:** Surf's up at this laidback end-of-the-road town (page 137).

★ **Horne Lake Caves:** Adventurous travelers head underground (page 150).

★ **Hornby Island:** A wonderful stretch of white sand backed by old-growth forest makes visiting this island a must (page 152).

Central Vancouver Island

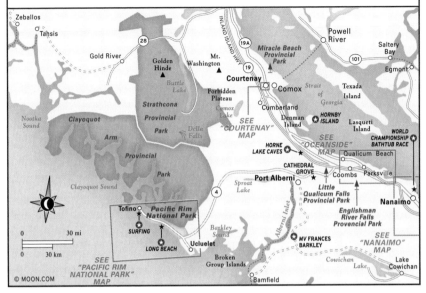

Visitors leaving Nanaimo are faced with two options. They can head west along Highway 4 to Port Alberni and Pacific Rim National Park, or travel north to Oceanside, where over 100 kilometers (60 miles) of coastline host towns and villages like Parksville and Qualicum Beach, brimming with action throughout summer, with crowds drawn by long sandy beaches and relatively warm ocean swimming.

At Parksville, Highway 4 provides the second option, turning away from the calm waters of the Strait of Georgia and leading up and over the forested Vancouver Island Ranges to the untamed west coast. Along this route, you'll pass a café best known for the family of goats that lives on its roof, a towering stand of 800-year-old trees, and crystal-clear lakes perfect for swimming and fishing. At the end of the road, you'll find picture-perfect fishing villages, driftwood-littered sand as far as you can see, and Pacific Rim

National Park, the island's only national park. Also on the west coast is Tofino, a favorite hangout for surfers as well as a base for sea kayaking and whale-watching on Clayoquot Sound.

PLANNING YOUR TIME

The east coast of Vancouver Island between Nanaimo and the Comox Valley is relatively compact. You could explore the entire region from a single campground or lodging, relaxing on the beaches, exploring the many parks, browsing the towns, and making short day trips to worthwhile destinations like **Horne Lakes Caves.** Day-tripping to the offshore islands is also possible, but to really get into island mode, an overnight stay is preferable, especially on the more remote choices like **Hornby Island.**

Plan on at least two nights on the west coast to take advantage of the sun, sand, and surf surrounding the west coast town of **Tofino**

Previous: Tofino; driftwood on Long Beach; Pacific Rim National Park.

and the adjacent **Long Beach** within Pacific Rim National Park, as well as take a cruise down Alberni Inlet aboard the **MV** *Frances Barkley.*

While Victoria is busy year-round, the travel seasons in the central section of Vancouver Island are more defined. July and August are very busy, especially along east coast Oceanside towns, around Tofino, and during special events like Nanaimo's **World Championship Bathtub Race.** If you are planning to travel to any of these regions during summer, it is imperative to make accommodations and camping reservations in advance. Travel in May, June, or September and you'll miss the crowds while saving money on accommodations. Winters are relatively mild, and although you wouldn't want to plan a camping trip to Parksville in winter, this is an excellent time of year to head to Pacific Rim National Park to watch storms batter the west coast.

Nanaimo and Vicinity

Nanaimo (pronounced na-NYE-mo) sprawls lazily up and down the hilly coastal terrain between sparkling Nanaimo Harbour and Mount Benson, on the east coast of Vancouver Island 110 kilometers (69 miles) north of Victoria. With a population of 92,000, it's the island's second-largest city and one of the six largest cities in British Columbia. It's also a vibrant city enjoying a rich history, mild climate, wide range of visitor services, and a direct ferry link to both of Vancouver's ferry terminals.

Visitors leaving Nanaimo are faced with three options: They can jump aboard a ferry to nearby Gabriola Island, head west along Highway 4 to Port Alberni and Pacific Rim National Park, or travel north to Parksville and Qualicum Beach. The **Nanaimo Parkway** bypasses the city to the west along a 21-kilometer (13-mile) route that branches off the original highway 5 kilometers (3 miles) south of downtown, rejoining it 18 kilometers (11 miles) north of downtown.

Five First Nations bands lived here (the name Nanaimo is a derivative from the Salish word Sney-Ny-Mous, or "Meeting Place"), and it was they who innocently showed dull, black rocks to Hudson's Bay Company employees in 1851. For most of the next century, mines in the area exported huge quantities of coal. Eventually, oil-fueled ships replaced the coal burners, and by 1949, most of the mines had closed. Surprisingly, no visible traces of the mining boom remain in Nanaimo, aside from a museum (built on top of the most productive mine) accurately depicting those times, and a sturdy fort (now a museum) built in 1853 in case of an attack by First Nations people.

Nanaimo was officially incorporated in 1874, which makes it the province's third-oldest town. When the coal mines closed, forestry and fishing became mainstays of the city. Today Nanaimo is also a major deep-sea shipping port.

SIGHTS

Downtown Nanaimo lies in a wide bowl sloping down to the waterfront, where forward thinking by early town planners has left wide expanses of parkland. Down near the water, the Civic Arena building makes a good place to park your car and go exploring on foot. Right in front of the Civic Arena is **Swy-A-Lana Lagoon,** a unique artificially constructed tidal lagoon full of interesting marinelife. A promenade leads south from the lagoon to a bustling downtown marina filled with commercial fishing boats and leisure craft. Beside the marina is a distinctive mastlike sculpture that provides foot access to a tiered development with various viewpoints. Up in downtown proper, many historical buildings still stand, most around the corner of Front and Church Streets and along

Nanaimo and Vicinity

To Horseshoe Bay (Vancouver)

To Parksville

HAMMOND BAY RD

Neck Point Park

Piper's Lagoon Park

LONGWOOD BREW PUB

RUTHERFORD RD

To Tsawwassen (Vancouver)

SMOKIN' GEORGE'S

BUZZ COFFEE HOUSE

DEPARTURE BAY RD

ISLAND HWY N

NANAIMO PKWY

Departure Bay Beach

Departure Bay

Beban Park

Saysutshun Marine Provincial Park

19

NANAIMO VISITOR CENTRE

BAILEY STUDIO

BOWEN RD

NANAIMO REGIONAL GENERAL HOSPITAL

BUCCANEER INN

Protection Island

DINGHY DOCK PUB

NANAIMO DIVE OUTFITTERS

BLUEBIRD MOTEL

Maffeo-Sutton Park

WORLD CHAMPIONSHIP BATHTUB RACE

Duke Point

Gabriola Island

JINGLE POT RD

Bus Depot

WESTWOOD LAKE

Westwood Lake

3RD ST

SEE "DOWNTOWN NANAIMO" MAP

Northumberland Channel

FITZWILLIAM
FRANKLYN
ALBERT

4TH ST

5TH ST

VICTORIA RD

NICOL ST

Nanaimo Harbour

7TH ST

Petroglyph Provincial Park

NANAIMO LAKES RD

LIVING FOREST OCEANSIDE

DUKE POINT HWY

To Crow and Gate Pub

19

19

CEDAR RD

0   1 mi

0   1 km

NANAIMO RIVER RD

Nanaimo River

····· Ferry Route

WILDPLAY

NANAIMO AIRPORT

HASLAM RD

To Victoria

© MOON.COM

Commercial Street. Look for hotels dating to early last century, the Francis Rattenbury-designed courthouse, and various old commercial buildings. Up Fitzwilliam Street are the 1893 St. Andrew's Church and the 1883 railway station.

Nanaimo Museum

In the heart of downtown, the **Nanaimo Museum** (100 Museum Way, 250/753-1821, 10am-5pm daily summer, 10am-4pm Mon.-Sat. fall-spring, adults $2, seniors $1.75, children $0.75) is a modern facility showcasing local and island history. Walk around the outside to appreciate harbor, city, and mountain views, as well as replica petroglyphs of animals, humans, and spiritual creatures. Then allow at least an hour for wandering through the displays inside, which focus on life in early Nanaimo and include topics such as geology, the First Nations, pioneers, and local sporting heroes. An exhibit on the coal-mining days features a realistic coal mine from the 1850s. Don't miss the impressive First Nations carvings by James Dick.

The Bastion

Overlooking the harbor at the junction of Bastion and Front Streets, and totally rebuilt in 2010, stands the Bastion, a well-protected fort built in 1853 by the Hudson's Bay Company to protect employees and their families against an attack by First Nations people. Originally used as a company office, arsenal, and supply house, today the fort houses the **Bastion Museum** (250/753-1821, 10am-3pm daily June-Aug., donation). A group of local university students dressed in appropriate gunnery uniforms and led by a piper parades down Bastion Street at 11:45am daily in summer. The parade ends at the Bastion, where the three cannons are fired out over the water. It's the only ceremonial cannon firing west of Ontario. For a good vantage point, be here early.

Saysutshun (Newcastle Island)

Saysutshun, formerly known as Newcastle Island, is a magnificent chunk of wilderness separated from downtown Nanaimo by a narrow channel. It is the traditional home of the Snuneymuxw people, who lived on the island each spring to harvest herring and also collect medicinal plants. When Europeans arrived and began mining coal, they displaced the Snuneymuxw. Coal was mined until 1883, and sandstone—featured on many of Nanaimo's

Nanaimo Harbour

Nanaimo

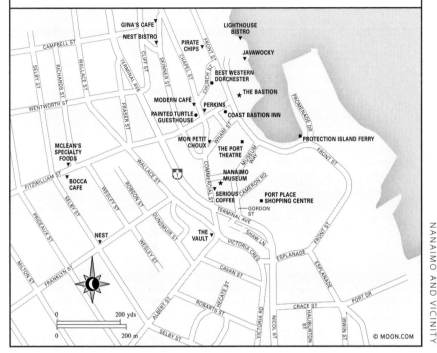

historical buildings—was quarried here until 1932. The pavilion and facilities near the ferry dock date to the 1940s. Back then, the island was a popular holiday spot, at one point even boasting a floating hotel. Today, protected as a marine park, the island is mostly forested, ringed by sandstone cliffs and a few short stretches of pebbly beach. Wildlife inhabitants include deer, raccoons, beavers, and more than 50 species of birds.

A 7.5-kilometer (4.7-mile) walking trail (allow 2-3 hours) encircles the island, leading to picturesque Kanaka Bay, Mallard Lake, and a lookout offering views east to the snowcapped Coast Mountains. The Saysutshun Ferry (250/755-6987, 9am-6pm daily May-Oct., $10 pp) departs for the island from Maffeo-Sutton Park every 20 minutes throughout summer, with fewer sailings in spring and fall. The only facilities

on the island are washrooms, a campground, and a food outlet serving surprisingly tasty and well-priced breakfasts, burgers, and fish-and-chips.

RECREATION
Parks
Along the Millstone River and linked by a trail to the waterfront promenade, 36-hectare (89-acre) Bowen Park remains mostly in its natural state, with stands of Douglas fir, hemlock, cedar, and maple. It's home to beavers and birds, and even deer are occasionally sighted within its boundaries. Street access is from Bowen Road.

On the road into downtown Nanaimo from the south, 2 kilometers (1.2 miles) north of the Nanaimo Parkway intersection, Petroglyph Provincial Park features a short trail leading to ancient petroglyphs (rock carvings).

Petroglyphs, found throughout the province and common along the coastal waterways, were made with stone tools, and they recorded important ceremonies and events. The designs at this park were carved thousands of years ago and are believed to represent human beings, animals (real and supernatural), bottom fish, and the rarely depicted sea wolf, a mythical creature that's part wolf and part killer whale.

West of downtown (take Wentworth St. and then Jingle Pot Rd. across the Nanaimo Pkwy.), 106-hectare (262-acre) **Westwood Lake Park** surrounds the crystal-clear waters of its namesake lake. Resident flocks of Canada geese and ducks, tame enough to snatch food from your fingers, inhabit the park. The lake's healthy population of cutthroat trout attracts anglers year-round.

Along Hammond Bay Road, north of downtown and beyond Departure Bay, is **Piper's Lagoon Park,** encompassing an isthmus and a rocky headland that shelter a shallow lagoon. A trail from the parking lot leads to the headland, with views of the mainland across the Strait of Georgia. Continuing north, more trails lead through **Neck Point Park** to rocky beaches and oceanside picnic areas.

Diving

A great variety of dives can be accessed from Nanaimo, including several vessels that have been sunk especially for diving enthusiasts, such as the HMCS *Cape Breton* and HMCS *Saskatchewan,* both 120-meter (400-foot) Navy destroyer escorts. The much smaller *Rivtow Lion,* a rescue tug, was scuttled in the shallow waters of Departure Bay, making it a popular spot for novice divers. Marinelife is also varied, with divers mixing with harbor seals, anemones, sponges, salmon, and "tame" wolf eels. **Nanaimo Dive Outfitters** (2205 Northfield Rd., 250/756-1863, www.nanaimodiveoutfitters.ca, 10am-5:30pm Mon.-Fri., 9am-5pm Sat.) is a well-respected island operation, offering sales, equipment rentals, and charters aboard *The Shepherd.* For nondivers, there is an option to go snorkeling with the local seal population.

Bungee Jumping

Nanaimo is home to **WildPlay** (35 Nanaimo River Rd., 250/716-7874, 10am-6pm daily summer), North America's only bridge-based commercial bungee jump. People flock here from afar to have their ankles tied and connected to "Bungee Bridge" by a long elastic rope. Next, they dive headfirst 42 meters (138 feet) down almost to the surface of Nanaimo River, rebounding until momentum dissipates. To receive this thrill of a lifetime, you have to part with $140, and if you have any cash left over, you'll find must-have T-shirts, hats, posters, videos, stickers, and other souvenirs to prove to the world that you really did it. At the same facility, other adrenaline rushes can be had by taking the Primal Swing ($100 pp) or the Zip Line ($30). All of the above are thoroughly entertaining to watch, with good viewing areas and plenty of parking provided. The site is 13 kilometers (8 miles) south of downtown.

ENTERTAINMENT AND EVENTS
★ **World Championship Bathtub Race**

On the last Sunday of every July, the waters off Nanaimo come alive for the World Championship Bathtub Race (250/753-7223, www.bathtubbing.com), the grand finale of the annual **Nanaimo Marine Festival.** Originally, competitors raced across the Strait of Georgia between Nanaimo and Kitsilano Beach, Vancouver. Today, they leave from downtown Nanaimo, racing around Entrance and Winchelsea Islands to the finish line at Departure Bay in a modified bathtub fitted with a 7.5-horsepower outboard motor. The racers are escorted by hundreds of boats of the more regular variety, loaded with people just waiting for the competitors to sink. Every

1: Commercial Street 2: Bowen Park 3: the Bastion 4: café on Commercial Street

bathtubber wins a prize—a golden plug for entering, a small trophy for making it to the other side of the strait, and a silver plunger for the first tub to sink. These days, the sport and the festivities around it have grown enormously, attracting tens of thousands of visitors to Nanaimo. And "tubbing," as the locals call it, has spread to other BC communities, where preliminary races qualify entrants for the big one.

Bars and Brewpubs

The best place in Nanaimo to enjoy a drink while soaking up harbor views is the **Lighthouse Pub** (50 Anchor Way, 250/754-3212, 11am-midnight daily), built out over the water in front of the main shopping district. At dock level is a restaurant, while the pub upstairs has nightly drink specials, a pool table, and a good selection of pub food (with the emphasis on seafood). Escape the pub atmosphere by requesting seating at the outside section of the restaurant.

Overlooking Matteo Sutton Park, **White Sails Brewing** (125 Comox Rd., 250/754-2337, 2pm-9pm Mon.-Thurs., noon-9pm Fri.-Sun.) is a modern, open-concept taproom with appropriate, locally sourced food (think chicken wings, salsa and chips, and cheeses) to accompany a delicious array of craft beers.

Nanaimo's original brewpub was **Longwood** (5775 Turner Rd., 250/729-8225, 11am-10pm daily). There's a pub downstairs and a restaurant upstairs, but the lagers and traditional British ales brewed in-house can be enjoyed in either section. Tours, with the obligatory tasting, are offered at 3pm Saturday. Longwood's is around five kilometers (three miles) north of downtown along Highway 19A (Island Hwy.); look for Turner Road on the right.

Find an outdoor table, order a traditional ale, soak up the sights and smells of well-tended gardens surrounding a Tudor-style building, and it is easy to believe you're in rural England at the **Crow & Gate Pub** (2313 Yellow Point Rd., 250/722-3731, 11am-10pm daily), south of the city limits. Crow & Gate is an extremely popular destination for locals on sunny weekends. It's located around 4 kilometers (2.5 miles) south along Cedar Road from the Duke Point Highway.

One of the most interesting places to go for a cold beverage on a warm summer day is **Dinghy Dock Pub** (Protection Island, 250/753-2373, 11:30am-8pm Sun.-Wed., 11:30am-10pm Thurs.-Sat.), accessible only from Nanaimo Boat Basin by ferry (every hour 8am-10pm daily, adults $10, children $5 round-trip, cash only). This floating restaurant is also a good place for a meal and hosts live entertainment on Friday and Saturday nights May to September.

The Arts

Lovers of the arts will find Nanaimo to be quite the cultural center, with the main focus being the **Port Theatre** (125 Front St., 250/754-8550, www.porttheatre.com). This magnificent 800-seat theater, in an architecturally pleasing circular concrete-and-glass building opposite the harbor, showcases theater productions, musicals, and music performances by a wide range of artists year-round. The **Nanaimo Theatre Group** (2373 Rosstown Rd., 250/758-7224, www.nanaimo-theatregroup.ca) presents live performances at the Bailey Studio. The **Nanaimo Art Gallery** (150 Commercial St., 250/754-1750, 10am-5pm Tues.-Sat., noon-5pm Sun., donation) displays and sells works by a diverse range of island artists.

FOOD

Nanaimo has a remarkably wide choice of dining options, including a dozen or more cafés and restaurants offering everything from local seafood to Middle Eastern cuisine.

Cafés

If you're wandering along the harbor and looking for a spot to relax with a hot drink, you won't do better than **Javawocky** (90 Front St., 250/753-1688, 8am-5pm Mon.-Fri., 9am-4:30pm Sat., lunches $8-12), overlooking the harbor. It offers all of the usual coffee drinks, great milkshakes, inexpensive cakes and pastries, and light lunchtime snacks.

Downtown, Commercial Street is lined with cafés. **Serious Coffee** (60 Commercial St., 250/591-1065, 8am-4pm Mon.-Sat., 9am-4pm Sun.), in the Nanaimo Museum complex, is one gathering spot for serious coffee lovers. Up the hill slightly, **Mon Petit Choux** (120 Commercial St., 250/753-6002, 8am-5pm Mon.-Sat., 9am-5pm Sun., lunch $6-8) seems to attract a slightly older crowd for in-house baking, such as delicious cheesecake brownies, while nearby **Perkins** (234 Commercial St., 250/753-2582, 7:30am-5pm Mon.-Fri., 8:30am-3pm Sat.-Sun.) serves up coffee and muffins to all types from within a heritage building.

At **The Vault Café** (499 Wallace St., 250/591-0776, 8am-10pm Mon.-Tues., 8am-midnight Wed.-Fri., 9am-2pm Sat., 10am-2pm Sun., lunches $10-15), across the highway from Commercial Street, it's all about the coffee throughout the day, but the wide-ranging menu is also notable, and there's often live music in the evenings. This place has a distinct European vibe within a historic commercial building designed by Francis Rattenbury, of Empress Hotel fame.

Up Fitzwilliam Street from the center of town in the Old Quarter is a concentration of quality eateries, including **Bocca Cafe** (427 Fitzwilliam St., 250/753-1797, 7am-6pm Mon.-Fri., 8am-5pm Sat., 9am-4pm Sun., lunch $8-12), an inviting little space that is a favorite with locals looking for a little style. From the delicious coffee and muffins in the morning to freshly made sandwiches at lunch, everything is delightful. Tables lining a covered walkway are especially popular.

Buzz Coffee House (4890 Rutherford Rd., 250/591-8310, 7am-5pm Mon.-Fri., 8am-5pm Sat.-Sun., lunch $13-21) is in the northern suburbs of Nanaimo, but if you're heading that way, it's well worth searching out for its bright, modern setting, delicious breakfasts and lunches, and healthy smoothies. From downtown, take Comox Road west along the

south side of Bowen Park for around three kilometers (two miles) and look for Dufferin Crescent to the left.

Gourmet Goodies

McLeans Specialty Foods (426 Fitzwilliam St., 250/754-0100, 10am-5pm Tues.-Sat.) is chock-full of local produce, in-house baking and soups, and an incredible selection of cheeses and gourmet foods from around the world.

Waterfront Dining

Dinghy Dock Pub (Protection Island, 250/753-2373, 11:30am-8pm Sun.-Wed., 11:30am-10pm Thurs.-Sat., $15-32) offers a unique dining experience; the floating restaurant is moored at nearby Protection Island. Well known for great food and plenty of sea-going atmosphere, the pub also hosts live entertainment on Friday and Saturday nights from May to September. To get to the restaurant, take a ferry (250/753-8244, 8am-10pm daily, adults $10, children $5 round-trip, cash only) from Nanaimo Boat Basin.

In the seaplane terminal on the waterfront (below the Bastion), the **Lighthouse Bistro** (50 Anchor Way, 250/754-3212, 11am-10pm daily, $15-28) is built over the water and has a large heated outdoor deck with sweeping harbor views. The salmon chowder is excellent, served with delicious bread. Also on the menu are tasty appetizers, salads, burgers, sandwiches, croissants, pasta dishes, and good daily specials. Upstairs is the **Lighthouse Pub,** with a similar menu and specials such as cheap wings on Wednesday.

Casual Dining

Near the top end of Commercial Street, **Modern Café** (221 Commercial St., 250/754-5022, 11am-11pm Tues.-Sat., 11am-9pm Sun., $14-32) has had a number of serious revamps since opening in 1946 that have seen changes to both the menu and decor, while leaving the distinctive neon sign out front in place. Mains run the gamut from mac and cheese to Australian lamb shanks.

Along the waterfront at the north end of downtown, ★ **Pirate Chips** (75 Front St., 250/753-2447, 11am-10pm Mon.-Thurs., 11am-midnight Fri.-Sat., 11am-8pm Sun., $12-20) is a funky little restaurant where you can load up hearty servings of fries with various toppings (including Dr. Pepper pulled pork), tuck into delicious seafood tacos, brave a peanut butter and bacon burger, and even try a deep-fried Nanaimo bar.

For some of the best Mexican food on Vancouver Island, head for **Gina's Mexican Cafe** (47 Skinner St., 250/753-5411, 11:30am-8pm Mon.-Thurs., 11:30am-9pm Fri.-Sat., noon-8pm Sun., $15-28), behind the courthouse north of Pirate Chips. Although it's on a back street, the building itself, a converted residence, is hard to miss—the exterior is painted shades of purple and decorated with a fusion of Mexican and maritime memorabilia.

Island Grown

★ **Nest Bistro** (77 Skinner St., 250/591-2721, 5pm-9pm Tues.-Sun., $18-26), one of Nanaimo's best restaurants, is a space that many visitors miss, yet it is just a couple of blocks from the bustle of Commercial Street. The ambience is friendly and inviting, with the chef-owners always present. A great deal of effort goes into sourcing local seafood, game, and produce, which is found in dishes such as arugula Caesar salad, sambuca prawn spaghetti, and a variety of thin-crust pizzas.

Beyond Downtown

South of the city, **Crow & Gate Pub** (2313 Yellow Point Rd., 250/722-3731, 11am-10pm daily, $14-24) mimics an English country pub, complete with exposed beams, a large fireplace, and expansive landscaped gardens dotted with outdoor table settings. Go to the bar to order traditional dishes such as Ploughman's lunches and steak and mushroom pie, or stay local with pan-fried oysters and a shrimp sandwich. To get there from town, head south out to the Duke Point ferry terminal and turn south onto Cedar Road just beyond the bridge over the Nanaimo River.

Cedar Road turns into Yellow Point Road, and the pub is on the right after 4 kilometers (2.5 miles).

Along a nondescript commercial strip north of downtown, the setting of **Smokin' George's** (4131 Mostar Rd., 250/585-2258, 11am-7pm Tues.-Sun., $15-36) is a world away from the touristy waterfront, but for Southern-style cooking, this restaurant is well worth searching out. Whether you order a pulled pork sandwich or a two-person Feast, you won't be disappointed in the quality of meats and their delicious sauces. Prices are reasonable—a half rack of ribs, baked beans, coleslaw, and corn bread is just $22.

Further north, just south of where Highway 19A rejoins Highway 19 (Inland Island Hwy.), **Longwood Brew Pub** (5775 Turner Rd., 250/729-8225, 11am-10pm daily, $18-30) is a large modern facility with a menu filled with local produce and seafood. Starters include fish tacos topped with pineapple and mango salsa, while mains such as citrus-infused cedar plank salmon are all a very good value. From downtown, follow Highway 19A (Island Hwy.) north and turn left onto Turner Road after five kilometers (three miles).

Continuing north along Highway 19A from Longwood, **Simonholt** (6582 Applecross Rd., 250/933-3338, 11am-10pm Mon.-Thurs., 11am-midnight Fri.-Sat., 10am-10pm Sun., $18-32) is a busy, contemporary dining room with live entertainment on weekends and lots of outdoor tables for those warm summer evenings. The cooking reflects the modern decor—coconut-crusted prawns, beer-battered halibut-and-chips, and seafood fettucine representative of the seafood choices. To get there from downtown, follow Highway 19A; turn left onto Hammond Bay Road, and then take the first left (Applecross Rd.).

ACCOMMODATIONS
$100-150

Painted Turtle Guesthouse (121 Bastion St., 250/753-4432, www.paintedturtle.ca, dorms $50, $100-110 s or d) is in a restored heritage building in the heart of downtown and just one block from the harborfront. The hostel operates year-round, providing four-bed dorms, private rooms (family rooms have a queen and bunk beds), a large and modern kitchen, laundry facilities, a lounge area, and friendly hosts.

On an island of overpriced accommodations, the two-story ★ **Buccaneer Inn** (1577 Stewart Ave., 250/753-1246 or 877/282-6337, www.buccaneerinn.com, $110-230 s or d) stands out as being an excellent value. Across from the waterfront and within easy walking distance of downtown and the Departure Bay ferry terminal, the Buccaneer is bedecked by a nautical-themed mural and colorful baskets of flowers and surrounded by well-maintained grounds, a sundeck, picnic tables, and a barbecue facility. The rooms are spacious and brightly decorated, and each has a desk, coffee-making facilities, a small fridge, and an Internet connection. The smallest rooms are $110 s or d, while kitchen suites, some with gas fireplaces, start at $190 s or d.

On the main thoroughfare north of downtown, the pick of many older motels is the **Bluebird Motel** (995 Terminal Ave. N, 250/753-4151 or 877/764-3832, www.thebluebirdmotel.ca, $127-157 s or d), which stands out for clean and comfortable rooms that are regularly revamped.

$150-200

As you'd expect, accommodations right downtown are more expensive than those farther out. A bit nicer than you'd expect from the bland exterior, the **Best Western Dorchester Hotel** (70 Church St., 250/754-6835 or 800/661-2449, www.dorchesternanaimo.com, $180-260 s or d) offers water views and a rooftop terrace from a central location. Rooms in this historical building won't win any design awards, but they are relatively modern, and many have water views. The hotel also has a fitness room, rooftop patio, and two restaurants.

Over $200

Also right downtown, the **Coast Bastion Inn** (11 Bastion St., 250/753-6601 or 800/716-6199, www.coasthotels.com, from $330-450 s or d) is a full-service, 179-room modern hotel with an exercise room, a day spa, the contemporary Minnoz Restaurant and Lounge, and harbor views from every room.

Camping

Two commercial campgrounds are within 10 kilometers (6 miles) of the city center, but the nicest surroundings are in the campground out on **Saysutshun** (www.saysutshun.ca, $20). It is a tents-only facility, and you will need reservations, which can be made through the **BC Parks** booking system (519/858-6161 or 800/689-9025, https://camping.bcparks.ca). The island is connected to downtown by regular passenger-only ferry service. Facilities include washrooms, picnic tables, and a barbecue shelter, while the island is also home to a concession that serves basic breakfasts, burgers, and other light meals to-go.

The closest of the commercial campgrounds to downtown is **Westwood Lake Campgrounds** (380 Westwood Rd., 250/753-3922, www.westwoodlakecampgrounds.com, tents $40, hookups $50, very basic cabins $650 s or d per week), set on the edge of beautiful Westwood Lake. Amenities include a sandy beach with canoe rentals, a barbecue area, a game room, laundry facilities, and hot showers.

Living Forest Oceanside RV & Campground (6 Maki Rd., 250/755-1755, www.campingbc.com, $40-65) is on 20 hectares (49 acres) of coastal forest at the braided mouth of the Nanaimo River south of downtown. The location is delightful and facilities are modern, including a laundry room, a general store, a game room, and coin showers.

INFORMATION AND SERVICES

Nanaimo is promoted to the world by **Tourism Nanaimo** (250/751-1556, www.tourismnanaimo.com). The main **Nanaimo Visitor Centre** (2450 Northfield Rd., 9am-5pm daily summer, 10am-4:30pm Tues.-Sat.

the rest of the year) is in a small but architecturally eye-catching structure at the north entrance to town (if you're traveling up-island from Victoria, stay on the main highway north; the center is well signed).

For emergencies, head to **Nanaimo Regional General Hospital** (1200 Dufferin Cres., 250/755-7691). A centrally located pharmacy is **London Drugs** (Port Place Shopping Centre, 650 Terminal Ave. S, 250/753-5566, 8am-9pm Mon.-Fri., 9am-9pm Sat., 10am-8pm Sun.).

GETTING THERE AND AROUND

It's possible to get to Nanaimo by airplane or bus, but most people arrive by ferry from Vancouver, or by vehicle up Highway 19 from Victoria; allow 90 minutes for the 110-kilometer (68-mile) trip.

BC Ferries (250/386-3431 or 888/223-3779, www.bcferries.com) operates regular services between Vancouver and Nanaimo along two different routes. Ferries leave Vancouver's Tsawwassen terminal up to eight times a day for the two-hour trip to Nanaimo's **Duke Point** terminal, 20 minutes south of downtown and with direct access to the highway that bypasses the city. Through downtown, at the north end of Stewart Avenue, is the **Departure Bay** terminal. This facility contains a large lounge area with a café and large-screen TVs. Ferries from Vancouver's Horseshoe Bay terminal leave up to 11 times a day for Departure Bay. Fares on both routes are the same: peak one-way travel costs adults $17.60, children $8.80, vehicles $59.50. Limited reservations are taken via the website ($17 plus ferry fare).

Harbour Air (250/714-0900, www.harbourair.com) flies daily between downtown Vancouver (just west of the convention center) and the seaplane base in downtown Nanaimo ($110-162 one-way). **VI Connector** buses (866/986-3466, www.viconnector.com)

1: Gabriola Sands Provincial Park 2: Nanaimo Visitor Centre

make stops at Port Place Shopping Centre, Departure Bay ferry terminal, and Nanaimo Airport on routes from Victoria that extend as far north as Campbell River and west to Tofino.

Nanaimo Regional Transit System (250/390-4531) buses run daily. The main routes radiate from downtown's Prideaux Street Exchange north to Departure Bay, west to Westwood Lake, and south as far as Cedar. An all-day pass is $5. Rental car agencies in Nanaimo include **Budget** (250/760-7368) and **National** (250/758-3509), both with desks at the airport.

GABRIOLA ISLAND

From Nanaimo, visitors can jump aboard a ferry to the nearby rural oasis of Gabriola Island. Geologically linked to the Southern Gulf Islands immediately to the south, Gabriola is partly residential, but it also holds large expanses of forest, abundant wildlife, and long stretches of unspoiled coastline. With an area of 57 square kilometers (22 square miles), it's one of the larger islands in the group and is separated from Vancouver Island by a narrow straight south of Nanaimo.

Petroglyphs were carved on island cliffs by Snuneymuxw people who lived on the island for at least 1,000 years prior to Spanish explorers making landfall in 1791. By the 1850s, European settlers arrived from Nanaimo and established farms. The island population remained low until the 1960s and 1970s, when the counterculture movement discovered the charms of Gabriola. The population has doubled in the last 30 years to 4,200 year-round residents.

Sights and Recreation

Many scenic spots invite you to pull off—at petroglyphs, secluded bays, and lookouts. The North and South Roads encircle the island, combining for a 30-kilometer (18.6-mile) loop that's perfect for a leisurely day-long bike ride.

Take Taylor Bay Road north from the ferry terminal to access the island's best beaches, including **Gabriola Sands Provincial Park,** a short stretch of fine white sand bookended by forest. Aside from a few picnic tables and restrooms, the park has no services—the beach is simply a wonderful place to spend a summer's day.

Drive out to the park's southern headland through stands of Garry oak and arbutus protected by **Drumbeg Provincial Park.** From the end of the road, walk out onto the grassy headland for sweeping views across Gabriola Passage and the opportunity for viewing whales, seals, and sea lions. On the loop back to the ferry dock, the South Road passes **Gabriola Island Golf Club** (825 South Rd., 250/247-8822, $29), a friendly little nine-hole set around Hoggan Lake. Facilities include rentals, a driving range, and a clubhouse with inexpensive meals.

Food and Accommodations
On the island's southeast coastline, **Page's Resort and Marina** (3350 Coast Rd., 250/247-8931, www.pagesresort.com, campsites $38-45, cottages $270-305 s or d) has a small campground surrounded by mature trees and a few comfortable one- and two-bedroom self-contained cottages with decks. Down on the resort's waterfront is a full-service marina and a grocery store with hot drinks and lots of island produce. Immediately north of the ferry dock, **Descanso Bay Regional Park** (595 Taylor Bay Rd., 250/247-8255, $20-23) offers 32 unserviced campsites sloping down to a

rocky cove. Reserve a campsite online at www. rdn.bc.ca.

Basic services are available less than one kilometer (0.6 miles) uphill from the ferry terminal on North Road. Here you'll find gas, groceries, and **Mad Rona's Coffee Bar** (500 North Rd., 250/247-0008, 7:30am-3:30pm daily, lunch $9-15), a modern café that opens to landscaped gardens filled with seating. The food is typical island café fare—breakfast burritos, freshly made sandwiches, and mostly healthy pastries. Adjacent to Mad Rona's is ★ **Woodfire** (500 North Rd., 250/247-0095, 4pm-9pm daily, $13-30), a stylish dining room that is the perfect setting to enjoy gourmet pizza and classic pastas such as butternut squash ravioli.

Information
Gabriola Visitor Centre (480 North Rd., 250/247-9332, www.gabriolaisland.org, 10am-2pm Thurs.-Sat.) is less than one kilometer (0.6 miles) east of the ferry terminal.

Getting There
BC Ferries (250/386-3431) schedules 15 sailings daily between the terminal off Front Street in Nanaimo (downtown, across from Harbour Park Mall) and Gabriola Island. The trip takes 20 minutes one-way, and reservations are not taken. The round-trip fare is adults $9.90, children $4.95, vehicles $23.45. For a taxi on the island, call **Gabriola Island Taxi** (250/247-0049).

Highway 4 to the West Coast

From Nanaimo, it's 35 kilometers (22 miles) northwest up Highway 19 to one of Vancouver Island's main highway junctions, where Highway 4 spurs west to Port Alberni and the island's west coast. The map shows a distance of 84 kilometers (52 miles) between Nanaimo and Port Alberni along Highway 4, but it's a winding highway, with lots of slower truck

traffic, so allow at least one hour. Follow Highway 4 to its end to reach **Pacific Rim National Park,** a long, narrow park protecting the wild coastal strip and some magnificent sandy beaches, and **Tofino,** a picturesque little town that makes the perfect base for surfing, sea kayaking, whale-watching, or fishing excursions.

ENGLISHMAN RIVER FALLS PROVINCIAL PARK

After turning off Highway 19 north of Nanaimo, make your first stop here, where Englishman River—full of cutthroat and rainbow trout—cascades down from high in the Beaufort Range over two photogenic waterfalls within an old-growth forest of Douglas fir, western red cedar, and hemlock. At the end of the park access road is a forested picnic area surrounded by lush ferns, easy hiking trails to both the upper and lower falls, and, downstream of the lower falls, a crystal-clear swimming hole. Back along the access road is a 94-site campground (no hookups or showers, May-Sept., $23) enclosed by the same forested setting. A short walking trail links the campground to the **waterfalls.** For campsite reservations, contact **BC Parks** (519/858-6161 or 800/689-9025, https://camping.bcparks.ca).

To get to the park, turn off Highway 4 on Errington Road, three kilometers (two miles) west of the Highway 19 junction, and continue another 9 kilometers (5.5 miles), following signs.

COOMBS

What started in the mid-1970s as a simple produce stand has grown into the **Old Country Market** (2310 Alberni Hwy., 250/248-6272, 9am-8pm daily in summer), the lifeblood of Coombs, along Highway 4A west of Highway 19. Before moving inside the market buildings, you'll want to stand out front and look upward, where several goats can be seen contentedly grazing along the roof line, seemingly oblivious to the amused, camera-clicking visitors. Inside the main building is a selection of goodies of epic proportions—a bakery, a deli, an ice cream stand, and a wealth of healthy island-made produce. Behind the main building and in an adjacent property are rows of arty shops selling everything from pottery to jewelry to kites.

On the west side of Coombs, at the junction of Highways 4 and 4A, is **Creekmore's**

Coffee (2701 Alberni Hwy., 250/752-5343, 7:30am-4pm Mon.-Fri., 8am-4pm Sat.), an unassuming place that pours freshly roasted coffee as good as any on the island.

LITTLE QUALICUM FALLS PROVINCIAL PARK

This 440-hectare (1,090-acre) park lies along the north side of the highway, 10 kilometers (6 miles) west of Coombs. The park's main **hiking trail** leads alongside the Little Qualicum River to a series of plummeting **waterfalls,** both upstream and downstream of the main day-use area. Stay the night in a sheltered riverside campsite (519/858-6161 or 800/689-9025, https://camping.bcparks.ca, May-Sept., $23,) although there are no hookups or showers. The source of the Little Qualicum River is **Cameron Lake,** a large, deep-green, trout-filled body of water just outside the western park boundary.

CATHEDRAL GROVE

At the west end of Cameron Lake, Highway 4 dives into one of the last remaining easily accessible stands of old-growth forest remaining in British Columbia. The tallest trees are protected by **MacMillan Provincial Park.** Highway 4 through the park is extremely narrow, and traffic within Cathedral Grove can get extremely congested in summer, so take extra care pulling into and out of the roadside parking lot. The park protects a majestic stand of 200- to 800-year-old Douglas firs that rise a neck-straining 70 meters (230 feet) from the forest floor and have a circumference of up to nine meters (30 feet). The trees have been a popular stop along the road to Port Alberni for almost 100 years and were officially afforded protection when one of the island's major logging companies donated the land to the government. Short trails lead from the parking lot on both the north and south sides of the highway, with the Old Growth Trail, on the south side, leading to Cameron Lake.

Port Alberni and Vicinity

If you hit Port Alberni, 84 kilometers (52 miles) west of Nanaimo, on a cloudy day, you won't know what you're missing until the sky lifts. Then beautiful tree-mantled mountains suddenly appear, and Alberni Inlet and the Somass River turn a stunning deep blue. Situated at the head of the island's longest inlet, Port Alberni is a busy town of 17,600, centered around the forestry industry. The town's three mills—lumber, specialty lumber, and pulp and paper—are its main sources of income. The town is also a port for pulp and lumber freighters, deep-sea vessels, and commercial fishing boats.

Despite all the industry, Port Alberni has much to offer, including interesting museums, nearby provincial parks, and a modern marina filled with both charter fishing boats and tour boats.

SIGHTS

Follow the signs from Highway 4 to brightly decorated **Alberni Harbour Quay** at the end of Argyle Street. For a great view of the quay, harbor, marina, inlet, and surrounding mountains, climb the clock tower. Off Argyle Street is Industrial Road, which leads to the **Maritime Discovery Centre** (2750 Harbour Rd., 250/723-6164, 10am-4pm Mon.-Fri., 9:30am-4:30pm Sat.-Sun. June-early Sept., donation), ensconced in a red-and-white lighthouse. Children will love the hands-on displays that explore the importance of the ocean to the town's history.

Originally linked to Alberni Harbour by rail, **McLean Mill National Historic Site** (5633 Smith Rd., 250/723-1376, dawn-dusk, free) boasts Canada's only remaining steam-powered sawmill. Guided tours are offered in summer (adults $18, seniors $12, children $9) and on-site is a café and gift shop.

1: Little Qualicum Falls Provincial Park 2: Alberni Harbour Quay 3: Cathedral Grove

Find out more about the origins of the famous West Coast Trail, see a collection of Nuu-chah-nulth artwork, or tinker with a variety of operating motorized machines from the forestry industry at the **Alberni Valley Museum** (4255 Wallace St., 250/720-2863, 10am-5pm Mon.-Sat. July-Aug., 10am-5pm Tues.-Sat. the rest of the year, donation).

SPROAT LAKE

A short drive west from Port Alberni, Highway 4 skirts the north shore of Sproat Lake, whose clear waters draw keen anglers. Along the highway, there is camping and a popular beachside day-use area at **Sproat Lake Provincial Park**. Provided they're not out squelching a fire, you can also see the world's largest water bombers—Martin Mars Flying Tankers—tied up here. Originally designed as troop carriers for World War II, only four were ever built and only two remain, both here at Sproat Lake. Used to fight wildfires, these massive flying beasts—36 meters (118 feet) long and with a wingspan of more than 60 meters (200 feet)—skim across the lake, each filling its tank with 26,000 liters (7,200 gallons) of water.

DELLA FALLS

In the remote southern section of **Strathcona Provincial Park,** difficult-to-reach Della Falls is accessible only from Port Alberni. The 440-meter (1,440-foot) waterfall northwest of town is one of the highest in North America, and getting to it requires a lot of effort: first by road from Port Alberni to Great Central Lake RV Resort, then by boat along Great Central Lake, then by a 16-kilometer (10-mile) hike (seven hours one-way) up the Drinkwater Creek watershed. Get to the trailhead with **Della Falls Water Taxi** (250/723-4720, www.dellafallswatertaxi.com, $165 pp round-trip), which departs from Great Central Lake RV

Resort at the end of Great Central Lake Road mid-May to mid-September.

FISHING

Port Alberni is one of three towns claiming to be the "Salmon Capital of the World" (the others are Campbell River and Ketchikan, Alaska), but is probably no better than a handful of other places on the island. The main salmon runs occur in fall, when hundreds of thousands of salmon migrate up Alberni Inlet to their spawning grounds. Check the **Port Alberni Visitor Centre** website (www.albernichamber.ca) for a list of local operators and expect to pay from $1,000 for a full day of salmon fishing.

FOOD

SteamPunk Cafe (3025A 3rd Ave., 778/421-3000, 7am-4pm Mon.-Fri., 7am-3pm Sat., $9-14) is in the downtown core, with outside tables and an interior divided into a main area and quieter section with a library of books. The coffee drinks are all excellent, and the food, such as salads, made from scratch.

If you're looking for fish-and-chips, it's hard to go past **Bare Bones Fish & Chips** (4824 Johnston Rd., 250/720-0900, 11:30am-8pm daily, $10-18), in a converted church on Highway 4 through town, three blocks east of the harbor. It's a smallish space with a funky decor that includes lots of fish-bone artwork. Local fish such as halibut, lingcod, and salmon are cooked in a variety of ways (grilled, battered, in tacos, etc.) and come with your choice of sides.

Another good choice for seafood in a casual setting, the **Clam Bucket** (4479 Victoria Quay, 250/723-1315, 11:30am-8pm daily, $15-32) is one of the most popular places in town. Although many seafood dishes are deep-fried, there are plenty of other choices, and portions are generous and well-priced. It's located on the north side of downtown, near where Highway 4 jogs west at the riverfront.

On the south side of downtown is Alberni Harbour Quay, which juts into the inlet and has a number of casual places to eat and lots of outdoor seating, although you are sacrificing food quality for the waterfront setting. At the very end of the quay, at **Starboard Grill** (5440 Argyle St., 778/421-2826, 11am-7pm daily, later hours in summer, $14-26), you'll find a large outdoor patio with uninterrupted views across the harbor. Food is fairly standard—salads, sandwiches, and burgers, but the setting can't be beat. At the entrance to the quay is **Blue Door Cafe** (5405 Argyle St., 250/723-8811, 8am-3pm daily, lunch $10-20), a small old-style place that's a real locals' hangout. Breakfasts are huge; an omelet with all the trimmings goes for $10-16.

For fresh cooking and an inviting ambience, if you're heading west from Port Alberni, **Dellas Cafe** (10695 Lakeshore Rd., 250/723-2722, www.sproatlakelanding.com, 8am-4pm daily mid-May-Oct., lunch $10-16) is a great place to stop for breakfast or lunch. As a bonus, it has a gift store stocked with local food, including smoked salmon. Dellas is 15 km (9.3 miles) from town at Sproat Lake Landing Resort.

ACCOMMODATIONS AND CAMPING

Port Alberni motels are generally more expensive than those on the east side of the island, but if you're heading to the west coast, they are cheaper. Aside from a Best Western, there are no chains in town, but rather a string of older independent park-at-your door motels.

Right downtown, you get what you pay for at the **Bluebird Motel** (3755 3rd Ave., 250/723-1153, $75-90 s or d), the cheapest place in town, but many visitors will be happy to pay double at the centrally located **Riverside Motel** (5065 Roger St., 250/724-9916, $159-249 s or d), where many of the rooms have kitchenettes.

Sproat Lake Landing Resort (10695 Lakeshore Rd., 250/723-2722, www.sproatlakelanding.com, mid-May-Oct., $329-549 s or d) is on a large lake of the same name

---

1: Alberni Inlet 2: Port Alberni waterfront

15 km (9.3 miles) west of Port Alberni on the highway leading to the west coast. The resort oozes West Coast contemporary charm, with exposed woodwork throughout and stylish furnishings that extend through public areas to the spacious guest rooms, all of which have balconies. Guests have complimentary use of canoes, kayaks, and paddleboards. Throw in an excellent café and an upscale restaurant specializing in local seafood, and there is no reason to leave during your stay.

The best camping is out of town, at **China Creek Campground** (250/723-9812, $34-52) right on Alberni Inlet. Choose between open and wooded full-facility sites in a relatively remote setting with sweeping views of the inlet from a sandy log-strewn beach. To get here, take 3rd Avenue south to Ship Creek Road and follow it for 14 kilometers (9 miles).

The campground within **Stamp River Provincial Park** (519/858-6161 or 800/689-9025, https://camping.bcparks.ca, Apr.-mid-Nov, $18), northwest of Port Alberni, enjoys a beautiful location on the river of the same name. A park highlight occurs each fall, when thousands of migrating salmon swim up river and over artificial fish ladders around Stamp Falls. From the campground, it's a short walk down to the river, or lace up your hiking boots for the more serious 7.5-kilometer (4.7-mile) Stamp Long River Trail that leads upstream past a succession of rapids. To get to the park, follow Highway 4 through town, and immediately after crossing Kitsuksus Creek, take Beaver Creek Road north for 14 kilometers (9 miles).

INFORMATION

On the rise above town to the east is **Port Alberni Visitor Centre** (2533 Port Alberni Hwy., 250/724-6535 or 866/576-3662, www.albernichamber.ca, 9am-6pm daily summer, 9am-5pm Mon.-Fri. fall-spring). This excellent facility is a great source of local information, as well as details for Pacific Rim National Park, transportation options to Bamfield, and all west coast attractions.

★ MV FRANCES BARKLEY

The *Frances Barkley* (250/723-8313 or 800/663-7192, www.ladyrosemarine.com), a vintage Norwegian ferry, serves the remote communities of Alberni Inlet and Barkley Sound, but because of the spectacular scenery along the route, the day cruise is also one of the island's biggest tourist attractions. Depending on the time of year, orcas and gray whales, seals, sea lions, porpoises, river otters, bald eagles, and all sorts of seabirds join you on your trip through magnificent Barkley Sound. The vessel is also a great way to reach the remote fishing village of Bamfield.

Year-round, the MV *Frances Barkley* departs Alberni Harbour Quay at 8am Tuesday, Thursday, and Saturday, reaching Kildonan at 10am and Bamfield at 12:30pm, then departs Bamfield at 1:30pm and docks back in Port Alberni at 5pm. Inquire about summer stops for kayakers in the Broken Group Islands. If you want to stay longer in Bamfield, accommodations are available. One-way fares from Port Alberni are Kildonan $38.50, Bamfield $47.50. Children under age 16 travel for half price. In summer, the *Frances Barkley* does a roaring business—book as far ahead as possible.

BAMFIELD

One of the island's remotest communities, this tiny fishing village lies along both sides of a narrow inlet on Barkley Sound. Most people arrive here aboard the MV *Frances Barkley* from Port Alberni, but the town is also linked to Port Alberni by a rough 100-kilometer (60-mile) logging road. It's well worth the trip out to go fishing, explore the seashore, or just soak up the atmosphere of this picturesque boardwalk village. Bamfield is also the northern terminus of the **West Coast Trail.**

Practicalities

On the boardwalk, but across the channel from the road side of the village, **Bamfield**

Lodge (250/728-3419, www.bamfield-lodge.com, $120-230 s or d) comprises self-contained cabins set among trees and overlooking the water. Sleeping up to five people, each has a kitchen and barbecue. Rates include boat transfers from across the channel. The lodge owners also operate a waterfront restaurant and a charter boat for fishing and wilderness trips.

WEST FROM PORT ALBERNI

Highway 4 west from Port Alberni meanders through unspoiled mountain wilderness, and you won't find a gas station or store for at least a couple of hours. Ninety-one kilometers (57 miles) from Port Alberni, Highway 4 splits, leading 8 kilometers (5 miles) south to Ucluelet or 34 kilometers (21 miles) north through Pacific Rim National Park to Tofino.

Ucluelet

A small town of 1,700 on the northern edge of Barkley Sound, Ucluelet (pronounced yoo-CLOO-let, although known locally as "Ukee") has a wonderfully scenic location between the ocean and a protected bay. You can enjoy all of the same pursuits as in Tofino—beachcombing, whale-watching, sea kayaking, and fishing—but in a more low-key manner.

The Nuu-chah-nulth people lived around the bay where Ucluelet now sits for centuries before the arrival of Europeans (in the Nuu-chah-nulth language, the town's name means "People of the Safe Harbor"). During the 20th century, Ucluelet was also a fur sealers' trading post and a logging and sawmill center, but fishing remains the steady mainstay, as evidenced by the town's resident fishing fleet and several fish-processing plants.

SIGHTS AND RECREATION

Down on the harbor, Ucluelet Aquarium (180 Main St., 250/726-2782, 10am-4:30pm daily Mar.-Nov., adults $16, seniors $12, children $9) is a dynamic facility, built on piers over the water and designed in the shape of a fish. Operated by a local non-profit, the facility is unique in that it is catch-and-release—every February specimens are collected from local waters, and all are released at the end of the season. The building is anchored by a massive low-profile aquarium, allowing visitors to peer in the glass sides and also over the top.

Touch tanks, interpretive displays, and fish-themed art round out this very special facility.

The Wild Pacific Trail is an ambitious project that will eventually wander along the coastline all the way to Pacific Rim National Park. Through the hard work of local oyster farmer "Oyster Jim," two sections totaling 9 kilometers (5.5 miles) of beautifully maintained coastal trail have currently been completed. One section, the 2.6-kilometer (1.6-mile) Lighthouse Loop, starts from He-tin-kis Park, hugging the rugged and rocky coastline to a lighthouse that is not the world's most photogenic, but it gets the job done—keeping ships from running ashore along this stretch of particularly treacherous coastline. The second section of the Wild Pacific Trail starts from Marine Drive south of downtown and follows the coast for eight kilometers (five miles) to Rocky Bluffs, with the option to loop inland through a forest of ancient cedars.

Many visitors who choose to stay in Ucluelet do so for the fishing, particularly for chinook salmon (Feb.-Sept.) and halibut (May-July). The fall runs of chinook can yield fish up to 20 kilograms (44 pounds), and the town's busy charter fleet offers deep-sea fishing excursions as well as whale-watching trips.

FOOD

Get your morning caffeine fix along with cakes and pastries made from scratch at Zoe's Bakery and Cafe (250 Main St.,

250/726-2253, 8am-3pm daily mid-Mar.-Dec., lunch $9-12). The selection of baked goods is extensive, and includes delicious breakfasts, daily sandwich specials, and soups, all created using island-sourced ingredients whenever possible. At **Barkley Cafe** (1620 Peninsula Rd., 250/726-2999, 7am-3pm daily, lunch $10.50-11.50), along the main road through town, the specialty coffee drinks are all delicious, and sandwiches and paninis are made daily with fresh ingredients. Also of note, the Barkley opens at 7am, so if you're looking for an early start to the day, begin it here with coffee and a breakfast ciabatta.

Seafood is a local specialty and is available at most local restaurants. One of the best choices for truly local fish is ★ **Jiggers Fish & Chips** (1685 Peninsula Rd., 250/726-5400, noon-8pm Fri.-Tues., $15-25), a food truck along the main street with a few picnic tables out front. It's not particularly cheap, but the fish is as fresh and delicious as anywhere on Vancouver Island. When halibut is in season, I encourage you the pay the extra dollars for this delicious treat.

Another casual dining option is **Ukee Dogs Eatery** (1571 Imperial Lane, 250/726-2103, 8am-8pm daily in summer, 10am-4pm daily the rest of the year, $6-18), down by the harbor. Here, in a renovated garage, the day starts with freshly baked breakfast muffins, then moves on to a wide variety of hot dogs, tacos, and burritos. Along the main street, but with water views from outside tables, **Blue Room Bistro** (1627 Peninsula Rd., 250/726-4464, 8am-4pm daily, lunch $12-20) has a good selection of simple breakfasts and lunches, including smoked salmon eggs Benedict and a crispy cod burger.

For its creative presentation of local specialties and an inviting ambience, ★ **Pluvio** (1714 Peninsula Rd., 250/726-7001, 5:30pm-9pm daily mid-Feb.-Dec., $85-105 for 3 to 5 courses) is one of the island's best restaurants, including those in Victoria. The offerings are very seasonal, with seafood purchased daily from local fishing boats, a vast majority of produce sourced from the island, and some ingredients, such as mushrooms and cynamoka berries, foraged from local forests. Simple cooking styles allow flavors to shine through, and combined with immaculate presentation, dining at Pluvio will be a vacation highlight for foodies.

ACCOMMODATIONS

Accommodations and campsites in Ucluelet are somewhat limited, especially if you're looking to stay somewhere inexpensive, so plan ahead by making reservations.

$100-200

If you're looking at sharing inexpensive accommodations with a younger, outdoorsy crowd, reserve a bed at **Ucluelet Hostel** (2081 Peninsula Rd., 250/726-7416, www.cnn-backpackers.com, mid-June-mid-Oct., dorms $45, $175 s or d), a rambling three-story house with a large backyard that extends all the way down to the water, just before reaching town. The lower floor is set aside for a large communal kitchen, while the middle floor has a lounge area and couple of private rooms and the top floor is divided into male and female dorms.

Island West Resort (160 Hemlock St., 250/726-7515, www.islandwestresort.com, $160-180 s or d) has its own marina right on the inlet and serves as the base of operations for a wide range of charter boats. The resort also has a good restaurant and pub. In the height of summer, rooms—each with full kitchen—run from a reasonable $160 s or d.

$200-300

Surfs Inn (1874 Peninsula Rd., 250/726-4426, www.surfsinn.ca, from $220 s or d) comprises a number of different buildings on a forested property along the main road, including a couple of cabins that sleep two to four people, and four-bedroom Surfs Inn guesthouse, which sleeps up to 10 guests.

The road leading to the lobby of the ★ **Black Rock Oceanfront Resort** (596 Marine Dr., 250/726-4800 or 877/226-2559, www.blackrockresort.com, $269-589 s or d)

The Broken Group Islands

These 100 or so forested islands in the mouth of Barkley Sound, south of Ucluelet, are mostly protected by Pacific Rim National Park. They were home to the Nuu-chah-nulth people for many thousands of years prior to the arrival of Europeans, and today their descendants work with Parks Canada on conserving their future as a natural and cultural destination. Although trading posts were established by the Europeans in the early 1900s, now they're inhabited only by wildlife and visited primarily by campers paddling through the archipelago in canoes and kayaks. The islands offer few beaches, so paddlers come ashore in the many sheltered bays.

Marinelife abounds in the cool and clear waters: Seals, porpoises, and gray whales are present year-round. Birdlife is also prolific: Bald eagles, blue herons, and cormorants are permanent residents, and large numbers of loons and Canada geese stop by on their spring and fall migration routes.

The archipelago extends almost 15 kilometers (9 miles) out to sea from Broken Islands Lodge, the starting point for most kayakers. The protected islands of Hand, Gibraltar, Dodo, and Willis all hold campsites and are good destinations for novice paddlers. Farther out, the varying sea conditions make a higher level of skill necessary. Predictably, a westerly wind blows up early each afternoon through summer, making paddling more difficult.

The starting point for most kayaking trips is Sechart, the site of a whaling station and now home to Broken Islands Lodge (250/466-5663, www.brokenislandslodge.com, $299-349 s, $369-409 d), in a delightful cove far removed from civilization. Originally an office building for a local forestry company, the lodge was barged to the site and converted to comfortable guest rooms and a dining room. All meals are included in the rates, and single and double kayaks can be rented, whether you are guest or not, for $69-99 per day. Beyond the lodge, kayakers will need to plan ahead by reserving campsites on the remote islands through the Parks Canada (877/737-3783, www.reservation.pc.gc.ca).

The best way to reach the lodge and the Broken Group Islands is by water taxi from Secret Beach Marina. To get to the marina, head west from Port Alberni for 80 kilometers (50 miles) and turn left onto Toquaht Bay Road. Stay left at all intersections, and after 15 kilometers (9.3 miles), you reach the marina and a campground (250/726-8349, www.secretbeachcampground. com, mid-June-mid-Sept., $40). The only scheduled departures head to Broken Islands Lodge at 10:15am and 4pm daily between mid-June and mid-September, but the boat can be chartered from the marina and from the lodge for departures further into the archipelago.

doesn't even hint at the sweeping oceanfront views enjoyed by guests who upgrade to an Oceanview room at the contemporary lodging set on a rocky headland just south of town. Public areas are dominated by striking steel, rock, and wood architecture, while the 133 rooms take full advantage of the setting with floor-to-ceiling windows. Amenities include an oceanfront restaurant with outdoor patio, and a day spa.

North of town, my favorite lodging at **Wya Point Resort** (2460 Willowbrae Rd., 250/726-2625, www.wyapoint.com, yurts $249-299 s or d, private lodges from $600 s or d) are the yurts, on wooden platforms overlooking the ocean—perfect for campers who want the experience without having to buy the equipment. The yurts share baths, but each is very spacious and has a large deck with barbecue, comfortable beds, kitchen equipment, and lounge chairs. The resort also has private lodges, each with one or two separate bedrooms in a variety of configurations, but all are airy and spacious, with lots of exposed woodwork and large windows. They also have full kitchens. To get here, head north from Ucluelet and look for Willowbrae Road to the left.

Over $300

Terrace Beach Resort (1002 Peninsula Rd., 778/762-3600, www.terracebeachresort.ca,

$500-900 s or d) was the first Tofino-style lodging in Ucluelet. The weathered "eco-industrial" exterior is a little deceiving, as the guest rooms feature West Coast contemporary styling throughout livable units that range from one-bedroom suites to multistory oceanfront cabins with decks and hot tubs. Winding through the property are elevated boardwalks enclosed in an old-growth forest. In the off-season, rooms sell for as little as $160 and cabins for $250, an excellent value.

Camping

The best camping is north of town, on the southern edge of Pacific Rim National Park. Here you'll find **Wya Point Resort** (2460 Willowbrae Rd., 250/726-2625, www.wyapoint.com, $55-75), where the least expensive campsites are set among towering trees of the coastal rainforest. The more expensive ones overlook the ocean and a short stretch of sandy beach, which often has good waves for surfing.

Options closer to town include **Ucluelet Campground** (260 Seaplane Base Rd.,

250/726-4355, www.uclueletcampground. com, $50-72), which is set around a forested cove at the west end of Ucluelet Harbour, and the downtown waterfront **Island West Resort** (160 Hemlock St., 250/726-7515, www. islandwestresort.com, $52-55 s or d), which is for RVs only.

INFORMATION

Ucluelet itself doesn't have a visitors center. Instead, stop at **Pacific Rim Visitor Centre** (2791 Pacific Rim Hwy., 250/726-4600, www. discoverucluelet.com, 10am-5pm daily May-mid-Oct.), where Highway 4 spurs north to Tofino and Peninsula Road heads south to Ucluelet.

GETTING THERE

VI Connector buses (866/986-3466, www. viconnector.com) stop at Ucluelet on their daily run between Victoria and Tofino, with stops made at both Nanaimo ferry terminals. The fare to Ucluelet from Victoria is $100, and from Nanaimo, $65. The fare between Tofino and Ucluelet is $20 one-way.

Pacific Rim National Park

Named for its location on the edge of the Pacific Ocean, this park encompasses a long, narrow strip of coast that has been battered by the sea for eons. The park comprises three units, each different in nature and accessed in different ways. The section at the end of Highway 4 is the **Long Beach Unit,** named for an 11-kilometer (7-mile) stretch of beach that dominates the landscape. Accessible by vehicle, this is the most popular part of the park and is particularly busy in July and August. To the south, in Barkley Sound, the **Broken Group Islands Unit** encompasses an archipelago of 100 islands, accessible by the MV *Frances Barkley* from Port Alberni. Farther south still is the **West Coast Trail Unit,** named for the famous long-distance

hiking trail between Port Renfrew and Bamfield.

You're not charged a fee to just travel straight through the park to Tofino, but if you stop anywhere en route, a strictly enforced charge applies. A one-day permit is adults $10.50, seniors $9, to a maximum of $21 per vehicle. Stock up on supplies in either Port Alberni or Tofino before heading out into the park, as the only facilities are a campground and day-use areas.

PLANTS AND ANIMALS

Like the entire west coast of Vancouver Island, Pacific Rim National Park is dominated by littoral (coastal) rainforest. Closest to the ocean, clinging to the rocky shore, a narrow

Pacific Rim National Park

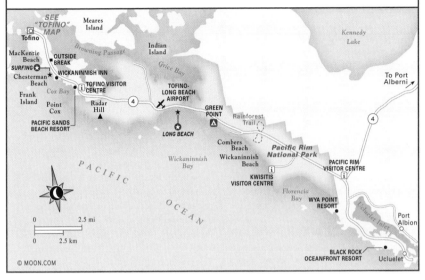

windswept strip of Sitka spruce is covered by salty water year-round. These forests of spruce are compact and low-growing, forming a natural windbreak for the old-growth forests of western hemlock and western red cedar farther inland. The old-growth forests are strewn with fallen trees and lushly carpeted with mosses, shrubs, and ferns.

The ocean off western Canada reputedly holds more species of marinelife than any other temperate coast. Gray whales migrate up the coast each spring, seals and porpoises inhabit the park's waters year-round, sea lions overwinter on rocky offshore outcrops, and salmon spawn in the larger creeks through late fall. The tidal zone is the best place to search out smaller sea creatures such as anemones, shellfish, and starfish—all colorful residents of the rocky shoreline.

The park's largest land mammal is the black bear, some of which occasionally wander down to the beach in search of food. Also present are black-tailed deer, raccoons, otters, and mink. Bald eagles are year-round residents. The migratory birds arrive in the largest numbers in spring and fall, when thousands of Canada geese, pintails, mallards, and black brants converge on the vast tidal mudflats of **Grice Bay,** in the north of the park beyond the golf course.

★ LONG BEACH

Ensconced between rocky headlands is more than 11 kilometers (7 miles) of hard-packed white sand, covered in twisted driftwood, shells, and the occasional Japanese glass fishing float. Dense rainforest and the high snowcapped peaks of the Mackenzie Range form a beautiful backdrop, while offshore lie craggy surf-battered isles home to extensive marinelife.

Through summer, Long Beach attracts hordes of visitors. Most just wander along the beach soaking up the smells and sounds of the sea, but some brave the cool waters for swimming or surfing. The waves here are reputed to be Canada's best; rent boards and wetsuits in Ucluelet and Tofino. In winter, hikers dress for the harsh elements and walk the surf-pounded beach in search of treasures,

Coastal Climate

Weather patterns on the west coast of Vancouver Island are dominated by eastward-moving air masses that hit the coastline and cool quickly, releasing moisture that equates to over 3,000 millimeters (120 inches) of rainfall annually. This pattern leads to relatively minimal changes in temperatures throughout the year. Additionally, west coast weather can only be described as extremely changeable, especially in summer. It can be windy and wet in the morning, yet warm and dry in the afternoon, so always carry extra clothes and raingear while exploring Pacific Rim National Park. In summer, when the average temperature daily high is 19°C (66°F), dense fog is common, especially in the morning.

In winter, Pacific Rim experiences a good proportion of its annual rainfall, and the average temperature is 6°C (43°F). In spring, you can expect 10°C (50°F) days, 6°C (43°F) days in autumn.

admiring the ocean's fury during the many ferocious storms.

KWISITIS VISITOR CENTRE

You can access the beach at many places, but first stop at the **Kwisitis Visitor Centre** (Wickaninnish Rd., 250/726-4212, 10am-5pm daily May-mid-Oct., 10am-5pm Fri.-Sun. mid-Oct.-Apr., free with proof of park entry payment), which overlooks Long Beach from a protected southern cove near the south end of the park. This is the place to learn about the natural and Nuu-chah-nulth peoples history of both the park and the ocean through exhibits, First Nations artwork, and spectacular hand-painted murals.

TOP EXPERIENCE

HIKING

The most obvious place to go for a walk in Pacific Rim National Park is along the beach. From the Kwisitis Visitor Centre at the end of Wickaninnish Road, Long Beach extends north for around 11 kilometers (7 miles). With the ocean on one side and piles of driftwood pushed up against lush rainforest on the other, you'll never tire of the scenery.

Don't be put off by the unappealing name of the **Bog Trail** (allow 20 minutes), which makes a short loop off the road between the Pacific Rim Highway and the Kwisitis Visitor Centre. Poor drainage has created

a buildup of sphagnum and stunted the growth of trees such as shore pine that struggle to absorb nutrients from the waterlogged soil. From the Kwisitis Visitor Centre, an 800-meter (0.5-mile) trail (15 minutes one-way) leads south around a windswept headland, passing small coves and Lismer Beach, then descending a boardwalk to pebbly **South Beach.** Back up the hill, the **Wickaninnish Trail** leads 2.5 kilometers (1.6 miles) over to Florencia Bay; allow 50 minutes one-way. The beach along the bay can also be accessed by road off the Kwisitis Visitor Centre access road. Continuing northwest toward Tofino, the **Rainforest Trail** traverses an old-growth littoral rainforest in two 1-kilometer (0.6-mile) loops (allow 20 minutes for each). Farther north, at the back of the Combers Beach parking lot, is the trailhead for the 1.6-kilometer (1-mile) **Spruce Fringe Loop.** This trail leads along the beach past piles of driftwood and through a forest of Sitka spruce.

CAMPING

Green Point Campground (mid-Mar.-mid-Oct., $29-34.50, OTENTiks $128 s or d) has a marvelous location behind Long Beach. Facilities include drive-in sites, restrooms, picnic tables, an evening interpretive program, plenty of firewood, and a few sites

1: Pacific Rim National Park **2:** surfer at sunset on Long Beach **3:** Wild Pacific Trail

with power hookups. Demand for these sites at Green Point is extremely high, so make reservations through the **Parks Canada** (877/737-3783, www.reservation.pc.gc.ca) as soon as the system opens in January for the upcoming summer.

INFORMATION AND SERVICES

Kwisitis Visitor Centre (Wickaninnish Rd., 250/726-4212, www.pc.gc.ca/pacificrim, 10am-5pm daily May-mid-Oct., 10am-5pm Fri.-Sun. mid-Oct.-Apr.) is a worthwhile stop in itself, but is also the best source of park information. On the road into the park, **Pacific Rim Visitor Centre** (2791 Pacific Rim Hwy., 250/726-4600, www.discoverucluelet.com, 10am-5pm daily May-mid-Oct.) sits where Highway 4 meets the road from Port Alberni. There are no stores or gas stations in the park, but supplies and gas are available in Ucluelet and Tofino.

Tofino

The bustling tourist town of Tofino sits at the end of a long narrow peninsula, with the only road access to the outside world being winding Highway 4. Originally the site of a First Nations Clayoquot village, Tofino was one of the first points in Canada to be visited by Captain Cook. It was named in 1792 for Don de Vincent Tofino, a hydrographer with a Spanish expedition. Aside from contact with fur traders and whalers, the entire district remained basically unchanged for almost 100 years.

Fishing has always been the mainstay of the local economy, but Tofino is also a supply center for the several hundred hermits living along the secluded shores of the sound and for the hordes of visitors who come in summer to visit Pacific Rim National Park, just to the south. In winter, it's a quiet, friendly community with a population of fewer than 2,000. In summer, the population swells to several times that size, and the village springs to life: Fishing boats pick up supplies and deposit salmon, cod, prawns, crabs, halibut, and other delicacies of the sea, and cruising, whale-watching, and fishing boats, along with seaplanes, do a roaring business introducing visitors to the natural wonders of the west coast.

The town lies on the southern edge of sheltered **Clayoquot Sound,** known worldwide for an ongoing fight by environmentalists to save the world's largest remaining coastal temperate forest. Around 200,000 hectares (494,000 acres) of this old-growth forest remain; several parks, including Clayoquot Arm Provincial Park, Clayoquot Plateau Provincial Park, Hesquiat Peninsula Provincial Park, Flores Island Provincial Park, and Maquinna Marine Provincial Park have resulted from the Clayoquot Sound Land Use Decision. An influx of environmentally conscious residents over the last two decades has added flavor to one of the west coast's most picturesque and relaxing towns, and because many aware residents like Tofino exactly the way it is, it's unlikely that high-rise hotels or fast-food chains will ever spoil this peaceful coastal paradise.

SIGHTS
Tofino Botanical Gardens

Tofino is best known for whale-watching, kayaking, and the long sandy beaches south of town, but a couple of interesting diversions are well worth a stop. The first is **Tofino Botanical Gardens** (1084 Pacific Rim Hwy., 250/725-1220, 9am-dusk daily, adults $12, students $8, under age 13 free), just before town. Developed by knowledgeable locals, it showcases local flora with the emphasis on indigenous culture. One garden is devoted to native species you would find in the adjacent national park, and another to plants you can

Tofino

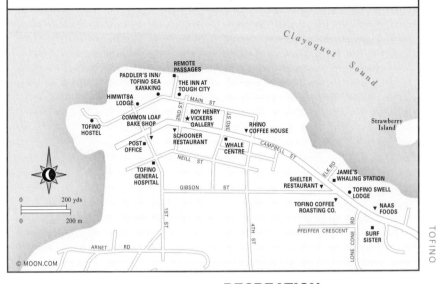

© MOON.COM

eat. This is the only botanical garden I've visited where a colorfully painted camper van from the 1970s is incorporated into a display. Another botanical point of interest is the massive cedar tree on the right-hand side of the road as you enter town. Estimated to be more than 800 years old, the tree is kept from toppling over by wire stays.

Roy Henry Vickers Gallery

Roy Henry Vickers Gallery (350 Campbell St., 250/725-3235, 10am-5pm daily in summer, 11am-4pm Thurs.-Mon. the rest of the year, free) features the eye-catching paintings, prints, and sculptures of Roy Henry Vickers, a well-known and highly respected Tsimshian artist. You can watch a video about the artist and then browse among the artworks, primarily First Nations designs and outdoor scenes with clean lines and brilliant colors. If you fall for one of the most popular paintings but can't afford it, you can buy it in card or poster form. The gallery is built on the theme of a west coast First Nations longhouse, with a carved and painted exterior and interior totem poles.

RECREATION

TOP EXPERIENCE

★ Surfing at Tofino

If you fancy a long walk along a fabulous shell-strewn stretch of white sand, like to sit on craggy rocks watching the waves disintegrate into white spray, or just want a piece of sun all your own to lie in and work on your tan, head for **Chesterman Beach,** just south of Tofino. From that beach, at low tide you can walk all the way out to **Frank Island** to watch the surf pound the exposed side while the tide creeps in and cuts you off from civilization for a few hours. The turnoff (not marked) to Chesterman Beach is Lynn Road, on the right just past the Dolphin Motel as you leave Tofino. Follow the road and park at one of three small parking lots; the parking lot at the corner of Lynn and Chesterman Beach Roads is closest to Frank Island.

Surfers wanting to hit the water should head south of town to **Live to Surf** (Outside Break, 1180 Pacific Rim Hwy., 250/725-4464, www.livetosurf.com). The shop rents surfboards for $38 per day and wetsuits for $30, and offers lessons for $75 pp, including rentals. The staff will also tell you where the best surf can be found, and if there's no surf, they'll tell you how good it was last week. The shop is within Outside Break, a group of like-minded local businesses on the road leading into town. It's the perfect place to shop for surf apparel and local arts, or to just relax over a coffee. Check the website for west coast surf reports. Back in town, **Surf Sister** (625 Campbell St., 250/725-4456 or 877/724-7873, www.surf-sister.com) is Canada's only all-women surf school, which charges around $100 per day for lessons and surfboard/wetsuit rental.

Kayaking

Aside from surfing, exploring the waters around Tofino by sea kayak is the most popular recreation activity in Tofino. **Tofino Sea Kayaking** (320 Main St., 250/725-4222, www.tofinoseakayaking.com) has designed tours to meet the demand and suit all levels of experience. Excursions range from a three-hour harbor paddle ($69 pp) to a six-hour ocean paddle along the open ocean coastline ($124 pp). The company's experienced staff will also help adventurous, independent paddlers plan an itinerary—many camping areas lie within a one-day paddle of Tofino. Single kayak rentals are $80 for one day or $60-70 per day for two or more days; double kayaks are $140 or $110-120. Rental prices include all accessories. The company base, right on the harbor, has a shop selling provisions, accessories such as marine charts, and a wide range of local literature; a cafe; and a few upstairs guest rooms ($135-155 s or d).

Whale-Watching

Each spring around 20,000 Pacific gray whales migrate between Baja and Alaska, passing through the waters off Tofino between March and May. Most of them continue north, but some stay in local waters throughout summer. Their feeding grounds are north of Tofino within **Maquinna Marine Park.** During the spring migration and some feeding periods,

gray whales are also frequently sighted in the calm inland waters around **Meares Island,** just off Tofino.

Whale-watching is one of the most popular activities in town, and companies search out whales to watch them cruise up the coast, diving, surfacing, and spouting. On the whale-watching trips, you'll likely spy other marinelife as well; look for sea lions and puffins sunning themselves on offshore rocks, dolphins and harbor seals frolicking in the bays and inlets, and majestic bald eagles gracefully swooping around in the sky or perching in the treetops. Trips depart mid-March to early November and generally last 2-3 hours. Expect to pay $120-130 pp.

Cruises and Charters

The streets of downtown Tofino hold a profusion of charter operators offering a wide variety of trips. All of those listed below go whale-watching and head out to Hotsprings Cove. Other options include a tour of Meares Island and fishing charters. For details, head to any of the following: **Jamie's** (606 Campbell St., 250/725-3919 or 800/667-9913, www.jamies.com), **Remote Passages** (51 Wharf St., 250/725-3330 or 800/666-9833, www.remotepassages.com), or the **Whale Centre** (411 Campbell St., 250/725-2132 or 888/474-2288, www.tofinowhalecentre.com), where a gray whale skeleton is on display. Even with all these operators, business is brisk, so book ahead if possible.

Hot Springs

Pamper yourself and take a boat or floatplane to **Hotsprings Cove,** Vancouver Island's only hot spring. Water bubbles out of the ground at a temperature of 87°C (189°F), tumbles over a cliff, and then drops down through a series of pools—each large enough for two or three people—and into the sea. Lobsterize yourself silly in the first pool, or go for the ultimate in hot-cold torture by immersing yourself in the

---

1: Chesterman Beach 2: the Inn at Tough City
3: Wickaninnish Inn 4: kayaking along the coast

last pool, where at high tide you'll be slapped by breathtakingly refreshing ocean waves.

Each of the companies listed above under Cruises and Charters offer excursions out to the hot springs, and although prices vary slightly, expect to pay around $170 for a six- to seven-hour trip departing around 10am, with about three hours ashore at the hot springs and the chance to see whales en route. **Tofino Air** (250/725-4454, www.tofinoair.ca), based at the 1st Street dock, offers a scenic 20-minute flight to the hot springs by floatplane (minimum 3 people, $220 pp round-trip).

EVENTS

Tofino and Ucluelet join together each spring to put on the annual **Pacific Rim Whale Festival** (www.pacificrimwhalefestival.com), which features educational shows and special events in the adjacent national park, a First Nations song and dance festival, a parade, crab races, plays at the local theater, dances, concerts, and a multitude of events and activities in celebration of the gray whale spring migration. The festival takes place the last two weeks of March.

FOOD
Cafés and Cheap Eats

For basic groceries, Tofino has a midsize **Co-op Food Store** (140 1st St., 250/725-3226, 8:30am-7pm daily) at the far end of the main street into town. For the very freshest seafood, stop by **Naas Foods** (630 Campbell St., 250/266-8556, 10am-7pm daily), which, in addition to fresh local fish (halibut, cod, salmon, and rockfish), also sells kelp. This seaweed can be purchased dried or smoked and is most often used in salads, but can also be enjoyed as a snack.

Common Loaf Bake Shop (180 1st St., 250/725-3915, 7am-7pm daily summer, 8am-3pm Tues.-Sat. the rest of the year) is a longtime favorite with locals (delicious cinnamon rolls for $5); sit outside or upstairs, where you'll have a magnificent view down Tofino's main street and across the sound.

Also an established part of the café scene is **Rhino Coffee** (430 Campbell St., 250/725-2558, 7:30am-4pm daily, lunch $9-13.50), which has a chill surfer vibe, along with excellent coffee that is roasted in-house. Food offerings include generously filled breakfast wraps, sandwiches, and salads. On the road into town, the emphasis at **Tofino Coffee Roasting Co.** (605 Gibson St., 250/726-6016, 7am-3pm daily) is on high-quality coffee, roasted in-house daily.

Perfectly reflecting the Tofino lifestyle is **Outside Break** (1180 Pacific Rim Hwy.), a collection of locally operated eateries, boutiques, and the coast's original surf shop, surrounded by coastal rainforest on the road into town between Lynn Road and Hellesen Drive. At the front of the complex is the **Tofitian** (250/725-2631, 7am-4pm daily April-Sept., 7am-3pm daily Oct.-March), which is a welcoming café with an amazing array of coffee drinks, a wide range of loose-leaf teas, and an in-house bakery. The orange van at the back of Outside Break is ★ **Tacofino** (250/725-8228, 11am-6pm daily, $7-15), a brightly painted food truck that possibly has the best fish tacos on Vancouver Island. They are fresh, filled with local fish, and reasonably priced. After being served with a smile, enjoy your feast at one of the surrounding picnic tables.

Even if staying at the upscale Wickaninnish Inn is outside your budget, the resort's **Driftwood Cafe** (Wickaninnish Inn, Osprey Lane, Chesterman Beach, 250/725-3100, 7am-9pm daily, lunch $12-15) is a wonderful spot for guests and nonguests alike, especially after a morning walk along Chesterman Beach. The café itself has sweeping ocean views and is anchored by an impressive bar made from a large piece of driftwood. The menu includes a wide range of coffee drinks, fruit smoothies, and light breakfasts. Lunch is highlighted by clam chowder, salads, and a cheese platter.

Restaurants

Schooner Restaurant (331 Campbell St., 250/725-3444, 9am-9pm Wed.-Sun., $22-44) has been dishing up well-priced seafood for over 70 years. Over time the menu has gotten more creative (crab, shrimp, and brie cheese-stuffed halibut), but old favorites (cedar-planked salmon) still appear. Also of note is the service, which is remarkably good for a tourist town.

In an unassuming building near the entrance to town, **Shelter Restaurant** (601 Campbell St., 250/725-3353, noon-10pm daily, $18-35) brings some big-city pizzazz to tiny Tofino. Inside you'll find an open dining room with imaginative treats such as Southwestern-spiced calamari and an Asian-inspired seafood bowl.

South of Tofino, the ★ **Pointe Restaurant** (Wickaninnish Inn, Osprey Lane, Chesterman Beach, 250/725-3100, 8am-9pm daily, $42-58) is simply superb in every respect. Built on a rocky headland, the circular dining room provides sweeping ocean views as good as those at any restaurant in Canada (ask for a window table when reserving). At breakfast, mimosas encourage holiday spirit, or get serious by ordering eggs Benedict with smoked salmon. The lunch and dinner menus highlight seafood and island produce. Lunch includes seafood chowder and a wild salmon BLT. A good way to start dinner is with potato-crusted oysters or endive and berry salad before moving on to the seared wild salmon or butter-baked halibut. The impeccable service and a wine list that's dominated by Pacific Northwest bottles round out a world-class dining experience.

ACCOMMODATIONS

Tofino boasts plenty of accommodations, both in town and south along the beach-fringed coastline, but getting a room or campsite in summer can be difficult if you just turn up, so book as far ahead as possible. As elsewhere on the island, high-season rates apply July and August. Visit a month or two on either side of summer holidays and you'll enjoy big discounts when the weather is still warm enough to take advantage of Tofino's outdoor attractions. Winter in Tofino is known as the storm-watching season, when rates are reduced up

to 50 percent, although no one can guarantee the big storms.

$100-200

The town's least expensive lodging for single travelers is **Tofino Hostel** (81 West St., 250/725-3443, www.tofinohostel.com, dorms $55, $179-339 s or d). Affiliated with Hostelling International, it is a world away from hostels of old, appealing to all travelers. The building is a stylish log structure with a stunning waterfront location, of which the communal lounge area takes full advantage. Other facilities include a modern kitchen, a laundry room, a large deck with a barbecue, free wireless Internet, a game room, and bike rentals.

Paddler's Inn (320 Main St., 250/725-4222 or 800/863-4664, www.tofinopaddlersinn.com, $135-155 s or d) has a prime location along the downtown waterfront. Within the century-old Hotel Tofino, the five guest rooms are basic but comfortable and share two bathrooms. Guests also have use of a communal kitchen and living area. The Inn is operated by Tofino Sea Kayaking, which is based downstairs (10% discount for guests), along with a café that has a good choice of food perfect for a picnic lunch.

As you drive into town, **Tofino Swell Lodge** (341 Olsen Rd., 250/725-3274, www.tofinoswell.com, $175 s or d) is on the right above a busy marina. This seven-room motel offers older but well-decorated rooms, shared use of a fully equipped kitchen and living room (complete with a TV and telescope), a barbecue area, and pleasant gardens with incredible views of Tofino Inlet, tree-covered Meares Island, and distant snowcapped mountains.

$200-300

Out of town to the south are several oceanfront resorts. Of these, ★ **Middle Beach Lodge** (Mackenzie Beach Rd., 250/725-2900 or 866/725-2900, www.middlebeach.com, $210-500 s or d) does the best job of combining a unique west coast experience with reasonable prices. It comprises two distinct complexes: At the Beach, which is more intimate, with its own private beach; and At the Headlands, with luxurious self-contained chalets built along the top of a rugged headland. A short trail links the two, and guests are welcome to wander between them. Rates for At the Beach start at a very reasonable $165, but there are also rooms with ocean views and a balcony from $210, and all rates include a gourmet continental breakfast served in a magnificent common room. Breakfast is complimentary, while the resort also has a restaurant with a table d'hôte menu offered nightly.

Overlooking the water right downtown is the **Inn at Tough City** (350 Main St., 250/725-2021 or 877/250-2021, http://toughcity.com, $219-279 s or d), constructed with materials sourced from throughout the region. The bricks, all 30,000 of them, were salvaged from a 100-year-old building in Vancouver's historical Gastown, while stained-glass windows, hardwood used in the flooring, and many of the furnishings are of historical value. The rooms are decorated in a stylish heritage color scheme, and beds are covered in plush down duvets.

In the best location in town, right beside the main dock, is **Himwitsa Lodge** (300 Main St., 250/725-2017, www.himwitsa. com, $230-300 s or d). At street level is a First Nations art gallery, while the second floor comprises contemporary suites, each with a comfortable lounge, a fully equipped kitchen, and a private balcony with ocean views.

$400-500

The log cabins at **Crystal Cove Beach Resort** (250/725-4213, www.crystalcove.ca, $410-650 s or d), south of town, have direct access to MacKenzie Beach. All cabins have kitchens and decks, while many have separate bedrooms, and the most expensive have private hot tubs. Outside of summer, rates drop as low as $240 s or d.

Over $500

You'll find cheaper places to stay in Tofino, but you won't find a lodge like ★ **Pacific**

Sands Beach Resort (Cox Bay, 250/725-3322 or 800/565-2322, www.pacificsands.com, from $629 s or d), which is perfect for families and outdoorsy types who want to kick back for a few days. Set right on a popular surfing beach eight kilometers (five miles) south of town, guest units come in a variety of configurations, starting with one-bedroom, kitchen-equipped suites. Some of these hold a prime beachfront location—ask when booking. The best units are the newest: two-level timber-frame villas equipped with everything from surfboard racks to stainless steel kitchen appliances. The heated floors and gas fireplaces are a plus during the winter storm-watching season. Pacific Sands is a family-run operation, which translates to friendly service and repeat guests who have been visiting since childhood (and still bring their surfboards).

If you subscribe to one of those glossy travel mags, you've probably read about the ★ **Wickaninnish Inn** (Osprey Lane, Chesterman Beach, 250/725-3100, www.wickinn.com, from $580 s or d), which is regarded as one of the world's great resorts—and regularly features at the top of Top Ten lists. Just for good measure, the in-house Pointe Restaurant is similarly lauded. Everything you've read is true: If you want to surrender to the lap of luxury in a wilderness setting, this is the place to do it. Designed to complement the rainforest setting, the exterior post-and-beam construction is big and bold, while the interior oozes West Coast elegance. Public areas such as the restaurant, an upscale lounge, a relaxing library, and a downstairs TV room make the resort feel like a world unto itself, but the guest rooms will really wow you. Spread throughout two wings, the 76 rooms overflow with amenities, including fireplaces, oversize soaker tubs, super-comfortable beds, and furniture made from recycled old-growth woods, but the ocean views through floor-to-ceiling windows will captivate you most. The menu of spa treatments is phenomenal—think hot stone massage for two in a hut overlooking the ocean, a full-body exfoliation, or a sacred sea hydrotherapy treatment. The Wickaninnish is a five-minute drive south of Tofino; you won't want to leave.

Camping

All of Tofino's campgrounds are on the beaches south of town, but enjoying the great outdoors comes at a price in this part of the world, with some campsites costing more than $50 per night. The best of the bunch is **Bella Pacifica Campground** (250/725-3400, www.bellapacifica.com, Mar.-late Oct., $80-95), right on MacKenzie Beach and offering over 100 protected tent sites and full hook-ups, as well as coin-operated showers and a laundry room.

Along the same stretch of sand, **Crystal Cove Beach Resort** (250/725-4213, www.crystalcove.ca, $75-95, cabins $410-650) has modern facilities, a coffee and muffin bar, and direct access to MacKenzie Beach. Many of the sites are in a private, heavily wooded area, but tents are not allowed. Open year-round, outside of summer campsites are $55 and cabins start at $240.

INFORMATION AND SERVICES

Tofino Visitor Centre (1426 Pacific Rim Hwy., 250/725-3414, www.tourismtofino.com, 9am-7pm daily summer, 10am-5pm daily

fall-spring) is along the Pacific Rim Highway, eight kilometers (five miles) before town.

The **post office,** a **laundromat,** and **Tofino General Hospital** (250/725-3212) are all on Campbell Street.

Getting There

The closest town of any size to Tofino is Port Alberni, 130 kilometers (80 miles) to the east (allow at least 2.5 hours along a very narrow and winding road); Victoria is 340 kilometers (210 miles) distant.

VI Connector buses (866/986-3466, www.viconnector.com) run one bus daily between Victoria and Tofino, making pickups at both Nanaimo ferry terminals. The fare from Victoria is $85. Three times daily, this company runs a bus between Tofino and Ucluelet ($20 one-way), with stops made at lodges, beaches, and hiking trails along the way.

Pacific Coastal (604/273-8666 or 800/663-2872) flies from its base at Vancouver's South Terminal to Tofino year-round. **Harbour Air** (250/714-0900, www.harbourair.com) is a seaplane service between the Vancouver harborfront (just west of the convention center) and Tofino. Although it doesn't offer any scheduled flights, **Tofino Air** (250/725-4454), based at the foot of 1st Street, provides scenic floatplane flightseeing and charters.

Oceanside

Back on the east side of the island, Highway 19 (Inland Island Hwy.) north of the Highway 4 junction to the west coast bypasses a stretch of coastline that has developed as a popular holiday area, with many beaches, resorts, and waterfront campgrounds, known collectively as Oceanside.

PARKSVILLE

Unspoiled sand fringes the coastline between Parksville (pop. 12,500) and Qualicum Beach. Parksville Beach claims "the warmest water in the whole of Canada." When the tide goes

out along this stretch of the coast, it leaves a strip of sand up to 1 kilometer (0.6 miles) wide exposed to the sun. When the water returns, voilà—sand-heated water.

Sights and Recreation

Running parallel to Highway 19A (Island Hwy.) through town is **Parksville Beach,** with lots of driftwood and protected swimming. At low tide, there is a wide swath of sand where beachgoers relax and kids play in shallow pools. On warm days, as the tide comes in, the warm sand warms the water,

Oceanside

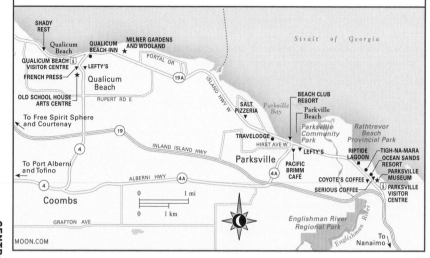

SHADY REST

Qualicum Beach · QUALICUM BEACH INN ★ · MILNER GARDENS AND WOOLAND

QUALICUM BEACH VISITOR CENTRE ℹ
FRENCH PRESS ★
Qualicum Beach
PORTAL DR
▾ LEFTY'S
19A

OLD SCHOOL HOUSE ARTS CENTRE
RUPERT RD E

To Free Spirit Sphere and Courtenay

19

4

To Port Alberni and Tofino
4
ALBERNI HWY
4A

Coombs

GRAFTON AVE

MOON.COM

INLAND ISLAND HWY

ISLAND HWY W

SALT PIZZERIA ▾

Parkville Bay

Strait of Georgia

BEACH CLUB RESORT
Parkville Beach

TRAVELODGE ●
HIRST AVE W
Parksville
▾ LEFTY'S
PACIFIC BRIMM CAFÉ
4A

Parksville Community Park

RIPTIDE LAGOON ■

COYOTE'S COFFEE ▾
SERIOUS COFFEE ▾

Rathtrevor Beach Provincial Park

TIGH-NA-MARA OCEAN SANDS RESORT
PARKSVILLE MUSEUM
ℹ PARKSVILLE VISITOR CENTRE

0   1 mi
0   1 km

Englishman River Regional Park

To Nanaimo

Englishman River

creating ideal swimming for all ages. Behind the beach is **Parksville Community Park** with a boardwalk, a large playground, a splash park, a skateboard park, exercise equipment that anyone is free to use, and lots of grassy areas to spread out a picnic.

Rathtrevor Beach Provincial Park, a 347-hectare (860-acre) chunk of coastline just south of the town center, features a fine 2-kilometer (1.2-mile) sandy beach, a wooded area of old-growth Douglas fir, signs of homesteaders dating to the 1880s, and easy walking trails. The birdwatching highlight occurs in March and April, when thousands of Brant geese stop by on their annual migration to Alaska, swooping into the water for a herring feast.

The children will probably want to stop at **Riptide Lagoon** (1000 Resort Dr., 250/248-8290, 9:30am-9:30pm daily mid-Mar.-mid-Oct.), near the park entrance. This over-the-top 36-hole mini-golf complex costs $9.25 per game for adults, $7 for children.

Although the beach is the focus for most people visiting Parksville, there is a small museum adjacent to the information center at **Parksville Museum** (1245 East Island Hwy., 250/248-6966, 10am-5pm daily May-Sept., donation), comprising historical buildings such as an 1888 post office, an example of a century-old holiday cottage, a one-room schoolhouse, and a church that is still used for weddings. Although the buildings are only open in summer, you can wander through the grounds year-round.

Events

Also known as Beachfest, the midsummer **Canadian Open Sand Sculpting Competition** (250/951-2678, www.parksvillebeachfest.ca) takes place along the greenspace at Parksville Community Park from mid-July to late August. Created by artists from across Canada who are given 30 hours over four days to complete their masterpieces, the sand sculptures are nothing short of amazing. But one of the good things about the event is that the sand sculptures remain on display 9am-9pm daily until mid-August, and entry to the compound is just $3. The event also features beachside concerts every Friday and Saturday evening throughout the festival.

Food

Step away from the beach scene at **Pacific Brimm Cafe** (123 Craig St., 250/248-3336, 8:30am-3:30pm Mon.-Sat., 8am-1pm Sun., lunch $9-14), an inviting café that's halfway between relaxed and refined. In addition to all the usual coffee choices, you'll find a good selection of loose-leaf teas, delicious over-size cinnamon buns, full breakfasts, and hot lunches, all at reasonable prices.

On the south side of town, toward down-town from the museum, are two good choices for coffee. **Serious Coffee** (Heritage Centre Mall, 1209 East Island Hwy., 250/586-0188, 6:30am-4pm Mon.-Fri., 7am-4pm Sat.-Sun.) is a Vancouver Island chain renowned for its quality drinks, but if you've already tried Serious elsewhere, search out nearby **Coyote's Coffee** (1499 Huntley Rd., 250/586-2204, 9am-5pm Mon.-Fri.), where ethically sourced beans are roasted in-house. Food is minimal; it's all about the coffee here, including excellent espressos.

Lefty's (280 Hwy. 19A, 250/954-3886, 11:30am-7pm, lunch $15-23) is a bistro-style restaurant along the main road through Parksville (beside Thrifty Foods). In addition to standard cooked breakfasts, there are delicious oatmeal pancakes made in-house. Lunch choices include cranberry quinoa salad, while in the evening, choices range from thin-crust pizza to slow-roasted back ribs.

Salt Pizzeria (897 Island Hwy. W, 250/586-2121, 3pm-8pm Wed.-Sun., $18-25) cooks up some of the island's best pizza from an unassuming shopfront on the north side of downtown. Thin-crust sourdough is topped with minimal sauces, allowing the tastes and smells of the very freshest ingredients to shine through. Our family had Prosciutto Fresco (prosciutto, arugula, and parmesan cheese) and West Coast (goat cheese, red onions, and smoked salmon), and we all agreed they were as good as we've had for many years.

After soaking up the elegance of the Grotto Spa at Tigh-Na-Mara Seaside Spa Resort, plan on moving upstairs to the resort's **Treetop Tapas & Grill** (1155 Resort Dr., 250/248-1838, noon-8pm daily), where you are encouraged to relax in your robe over an unlimited procession of creative tapas. The cost is $125 pp, which includes pool access. The resort's other restaurant, the **Cedar Room** (7:30am-9pm daily, $18-32), offers classic Pacific Northwest cooking at reasonable prices, including a delicious cedar-plank salmon, but also less expensive choices such as burgers.

Accommodations and Camping

Parksville's many accommodations have been developed for vacationing families—with weekly rentals of self-contained units within walking distance of the water.

Across from the main beach is a **Travelodge** (424 West Island Hwy., 250/248-2232 or 800/661-3110, wyndhamhotels.com, $229-309 s or d) with an indoor pool and hot tub. While you know exactly what you're getting with this mid-priced chain, it's in the off-season that this place shines, with rooms for under $100.

If you want to be right on Parksville Beach, make reservations at the **Beach Club Resort** (181 Beachside Dr., 250/248-8999 or 888/760-2008, $379-599), a modern, multistory hotel separated from the oceanfront promenade by a wide swath of greenspace. Amenities include an oceanfront restaurant, an indoor pool, and a fitness room. Guests also enjoy use of beachy toys, ranging from umbrellas to games to kayaks and paddleboards. The 149 guest rooms are studios, one-bedroom, or two-bedroom; although all have balconies, only the more expensive ones have ocean views.

Overlooking Craig Bay on the southeast side of town, **Ocean Sands Resort** (1165 Resort Dr., 250/954-0662 or 877/733-5969, www.oceansandsresort.ca, $319-419 s or d) is a good choice for families. Guests swim in the warm ocean water out front or in the smallish heated pool, while children make the most of the playground. Most of the units enjoy sweeping ocean views and separate bedrooms. All have full kitchens and comfortable living areas. Rates start at $170 outside of summer.

Guest rooms at beachfront **Tigh-Na-Mara Seaside Spa Resort** (1155 Resort Dr., 250/248-2072 or 800/663-7373, www.tigh-na-mara.com, from $349 s or d) range from garden view studios to two-bedroom ocean-facing suites. The resort itself is renowned for its day spa, while other amenities include two adventure playgrounds, mountain bike rentals, a large swimming pool, and two restaurants.

At **Rathtrevor Beach Provincial Park** (mid-Mar.-mid-Oct., $35), south of downtown off Highway 19A (take exit 46 from the south), campers choose the natural setting and a great sandy beach over modern facilities (no hookups). To be ensured of a campsite, make reservations by contacting BC Parks (519/858-6161 or 800/689-9025, https://camping.bcparks.ca).

Information

Traveling north from Nanaimo, take exit 46 from Highway 19 (Inland Island Hwy.) and follow Highway 19A (Island Hwy.) for just under 1 kilometer (0.6 miles) to reach **Parksville Visitor Centre** (123 East Island Hwy., 250/248-3613, www.visitparksvillequalicumbeach.com, 9am-5pm Mon.-Sat. July-Aug., 9am-5pm Mon.-Fri. Sept.-June).

QUALICUM BEACH

This beachside community (pop. 9,000) facing the Strait of Georgia is generally quieter than Parksville, but it shares the same endless sands and attracts the same droves of beachgoers, sun worshippers, anglers, and golfers on summer vacation. You can stay on Highway 19 (Inland Island Hwy.) to bypass Parksville and take the Memorial Avenue exit to reach the heart of the town, but a more scenic option is to continue along the old coastal highway through Parksville. This route is lined with motels, resorts, and RV parks. The attractive downtown area, locally known as "the Village," is away from the beach area up Memorial Avenue.

1: the Canadian Open Sand Sculpting Competition **2:** the wooden boardwalk in Horne Lake Caves Provincial Park **3:** Parksville Beach

Wide, sandy **Qualicum Beach** is most definitely the main attraction here. Park anywhere along its length and join the crowd walking, running, biking, or simply relaxing in one of the many cafés along the promenade. At low tide, the beach comes alive with people searching out sand dollars.

Sights

Between Parksville and Qualicum Beach, **Milner Gardens and Woodland** (2179 Island Hwy. W., 250/752-8573, 10am-4:30pm daily late Apr.-Aug., noon-4pm Thurs.-Sun. Apr. and Sept., adults $12, students $7) protects a historical oceanfront estate that includes a 24-hectare (60-acre) old-growth forest and over 500 species of rhododendrons. Whether you take afternoon tea (1pm-4pm daily, $9-30) in the drawing room of the main house or on the adjacent garden patio, you'll be paying a whole lot less than in Victoria.

If you appreciate high-quality arts and crafts, detour off the main drag at this point and head for the **Old School House Arts Centre** (122 Fern Rd. W., 250/752-6133, 11am-3pm Tues.-Sat., free). The gallery occupies a beautifully restored 1912 building, while working artist studios below allow you a chance to see wood carving, printmaking, pottery, weaving, painting, and fabric art in progress. Don't miss a stop at the gallery shop, where all kinds of original handcrafted treasures are likely to lure a couple of dollars out of your wallet.

Through town to the west, take Bayswater Road inland a short way to reach the government-operated **Big Qualicum Hatchery** (215 Fisheries Rd., 250/757-8412, dawn-dusk daily, free), where a wooded trail leads to an artificial spawning channel with a fish ladder and a holding pond. The best time of year to watch salmon ascending the channel ladder is mid-September to mid-November. Steelhead can be viewed February-April. The hatchery is one of many on Vancouver Island; this one produces around 25,000 cutthroat trout and 100,000 steelhead each year. To get here from Qualicum Beach, head northwest

on Hwy. 19A (Island Hwy.) for 11 kilometers (6.8 miles) and turn west at Fisheries Road, just past Horne Lake Caves Road.

The hatchery is the northern trailhead for the **Big Qualicum Regional River Trail,** a 10-kilometer (6.2-mile) gravel road (walking and biking only) that passes through old-growth forest, traverses a moss-covered log bridge, and ends at Horne Lake Caves Road.

Events

The year's biggest event is the Father's Day (mid-June) **Show & Shine** (www.seaside-cruizers.com), which sees Qualicum's streets filled with antique and hot rod cars from throughout North America.

Food

Take full advantage of Qualicum's beachfront by dining at **Shady Rest** (3109 West Island Hwy., 250/752-9111, noon-8pm daily, $15.50-26), a wooden hotel built on the oceanfront promenade in the 1920s. It's undergone many changes over the last century and is now a casual restaurant with a few outdoor tables and prices that are reasonable, considering the watery setting. As you may expect, the menu features lots of local seafood (the scallop, shrimp, and crab patty topped with guacamole makes for a delicious burger), but also has a few vegetarian options and a bison burger.

Downtown Qualicum is away from the water, and here you'll find excellent coffee at **French Press Coffee Roasters** (692 Primrose St., 250/594-4477, 8am-3pm Mon.-Sat.), where beans are roasted in-house and only the very best Belgian chocolate is used in their hot chocolate concoctions. Also downtown, and similar to its other location just to the south in Parksville, **Lefty's** (710 Memorial Ave., 250/752-7530, 11:30am-7pm, lunch $15-23) is a contemporary restaurant where the menu is filled with dishes made from fresh, locally sourced ingredients. At lunch, enjoy a mandarin and chicken wrap, while at dinner, mains such as mango ginger-glazed salmon

are mostly under $20. Adding to the appeal is friendly service and a row of outdoor tables.

Accommodations and Camping

Looking for a place to stay like no other you've ever experienced? Then make reservations at ★ **Free Spirit Spheres** (420 Horne Lake Rd., 250/757-9445, www.freespiritspheres.com, $334-374 s or d). Accommodations consist of three perfectly round, three-meter-wide (10-foot) wooden spheres hanging from towering old-growth trees. Handmade by the property owners, each comprises a small flat area, a shortish bed, windows, and a door that opens to a walkway connected to the ground. Baths are shared and also at ground level. Due to their popularity, you should reserve as far in advance as possible.

Qualicum Beach Inn (2690 Island Hwy. W., 250/752-6914, www.qualicumbeachinn.com, $259-429 s or d) is across the road from the ocean and within walking distance of Qualicum Beach Golf Club. The property features modern rooms, an indoor pool than opens to an oceanfront patio, and an excellent restaurant.

Give the central campgrounds a miss and continue 16 kilometers (10 miles) northwest from Qualicum Beach to **Qualicum Bay Resort** (5970 W. Island Hwy., 250/757-2003 or 800/663-6899, www.resortbc.com, tents $32, hookups $47-49, camping cabins that share bathrooms $55-105, motel rooms $129-229 s or d). Separated from the water by a road, this family-oriented resort has many facilities, including an artificially constructed swimming lake, a playground, a game room, an ice cream stand, and a restaurant.

Information

For the complete rundown on this stretch of the coast, stop in at **Qualicum Beach Visitor Centre** (2711 Island Hwy. W., 250/752-9532 or 866/887-7106, www.qualicum.bc.ca, 8:30am-6:30pm daily late May-early Sept., 9am-4pm Mon.-Fri. early Sept.-late May), on the promenade as you enter town from the southeast.

1: Qualicum Beach 2: Free Spirit Spheres

★ HORNE LAKE CAVES

If you can drag yourself away from the beach, consider a half-day detour inland to one of Vancouver Island's most intriguing natural attractions, Horne Lake Caves, which are protected as tiny **Horne Lake Caves Provincial Park. Horne Lake Regional Park,** protecting a wide swath of forest between the provincial park and Horne Lake itself, has a campground, picnic facilities, and a beach. To get there from Qualicum Beach, continue northwest along Highway 19A for 11 kilometers (7 miles) and turn west at Horne Lake Caves Road, following the road for 16 kilometers (10 miles) west to Horne Lake. When the road reaches Horne Lake, it follows the north shore to the cave staging area.

Exploring the Caves

Guided tours of the larger caves are offered. The two-hour Riverbend Explorer (May-Sept., $54 pp) includes a short walk as well as underground exploration and explanation of the major formations. For those looking for more adventure, other options include the three-hour Multi Cave Adventure ($75 pp) and the four-hour Max Depth Adventure (minimum age 13, July-Aug., $199 pp). At the time of publication, two small caves that have been open to the public in the past (10am-4pm daily year-round) were closed, but check the website for their status. If open, there's no charge, but you'll need a helmet and light source, which can be rented on-site. A private contractor (250/248-7829, www.hornelake.com) runs the tours using qualified guides.

Horne Lake Regional Park

In addition to the caves, a beautiful sandy beach with freshwater swimming, canoeing under the shadow of Mount Mark, and a well-manicured campground within Horne Lake Regional Park make the drive out to Horne Lake worthwhile. The **campground** (250/248-1134, April-Sept., $25-30) is beyond the main entrance to the park. Reservations can be made online (www.rlcparks.ca). Trails lead down to the Qualicum River from this point, while on the south side of the river mouth, the park is less built up and there are good opportunities for bird-watching. The campground operator rents canoes, kayaks, and SUPs, and operates an interpretive program during July and August.

Offshore Islands

If you can drag yourself away from the beaches of Oceanside, consider visiting one or more offshore islands, including Lasqueti, a larger island directly north that holds a degree of isolation, as there is no scheduled BC Ferries link; the rural oasis of Denman Island, just a short hop away from Vancouver Island; and Hornby Island, which is my favorite for its beaches and laid-back character.

LASQUETI ISLAND

Visitors who make the effort to reach Lasqueti Island are welcomed with open arms, but there is no tourism industry as such, and services are extremely limited. Residents generate their own electricity, paved roads are nonexistent, and there is no public transportation.

Lasqueti Island is across the Strait of Georgia from Oceanside communities, closer to Texada Island than Vancouver Island, but is linked to the latter by a small passenger ferry. Inhabited by First Nations people for thousands of years, it wasn't until Spanish explorers landed in 1791 that Lasqueti was marked on maps. By the 1860s, Europeans settlers had arrived with herds of sheep. The island's original settlement was on Tucker Bay; by 1916, a salmon cannery had been built at False Bay, and this began a commercial center. Today, the island has a year-round population of just 400 self-sufficient residents.

Sea kayaking is a major draw, but at press time there were no organized tours or rentals. Instead, rent from **Comox Valley Kayaks and Canoes** (2020 Cliffe Ave., Courtenay, 250/334-2628, 10am-5pm daily), which charges $46-65 for a single kayak and $82-110 for a double per day. They also rent dry bags and roof racks. Paddle trips along the island's protected north coast are an enjoyable way to spend the day, but experienced paddlers use Lasqueti as a jumping-off point for multiday trips to **Jedediah Island.** Now protected as a marine park, the island was settled in the 1880s and privately owned until 1994. Many signs of early homesteading remain, including boarded-up buildings, exotic trees, and wild sheep and goats.

Food and Accommodations

Lodging on the island is very limited, and there is no camping. Overlooking False Bay is the **Lasqueti Island Hotel** (1 Weldon Rd., 250/333-8503, www.lasquetihotel.com, $110-130 s or d), which has eight basic rooms and a restaurant (3pm-8pm daily) with live music on Friday night through summer.

Getting There

The passenger-only ferry to Lasqueti (three times daily Wed.-Mon., adults $12, children $6, one-way) departs from French Creek, between Parksville and Qualicum Beach, and takes around one hour to reach the island. It is operated by **Western Pacific Marine** (250/927-0431). Dockside parking at French Creek is $5 per day.

DENMAN ISLAND

Ten minutes after leaving Buckley Bay, 35 kilometers (22 miles) northwest of Qualicum Beach, you'll be driving off the ferry and onto this rural oasis, similar to the Southern Gulf Islands in appearance, sans crowds. Fishing, hiking, biking, bird-watching, and sea kayaking are prime draws here, and you'll also find good beaches, parks, and an artisanal community, all along narrow winding roads.

Sights and Recreation

Within walking distance uphill from the ferry dock is **Denman Village,** boasting several early-20th-century commercial buildings, including the 1908 general store. Across the island, 23-hectare (57-acre) **Fillongley Provincial Park** is a prime stretch of oceanfront that longtime island resident George Beadnell donated as parkland. Beadnell lived a surprisingly grand life on the island; remains of his home still stand, a variety of trees imported from England dot the park, and the open meadow just north of the parking lot was once a bowling green. The easy Homestead Trail leads through his former estate and into an old-growth forest, then back along the beachfront. The beach itself is a long stretch of sand and pebbles backed by driftwood.

The island's southern tip is protected by **Boyle Point Provincial Park,** where an 800-meter (0.5-mile) trail (20 minutes one-way) leads to a lofty lookout with views down to Chrome Island, where a classic red-and-white lighthouse stands. If you are visiting in winter, this vantage point is a good place to view sea lions.

Food and Accommodations

Turn left as you arrive on the island to reach **Ima's Kitchen** (1840 NW Rd., 250/650-8037, 9am-dusk), where different breads are baked each day, cinnamon buns are a staple, and the ice cream is a best-seller through summer.

Earth Club Factory (3806 Denman Rd., 250/335-2688, 7am-3pm Mon.-Fri., 8am-3pm Sat.-Sun., lunch $8-12) is a funky room attached to a budget lodging (see below). Coffee is roasted in-house, and all the food is cooked from scratch daily—when a menu item sells out, it's done for the day.

Most overnight visitors stay in week-long rental units, but for travelers looking to immerse themselves in island culture, **Earth Club Factory** (3806 Denman Rd., 250/335-2688, www.earthclubfactory.com, camping $20 pp, dorms $30-70 s, $50-70 d) is a memorable choice for its down-to-earth owners and magical setting. In a renovated

1912 farmhouse, the four rooms are simple yet comfortable (shared bath and the smallest doesn't have a window), while out on the grounds are two cabins, a "Tower" single room, and a few campsites.

At **Fillongley Provincial Park** (off Swan Rd., mid-Mar.-Oct., $23), the 10 primitive campsites are filled by campers that have made reservations (519/858-6161 or 800/689-9025, https://camping.bcparks.ca).

Getting There

Buckley Bay, 35 kilometers (22 miles) northwest of Qualicum Beach, is the departure point for ferries across Bayne Sound to Denman Island. Like all ferries through the Strait of Georgia, they are operated by **BC Ferries** (250/386-3431) and require no reservations. The service runs hourly 7am-11pm and costs adults $9.10, children $4.55, vehicles $21.10 round-trip.

TOP EXPERIENCE

★ HORNBY ISLAND

Beyond Denman Island, Hornby Island has my favorite beach in all of the Gulf Islands, as well as a distinct counter-cultural vibe that encourages visitors to relax and enjoy a slower pace of living—even if it's just for the few days you spend in this small piece of paradise. The island has attracted those looking to escape mainstream life since the first draft dodgers arrived at the onset of the Vietnam War. Today, the 1,000 year-round residents are mostly self-sufficient, relying on each other and the local cooperative to live as simple lives as possible, roasting their own coffee and growing their own fruit and vegetables; there's even a couple of small wineries. The best place to immerse yourself in the island lifestyle is **Ringside Market,** a collection of local businesses at the east end of Central Road by Tribune Bay Provincial Park. Here you'll find artisans, coffee roasters, a bike repair shop, kayak rentals, cafés, and a co-op, which was founded by island residents in 1955 and stocks everything from locally made pâté to hardware.

Sights and Recreation

A large chunk of the island is protected by **Mt. Geoffrey Escarpment Provincial Park,** including the highest peak and sea cliffs facing Denman Island, but most visitors gravitate to crescent-shaped Tribune Bay, where the longest stretch of sand is protected by 95-hectare (235-acre) **Tribune Bay Provincial Park.**

the beach at Tribune Bay Provincial Park

The sand is as white as you'll find on the Gulf Islands, the crowds minimal, and the water slightly warmer than other Vancouver Island beaches due to the protected bay.

St. Johns Point Road leads along the park's northern boundary to the entrance to **Helliwell Provincial Park.** Like Fillongley, this land was bequeathed to the people of British Columbia by an island resident. Stretching to Hornby's easternmost point, the park protects one of the few remaining old-growth forests of Douglas fir on the Gulf Islands. A five-kilometer (3-mile) trail loops through the forest to St. Johns Point and then back along high sea cliffs protecting Tribune Bay to the parking lot; allow 90 minutes to complete the circuit.

Food and Accommodations

Within walking distance of the beach at Tribune Bay is the commercial heart of the island, **Ringside Market** (Central Rd. and St. Johns Point Rd.) a collection of small, weathered buildings connected by gravel paths. Food outlets include **Lix** (8am-3pm daily), which is a gathering point for anyone looking for a caffeine fix and ice cream; **Forage Farm and Kitchen** (250/335-1487, 9am-3pm daily and 5pm-8pm Fri.-Sat. July-Aug., 10:30am-2:30 pm daily Sept.-June, lunch $14-17), serving up healthy cooking with much of the produce sourced from the owner's farm; and **Hornby Island Co-op** (250/335-1121, 250/335-1121, 9:30am-5:30pm daily), which stocks island-made goodies, fresh produce, and other basic groceries.

Overlooking the ferry dock from Hornby Island Resort is **Thatch Pub & Restaurant** (4325 Shingle Spit Rd., 250/335-2833, 11am-9:30pm daily summer, $15-23), built right over the water. Live music some weekend evenings draws the locals in.

Just north of Tribune Bay, on a north-facing stretch of coastline with sweeping water views, is **Sea Breeze Lodge** (5205 Fowler Rd., 250/335-2321, www.seabreezelodge.com). Spread across the 5-hectare (12-acre) property are 16 one- and two-bedroom cabins, a waterfront hot tub, a tennis court, and a dining room. In July and August, rates are adults $1,750, youth $1,000, and children $650 for a weeklong stay that includes all meals. The rest of the year, cabins are a very reasonable $160-240 s or d, with meals extra.

On the island's north side is **Isla de Lerena Vineyard** (1885 Central Rd., 250/335-2491, www.lerenavineyards.com, $165-245 s or d), where there are nine canvas glamping tents set in a forest at the end of the road beyond the main vineyard. The tents sleep 2-4 people, and all but the four-person tent share a bathroom. On the property is a pond with an island gazebo, a barbecue, fit pits, and wireless Internet. The winery has a tasting room (noon-5pm Tues.-Sat.) and lots of outside seating (including a massive U-shaped lounge) for enjoying wine and snacks.

Within the provincial park but operated separately, **Tribune Bay Campsite** (250/335-2359, www.tribunebay.com, mid-June-mid-Sept., $35-48) is adjacent to the beach and within walking distance of Ringside Market. Unlike most other Gulf Island campgrounds, Tribune Bay has powered sites, showers, and electric hookups.

Getting There

The journey over to Hornby from Vancouver Island begins with **BC Ferries** (250/386-3431) from Vancouver Island out to the dock on the west side of Denman Island (see above) and an eight-kilometer (five-mile) drive to Gravelly Bay, from where an even smaller ferry crosses Lambert Channel every hour between 8am-6pm daily, reaching Hornby Island in around 10 minutes. The round-trip fare to Hornby from Denman is adults $9.10, children $4.55, vehicles $21.10.

Comox Valley

The K'omoks people lived in the Comox Valley for thousands of years before the first Europeans arrived in the 1860s to set up farms and mine coal. Today, the three communities of **Courtenay, Cumberland,** and **Comox** are nestled between the Strait of Georgia and high mountains of the Vancouver Island Ranges to the west. The valley lies almost halfway up the island, 220 kilometers (137 miles) from Victoria. The three towns merge into one, but each has its own personality: Courtenay, the staid town with a compact downtown core and all the visitor services you need; Cumberland, away from the water but historically charming nonetheless; and Comox, a sprawl of retiree housing developments and golf courses that extends across a wide peninsula to the ocean.

COURTENAY

The valley's largest town and a commercial center for local farming, logging, fishing, and retirement communities, Courtenay (pop. 30,000) extends around the head of Comox Harbour. It's not particularly scenic but has a few interesting sights and plenty of highway accommodations. It was named for Captain George Courtenay, who led the original surveying expedition of the area in 1848. Almost 100 years later, on June 14, 1946, the worst earthquake recorded in Canada struck west of town and damaged much of Courtenay's downtown core.

As you enter Courtenay from the south, you pass a long string of malls, big-box stores, and older motels. Continue into the heart of downtown (continue straight ahead on Cliffe Ave. where 17th Ave. crosses the Courtenay River) and you come to the historic core of the city with its cobbled streets, old-fashioned lamps, brick planters full of flowers, and interesting shops.

From downtown, cross the bridge on 5th Street to the totem pole-flanked entrance to **Lewis Park,** at the confluence of the Puntledge and Tsolum Rivers. The two rivers join here to form the very short Courtenay River.

Sights

The main attraction downtown is the **Courtenay and District Museum** (207 4th St., 250/334-0686, 10am-5pm Mon.-Sat. and noon-4pm Sun. June-Aug., 10am-4pm Tues.-Sat. Sept.-May, donation). The highlight is a full-size replica of an *elasmosaur*. The original—12 meters (39 feet) long and 80 million years old—was found at the nearby Puntledge River. The museum leads tours out to the site (departs 9am Tues.-Sat. July-Aug.), on which you have the chance to dig for your very own fossil (adults $40, children $30).

Other museum exhibits include a series of realistic dioramas and a replica of a big house containing many First Nations artifacts and items, some formerly belonging to prominent chiefs. Finish up in the gift shop, which is well stocked with local arts and crafts.

Recreation

Vancouver Island is not usually associated with snow sports by outsiders, but locals know they don't need to leave their island home to enjoy world-class skiing and boarding at **Mount Washington Alpine Resort** (250/338-1386, www.mountwashington. ca), 35 kilometers (22 miles) northwest of Courtenay. The scope and popularity of the resort are remarkable—it ranks fourth in British Columbia for the number of skier days and has a modern base village with more than 3,500 beds—but not surprising, considering it receives an annual snowfall of 11 meters (33 feet) and temperatures that remain relatively warm compared to the interior of British Columbia. Six chairlifts serve 690 hectares (1,700 acres), with the vertical rise a respectable 500 meters (1,640 feet) and the longest

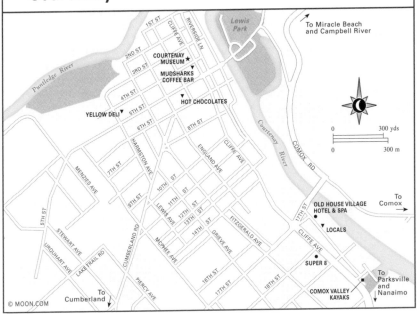

Courtenay

To Miracle Beach and Campbell River

To Comox

To Parksville and Nanaimo

To Cumberland

Lewis Park

Puntledge River

Courtenay River

COURTENAY MUSEUM

MUDSHARKS COFFEE BAR

HOT CHOCOLATES

YELLOW DELI

OLD HOUSE VILLAGE HOTEL & SPA

LOCALS

SUPER 8

COMOX VALLEY KAYAKS

© MOON.COM

run just under 2 kilometers (1.2 miles). Other facilities include a terrain park and a half-pipe. Lift tickets are adults $109, seniors $89, and children $56.

Between July and mid-October, the resort welcomes outdoor enthusiasts who come to hike through alpine meadows, ride the chairlift ($25 pp), mountain bike down the slopes, or go trail riding through the forest. A wealth of other activities are on offer—from mini golf to ziplining—making it a good place to escape the beachy crowd for a day or two. Inexpensive summer packages (see the website) encourage overnight stays.

Comox Valley Kayaks (2020 Cliffe Ave., 250/334-2628, www.cvkayaks.com, 10am-5pm daily in summer, 10am-4pm Tues.-Sat. the rest of the year) offers guided tours from $109 for three hours, sea-kayaking and paddleboard lessons for $79 pp, and full-day guided trips to Denman Island for $199. Or rent a kayak or paddleboard ($46-102 for 24 hours) for some exploration by yourself,

around the local waterways or out on nearby Denman and Hornby Islands. The company also rents canoes ($82 per day)—great for nearby Comox Lake. It's located along the highway just south of downtown.

Food

Branching west from Cliffe Avenue (the main thoroughfare through town), 5th Street has a number of good choices for local cuisine. At the top end of the street, **Yellow Deli** (596 5th St., 250/897-1111, noon-9pm Sun., 7am-9pm Mon.-Thurs., 7am-3pm Fri., lunch $8-11) is a friendly little place within a beautifully restored heritage house. Lattes, cappuccinos, and loose-leaf teas highlight the drinks menu, breakfasts include a vegetarian omelet and homemade granola, and lunches include a delicious cranberry-cashew salad. Everything is well-priced and the staff friendly and welcoming.

Or head down two blocks to **Hot Chocolates** (368 5th St., 250/338-8211,

8am-5pm Tues.-Sat.), which specializes in handcrafted chocolate treats and artisan baked goods. Hot Chocolates also has an in-house coffee bar and a covered patio.

At the lower end of downtown, across from the museum, **Mudsharks Coffee Bar** (244 4th St., 250/338-0939, 6:30am-4pm daily, lunch $12-16) has a tree-shaded courtyard that is the ideal place to enjoy fresh and healthy breakfast and lunches, including smoothies, an avocado breakfast wrap, or a Moroccan rice bowl.

Occupying one of Courtenay's original residences, **Locals** (1760 Riverside Lane, 250/338-5406, 11am-8pm Mon.-Fri., 10am-8pm Sat.-Sun., $19-34) sits among landscaped gardens of a much more modern Old House Hotel. The menu is filled with tempting yet well-priced Pacific Northwest choices, with produce and game sourced from local farms where possible. You could start with wild mushroom risotto, then move on to pan-seared halibut as a main.

Accommodations and Camping

Courtenay's motels are strung out along Highway 19 (known as Cliffe Ave. within city limits) as you enter town from the south. The 67-room **Super 8** (1885 Cliffe Ave., 250/334-2451, www.wyndhamhotels.com, $194-224 s or d) is typical of the mid-priced chains, with spacious rooms, breakfast, and some kitchenettes as a bonus.

Within easy walking distance of downtown is **Old House Hotel** (1730 Riverside Lane, 250/703-0202 or 888/703-0202, www.oldhousevillage.com, $290-445 s or d), a modern, three-story hotel with a fitness center, spa services, a restaurant, and a garden with a covered barbecue. Each of the 79 guest rooms is decorated in modern, earthy tones; kitchenettes and gas fireplaces add to the charm of the more expensive suites.

Overlooking Gartley Bay south of Courtenay is **Kingfisher Oceanside Resort** (4330 Island Hwy. S., 250/338-1323 or 800/663-7929, www.kingfisherspa.com,

$255-435 s or d), set around well-manicured waterfront gardens dotted with seating and firepits. The resort also holds an outdoor pool, a spa facility, a yoga lounge, a bar with outdoor seating, and a restaurant renowned for its West Coast cuisine (and a great Sunday brunch buffet). Lodging choices are in regular rooms, each with a private balcony, or newer beachfront suites, each with a fireplace, hot tub, and kitchen.

Information

The **Vancouver Island Visitor Centre** (3607 Small Rd., 855/400-2882, www.discovercomoxvalley.com, 9am-7pm daily summer, 9am-4pm daily fall-spring) is an architecturally striking building on the east side of Highway 19 (Inland Island Hwy.) at Exit 117 (Cumberland Rd.). In addition to the usual information services, the center has an interesting array of interpretive displays that tell the story of the Comox Valley, as well as free wireless Internet, a playground, and a picnic area.

Getting There

Courtenay in 105 kilometers (66 miles) north of Nanaimo, 215 kilometers (134 miles) north of Victoria, and 60 kilometers (38 miles) south of Campbell River. **VI Connector** (866/986-3466, www.viconnector.com) runs buses 3-5 times daily between Victoria and Courtenay, continuing north to Campbell River.

CUMBERLAND

This historic town of 3,800 lies on the west side of Highway 19 (Inland Island Hwy.) 7 kilometers (4.3 miles) southwest of downtown Courtenay. Its quiet streets are lined with mining-era cottages, with the main street leading past numerous brick commercial buildings.

Coal was first discovered in the Comox Valley in 1869, and by the mid-1880s, extraction of the most productive seam was going ahead under the direction of coal baron Robert Dunsmuir, who brought in hundreds of Chinese and Japanese workers.

Cumberland's Chinatown was once home to 3,000 people, second in size on North America's West Coast only to San Francisco's Chinatown. At the outbreak of World War II, the Japanese residents of Cumberland were all sent to internment camps scattered throughout mainland British Columbia.

Sights and Recreation

Cumberland Museum (2680 Dunsmuir St., 250/336-2445, 10am-5pm Mon.-Sat., 11am-4:30pm Tues.-Sat., adults $5, seniors $4) is a small but excellent facility, with interesting historical photos. On the museum grounds is a recreated mine shaft open to the public. Before leaving, pick up a heritage walking-tour brochure and ask for directions to the overgrown remains of the Chinese settlement, now protected as **Coal Creek Historic Park.** The park lies around 1.6 kilometers (1 mile) west of the museum along the road to Comox Lake.

The ocean beaches along the eastern flank of Comox Valley region are not as inviting as those farther south around Parksville and Qualicum Beach, so many locals head out to **Comox Lake,** three kilometers (two miles) west of Cumberland along Comox Lake Road. The swimming area is protected from motorized watercraft by a boom of large logs, and the beach has a concession and kayak and paddleboard rentals.

Accommodations and Camping

Instead of motels, Comox has one of Vancouver Island's best backpacker lodges, **Riding Fool Hostel** (2705 Dunsmuir St., 250/336-8250, www.ridingfool.com, dorm $35, private room $89-109 s or d). It has colorful common areas, family rooms, a female dorm, a large communal kitchen, and bike rentals.

West of town, **Cumberland Lake Park Campground** (1100 Comox Lake Rd., 250/702-8833, www.cumberlandlakepark.ca, $25-45) enjoys a lakefront setting, although there is no privacy between the best sites, which are right on the beach. Reservations are a must, especially for the powered sites.

COMOX

The population of Comox is quoted at 15,000, and there's certainly enough room for everyone, but you'd never know it, driving along forested roads that lead to golf courses, retirement communities, and a magnificent stretch of coastline. To reach Comox's small downtown area, take Comox Road eastward after crossing the Courtenay River along Highway 19.

Sights

Through downtown is a highlight of the valley, **Filberg Heritage Lodge and Park** (Comox Ave. at Filberg Rd., 250/339-2715, 8am-dusk daily, free), which was bequeathed to the people of Comox by logging magnate Robert Filberg in 1977. A high hedge hides the beautifully landscaped grounds, which stretch down to Comox Harbour, from the outside world. At the bottom of the garden is the main house (11am-3pm Wed.-Fri. summer), built in 1929 and filled with period antiques and quirky architecture.

Take Pritchard Road north from Filberg Lodge and you'll eventually reach the Canadian Forces Base, which doubles as the local airport for commercial flights. Cross Knight Road to reach **Comox Air Force Museum** (Ryan Rd., 250/339-8162, 10am-4pm Tues.-Sun., donation), at the entrance to Comox Air Force Base. The museum isn't huge, but it is chock-full of Air Force memorabilia. Once you've gone through the indoor displays, you'll want to wander down to Heritage Air Park, a 10-minute walk south, where a dozen planes from various eras are parked.

On the other side of the runway is **Kye Bay,** a wide strip of sand that is perfect for families. To the east, beyond the headland, are intriguing **white cliffs.** At the end of an ancient ice age, as the sheet of ice that covered this region retreated, it stalled, leaving behind a massive mound of finely ground glacial silt. Wind and water action in the ensuing years

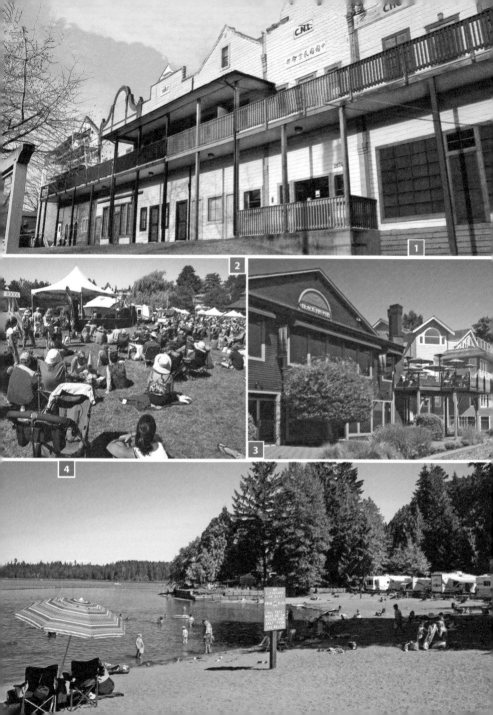

have uncovered the silt, forming white cliffs that stand in stark contrast to the surrounding bedrock. To reach Kye Bay from the airport, head east on Knight Road (past the entrance to the main terminal) and take Kye Bay Road around the south end of the runway.

Another interesting spot is **Seal Bay Nature Park,** north of the airport along Anderton and then Waveland Roads. The park protects one of the region's few undeveloped stretches of coastline. Trails lead through a lush forest of Douglas fir and ferns to a pleasant, rocky beach where bald eagles and seals are often sighted. On the way back from Seal Bay, plan on stopping at **40 Knots Winery** (2400 Anderton Rd., 855/941-8810, 11am-5pm Tues.-Sun.), one of the island's largest vineyards. In addition to a modern tasting room, there is a lounge, balcony, and covered terrace for visitors to relax with a glass of wine.

Events

The two major events are not run in conjunction with each other, but both are held on the first weekend of August. The **Filberg Festival** (250/339-2715, www.filbergfestival.com) features gourmet food, free entertainment, and unique arts and crafts from the best of British Columbia's artisans on the grounds of Filberg Heritage Lodge. Meanwhile, back along the waterfront toward downtown, **Comox Nautical Days** (www.comoxnauticaldays.ca) is a free festival centered on Marina Park, between downtown Comox and the harbor. The park fills each day of the August long weekend, when residents celebrate B.C. Day, starting in early morning for a pancake breakfast, while the rest of the celebration is focused on an arts and crafts fair, dragon boat races, a fishing derby, live outdoor music, and fireworks.

Food

While researching this edition, I stumbled upon **Red Wagon** (1466 Ryan Rd.,

250/339-6330, 7am-3pm Mon.-Fri., lunch $9-13), a tiny place along the main road leading to the airport. It offers up freshly made breakfast buns and daily specials such as pulled pork sandwiches and chili. The coffee is good and the tables out front perpetually busy when the weather is warm.

The most serene place to enjoy lunch is the landscaped gardens at Filberg Heritage Lodge, where the **Filberg Summer Kitchen** (61 Filberg Rd., 250/339-2750, 11am-4pm Thurs.-Sun. summer, lunch $21-34) offers picnic tables spread out under mature trees. A delightful setting and well-priced lunches and desserts make this a popular spot on sunny days.

Between April and early October, the parking lot at Marina Park, between downtown and the Comox waterfront, is dotted with food trucks serving up fresh and inexpensive meals that cover all tastes. Most are open 11:30am-7pm daily, with shorter hours outside of July and August. For delicious fish-and-chips, my fave is **Surfside** (250/207-7873), although they also sell corn dogs, clam chowder, and fish tacos.

Back up the hill in the heart of the commercial core, **Blackfin Pub** (132 Port Augusta St., 250/339-5030, 11am-9pm daily, $15-32) has unobstructed views across the harbor to the Vancouver Island Ranges. The interior has lots of polished woodwork, and the nautical theme is anchored by a small wooden boat hanging from the ceiling. The menu is best described as upscale pub fare, with choices that include baked cod coated in crumbled banana chips, coconut, and mango curry cream. A bonus is a wine list dominated by BC wines.

Even if you're not a golfer, consider lunch or dinner at the **Timber Room Bar and Grill** (Crown Isle Resort, 399 Clubhouse Dr., 250/703-5000, 11am-8pm daily, $20-32), which overlooks the resort's 18th green. A favorite with hungry locals on Friday and Saturday evenings is the prime rib with Yorkshire pudding, although burgers and sandwiches are just as tasty.

1: Cumberland Museum 2: Comox Nautical Days
3: Blackfin Pub 4: Comox Lake

Accommodations and Camping

Regular motel accommodations are limited in Comox, but for a resort-like atmosphere, it's hard to go past **Crown Isle Resort** (399 Clubhouse Dr., 250/703-5000 or 888/338-8439, www.crownisle.com, $300-400 s or d), a sprawling resort and residential estate set on 330 hectares (800 acres) north of Comox off Ryan Road. The standard rooms and one- and two-bedroom villas are comfortable and relatively spacious; some have kitchenettes and fireplaces. The best rates are available by purchasing a golf package. Other amenities include a fitness room and two restaurants.

Campers looking for a vacation vibe should make reservations at **Cape Lazo RV Park** (685 Lazo Rd., Comox, 250/339-3946, www.capelazo.com, $62), which is within easy walking distance of a sandy beach. Facilities include modern showers, a playground, and kayak and SUP rentals. Tents are not allowed. To get there from the highway, take Comox Road through downtown Comox and turn right onto Balmoral Avenue, which leads to Lazo Road.

Ferry to Powell River

BC Ferries (250/386-3431, www.bcferries.com) sail four times daily between Comox and Powell River, allowing mainlanders easy access to mid-island beaches and snow slopes, and saving visitors to northern Vancouver Island from having to backtrack down to Nanaimo or Victoria. To get to the terminal, stay on Highway 19 through Courtenay, then take Ryan Road east to Anderton Road. Turn left and follow the signs down Ellenor Road. The regular one-way fare for this 75-minute sailing is adults $13.80, children $6.90, vehicles $43.15.

HIGHWAY 19A

From Courtenay, it's an easy 30-minute drive north along Highway 19 (Inland Island Hwy.) to Campbell River. A more enjoyable way is the original route north, now known as Highway 19A (Island Hwy.), which provides many access points to the Strait of Georgia.

Miracle Beach Provincial Park

Miracle Beach Provincial Park, off Highway 19A (Island Hwy.) 23 kilometers (14 miles) north of Courtenay, is mostly about camping, but it has one of the nicest sandy beaches along this stretch of coastline, a few forested walking trails, and the opportunity to watch salmon spawning in Black Creek each fall. The park's Miracle Beach Nature House (10am-5pm daily summer, free) has interesting natural history displays, a shop selling gifts and books, and is the focus point for an interpretive program that includes walks and talks.

The 200-site **Miracle Beach Provincial Park Campground** ($33) is open March to October, but services such as hot showers are only available May to September. Ensure there is a campsite waiting for you by making reservations through **BC Parks** (519/858-6161 or 800/689-9025, https://camping.bcparks.ca).

Salmon Point

A short drive north of Miracle Beach and 18 kilometers (11 miles) south of Campbell River is **Salmon Point Resort** (2176 Salmon Point Rd., 250/923-6605 or 866/246-6605, www.salmonpoint.com, campsites $45-66, cabins $160-275 s or d), also offering great views across the Strait of Georgia to the snowcapped peaks of the Coast Mountains. Facilities are excellent: an outdoor swimming pool, a restaurant overlooking the water, a couple of recreation rooms (one for adults only), fishing guide service and tackle, a heated pool, and a laundry room. All campsites sit among small stands of pines.

Northern Vancouver Island

The northern section of Vancouver Island is

mountainous, heavily treed, dotted with lakes, riddled with rivers and waterfalls, and almost completely unsettled. For those seeking out a complete wilderness experience, northern Vancouver Island delivers.

Just one main highway, running along the east coast, serves the region, although thousands of kilometers of unpaved logging roads penetrate the old-growth and second-growth forests. The gateway to northern Vancouver Island is Campbell River, a small city of 35,000 that proudly calls itself the "Salmon Capital of the World." At Campbell River, Highway 28 cuts west to Gold River, passing through

Highlights

Look for ★ to find recommended sights, activities, dining, and lodging.

★ Cape Scott Provincial Park
Port Hardy
Holberg
Coal Harbour
Sointula
★ Alert Bay
Port McNeill
★ Whale-Watching
Telegraph Cove
Sayward
Port Alice

PACIFIC OCEAN

Kyuquot
Zeballos
Tahsis
★ Cruising Nootka Sound
Yuquot
Gold River

Salmon Fishing
Campbell River

Courtenay
Comox

0   15 mi
0   15 km

© MOON.COM

★ **Salmon Fishing:** Campbell River is one of the world's premier fishing towns. Try hooking a salmon using traditional Tyee Club methods (page 166).

★ **Cruising Nootka Sound:** Take to the same remote waters visited by Captain James Cook in 1788 on a day or overnight cruise (page 175).

★ **Alert Bay:** On Cormorant Island, Alert Bay is a hotbed of First Nations history. A cultural center and some of the world's tallest totem poles are highlights (page 179).

★ **Whale-Watching:** Catch a tour boat in search of orcas from Telegraph Cove, then wander around the postcard-perfect boardwalk village (page 181).

★ **Cape Scott Provincial Park:** Beyond the end of the road, this remote park protects a swath of rugged coastal wilderness—the domain of abundant wildlife and only the most adventurous visitors (page 188).

Northern Vancouver Island

enormous Strathcona Provincial Park, which is dotted with waterfalls and unspoiled lakes. North of Campbell River lies a surprisingly large area mostly untouched by civilization—in fact, today you can still find maps of the island that fizzle out above Campbell River. Unique Telegraph Cove, a boardwalk village known for its fishing and whale-watching activities, and intriguing Alert Bay on Cormorant Island are highlights of this undeveloped region. The main highway ends at Port Hardy, the largest community north of Campbell River and the terminus for ferries to Prince Rupert.

PLANNING YOUR TIME

The majority of visitors to northern Vancouver Island are drawn to the region for one or more of the following reasons: to go **salmon fishing** at Campbell River, to take a whale-watching tour from **Telegraph Cove,** or to catch the ferry at Port Hardy to head north to Prince Rupert. But there are other reasons to visit and explore the island's northern reaches. The wilderness is a major draw. At places like Strathcona Provincial Park, visitors can enjoy old-growth forests and unspoiled waterways without venturing too far from the road. The rugged west coast is

Previous: a grizzly bear on the shore of Johnstone Strait; Port Hardy harbour; sea stacks on San Josef Bay in Cape Scott Provincial Park.

accessible by those **cruising Nootka Sound** aboard a comfortable boat that delivers supplies to remote villages. For those seeking out a complete wilderness experience, northern Vancouver Island also delivers, whether it be a wilderness hike through **Cape Scott Provincial Park** or a sea kayaking adventure through the Broughton Archipelago. The region's human history is somewhat overshadowed by natural wonders, but plan on spending time at places such as **Alert Bay,** which is home to some of the world's tallest totem poles.

Lodging options throughout northern Vancouver Island are somewhat limited compared to elsewhere on the island, making reservations strongly recommended in July and August, and essential in Port Hardy the night before each ferry departure, so plan accordingly. If you're driving, plan to spend extra time reaching your destination. While the total distance from one end of the island to the other—from Victoria in the south to Port Hardy in the north—is 495 kilometers (308 miles), allow at least six hours.

Campbell River

A gateway to the wilderness of northern Vancouver Island, this city of 35,000 stretches along Discovery Passage 260 kilometers (162 miles) north of Victoria and 235 kilometers (146 miles) southeast of Port Hardy. Views from town—of tree-covered Quadra Island and the magnificent white-topped mountains of mainland British Columbia—are superb, but most visitors come for the salmon fishing. The underwater topography creates prime angling conditions; the Strait of Georgia ends just south of Campbell River, and Discovery Passage begins. The waterway suddenly narrows to a width of only two kilometers (1.2 miles) between Vancouver and Quadra Islands, causing some of the strongest tides on the coast, attracting bait fish and forcing thousands of migrating salmon to concentrate off Campbell River, much to every angler's delight.

SIGHTS AND RECREATION

Museum at Campbell River

One of the island's premier regional museums, Museum at Campbell River (470 Island Hwy., 250/287-3103, 10am-5pm daily mid-May-Sept., noon-5pm Tues.-Sun. Oct.-mid-May, adults $8, seniors $7, students $5) sits on 4 hectares (10 acres) overlooking Discovery

Passage. First check out the photos and interesting written snippets that provide a look at Campbell River's early beginnings. Then feast your eyes on mystical artifacts, a huge collection of masks, exciting artwork, baskets, woven articles, carved-wood boxes, colorful button blankets, petroglyphs, and totem poles in the First Nations Gallery. Other displays center on sportfishing and local pioneers. Worth watching in the museum's theater is *Devil Beneath the Sea,* a documentary cataloging the destruction of nearby Ripple Rock by the world's largest nonnuclear explosion. Finish up in the gift shop, where you can buy prints, masks, postcards, and other paraphernalia.

Discovery Pier

The best place to absorb some of the local atmosphere is **Discovery Pier.** The 180-meter (590-foot) pier is fun to walk on whether you're into fishing or not. Its benches and protected shelters allow proper appreciation of the marina, strait, mainland mountains, and fishing action, even on wet and windy days.

At the foot of Discovery Pier, the **Maritime Heritage Centre** (621 Island Hwy., 250/286-3161, 10am-4pm Mon.-Fri., adults $7, seniors $5, children $3.50) protects *BCP 45,* a salmon seiner that plied local waters for almost half

Campbell River

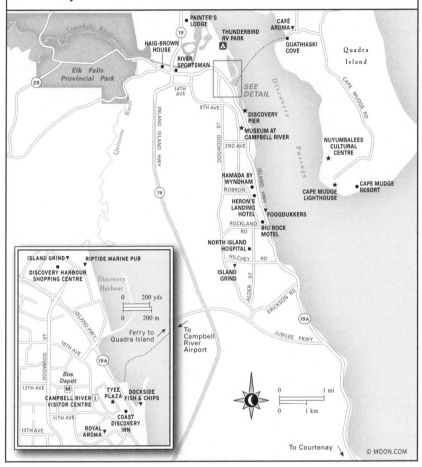

NORTHERN VANCOUVER ISLAND

CAMPBELL RIVER

a century. Now fully restored, it anchors the museum and is open for inspection.

Elk Falls Provincial Park

This 1,100-hectare (2,800-acre) park protects a salmon-rich stretch of the Campbell River as well as stands of old-growth forest. It extends from the western edge of the town of Campbell River to John Hart Lake and is cut in two by Highway 28, with the campground on the south side and the namesake Elk Falls farther west on the north side of the highway.

To get to the falls, continue west beyond the campground entrance for three kilometers (two miles) and turn north at the signed road. From the large day-use area, a short trail (allow 15 minutes) leads to a suspension bridge over the Campbell River and a viewpoint for the 25-meter-high (80-foot) waterfall. From the south side of the bridge, a trail loops upstream to two other waterfalls and the calm waters of the Dolphin Pool. Another highlight on this loop trail are towering stands of old-growth western red cedar and Douglas fir that escaped the eye of early logging operations.

Outside the park's southern boundary is **Quinsam River Hatchery** (4217 Argonaut Rd., 250/287-9564, 8am-4pm daily, free), one of Canada's largest salmon hatcheries. Between early August and mid-November, thousands of pink, coho, and chinook salmon swim up the Quinsam River to spawn at the hatchery. A glass-floored viewing platform makes observation easy, while interpretive boards describe the role the facility plays in maintaining Pacific salmon stocks. To get there, take Highway 28 west from downtown and turn left on Quinsam Road just after the Highway 19 intersection.

TOP EXPERIENCE

★ Salmon Fishing

Salmon fishing is the point of traveling to Campbell River for most visitors. The best thing about angling in the waters of adjacent **Discovery Passage** is that it can be enjoyed by all ages and on all budgets—and without a long boat ride through rough waters to reach the best spots. All five species of Pacific salmon are caught in local waters, including chinook (July-Sept.), pink (mid-July-Sept.), coho (July-Oct.), sockeye (mid-July-Aug.), and chum (mid-Sept.-Nov.).

Regardless of whether you're a first-timer or an old-timer, **Discovery Pier** in downtown Campbell River is a fantastic place to fish for salmon. The pier sports built-in rod holders, fish-cleaning stations, glassed-in shelters for nonanglers, and colorful signs describing the fish you're likely to catch. Anglers cast for salmon, bottom fish, and the occasional steelhead, hauling them up in nets on long ropes. When the salmon are running, the pier gets extremely busy, and for a reason—chinook salmon over 14 kilograms (30 pounds) are not uncommon. Rod rentals are available on the pier ($7 per hour, $15 per half day, $25 per day). Don't forget, you also need a tidal fishing license.

The marinas along this stretch of coast are filled with charter operators, but one that comes highly recommended is **Coastal Island Fishing Adventures** (250/203-1162 or 877/537-7678, www.coastalislandfishing.com), which charges $750 for a five-hour fishing trip for up to five people. Rates include transportation in a covered boat and fish cleaning and packaging. The local information center will help out with basic fishing and boat charter information, or head to the

Discovery Pier

Tyee Club

If you're fishing between July 15 and September 15, you may want to try qualifying for Tyee Club (www.tyeeclub.org) membership. This exclusive club, famous among anglers, has been dedicated to upholding the traditional methods of sportfishing since 1924. Several rules must be followed in order to become a member: You have to preregister your intent to fish under club rules; troll from a rowboat in the eddies at the mouth of the Campbell River; use a rod between six and nine feet long, an artificial lure, and a line of 20-pound test; then catch a trophy-size tyee (a Chinook salmon weighing over 30 pounds). Most tyee fishing is done at dawn and dusk. During the tyee season, most local charter operators offer the option of traditional tyee fishing, including **Coastal Island Fishing Adventures** (250/203-1162 or 877/537-7678 or 888/225-9776, www.coastalisland-fishing.com, $250 for two people). Guests at **Painter's Lodge** (1625 MacDonald Dr., 250/286-1102 or 800/663-7090, www.painterslodge.com) are charged a similar amount.

experts at the **River Sportsman** (2115 Island Hwy., 250/286-1017, 9am-6pm daily) for licenses, tackle, and maybe a few tips.

Although salmon fishing is the big draw in Campbell River, from November to March, the Quinsam River in Elk Falls Provincial Park is a hunting ground for hardy anglers chasing steelhead, and lakes throughout the interior are stocked with rainbow trout, cutthroat trout, and Dolly Varden.

FOOD

The best place to go for coffee is **Island Grind** (1416 Island Hwy., 778/418-4401, 7am-5pm Mon.-Fri., 8am-5pm Sat.-Sun., lunches $8-13), on the north side of town at the back of Discovery Harbour Shopping Centre. It also blends delicious smoothies, while lunches include salads and paninis. Island Grind's other location (801 Hilchey Rd., 778/418-4401, 7am-5pm Mon.-Fri., 8am-5pm Sat.-Sun., lunches

$8-13) is in a new subdivision on the city's southern edge—worth finding for its sun-drenched outdoor tables and ease of parking.

Around 4 kilometers (2.5 miles) south of downtown along Highway 19A is ★ **FoggDukkers** (907 S Island Hwy., 778/420-2030, 9am-5pm daily, lunches $7-12), serving coffee, tea, ice cream, and light meals from an oceanfront beach shack. An eclectic array of outdoor seating surrounds the main building, with complimentary binoculars supplied for whale-watching. A firepit keeps patrons warm on cooler days, or sit inside and keep warm around the wood stove.

For fresh seafood, head to **Dockside Fish and Chips** (1003 Dock C, Island Hwy., 778/346-3474, 11:30am-7pm Wed.-Sun.), on the waterfront at the Coast Marina. Halibut, salmon, and snapper—grilled or battered—it's all fresh and cooked to perfection. They also cook doughnuts in-house. Dine at the outdoor tables, or wander south along the promenade to one of many nearby grassy areas.

Royal Aroma (969 Alder St., 250/850-0785, 11am-9:30pm daily, $12-20) is a bright space in the heart of downtown. Using a traditional tandoor oven, the food is a step above the average small town Indian restaurant, with a huge selection of curries and vegetarian dishes.

At the back of the Discovery Harbour Shopping Centre (close to Island Grind—see above) is **Riptide Marine Pub** (1340 S. Island Hwy., 250/830-0044, 11:30am-10pm daily, $15-28), a good place for a full meal, although it doesn't take full advantage of its waterfront location (unless you score a table on the glassed-in patio). The sleek interior is a little nicer than you may imagine, while the food is exactly what you'd expect: standard pub fare mixed with fresh scallops, oysters, mussels, halibut, and salmon.

Continue north through town on Highway 19 and turn right on McDonald Road to reach two fishing resorts with excellent restaurants that welcome nonguests. The appetizer menu at **Legends Dining Room** (Painter's Lodge, 1625 MacDonald

Dr., 250/286-1102, 7am-11am and 5pm-9pm daily, $23-38) is dominated by seafood choices, and while mains include steak and lamb, it's hard to go past the halibut, cooked two different ways. Legends also offers a beautiful waterfront setting.

Just north of Painter's is **Anglers Dining Room** (Dolphins Resort, 4125 Discovery Dr., 250/287-3066, 8am-11am and 5pm-8pm daily, $32-43), a more rustic but equally inviting setting with a few outdoor tables. Local seafood is on the menu—oysters, lingcod, mussels, and salmon—but does not dominate.

ACCOMMODATIONS

Because Campbell River is a fish-centric resort town, every kind of lodging you could possibly want is here, from upscale fishing lodges to rustic campgrounds.

$50-100

Along Highway 19A (known as the South Island Highway through Campbell River) south of town, only the road separates several motels from Discovery Passage. If you want to save your money for a fishing charter, no worries—book a room at the 22-room **Big Rock Motel** (1020 S. Island Hwy., 250/923-4211 or 877/923-4211, www.bigrockmotel.com, $95 s or d, $130 with kitchen), your average two-story, cinder-block motel.

$100-150

Bed-and-breakfast accommodations are provided at **Haig-Brown House** (2250 Campbell River Rd., 250/286-6646, www.haig-brown.bc.ca, May-Oct., $110 s, $120 d), the modest 1923 riverside home of famed angler and author Roderick Haig-Brown. The old antiques-filled house has changed little over time, and the spacious grounds are a delightful place to relax. The three guest rooms share a bath. It's on the north side of Highway 28, just west of where Highway 19 spurs north to Port Hardy.

$150-200

Along the same strip of accommodations overlooking the water is **Heron's Landing**

Hotel (492 S. Island Hwy., 250/923-2848 or 888/923-2849, www.heronslandinghotel.com, $159-199 s or d), an older property that has undergone extensive renovations to create some of the nicest guest rooms in Campbell River. Standard rooms have one king bed or two twins, while the one-bedroom suites have kitchens. Rates include a cooked breakfast.

In the heart of downtown and across the road from a marina, 88-room **Coast Discovery Inn** (975 Shopper's Row, 250/287-7155 or 800/716-6199, www.coasthotels.com, $180-330 s or d) is a full-service hotel with bright and spacious rooms, many with water views, a fitness room, hot tub, and a restaurant. A hot buffet breakfast is also included in the rates.

Over $200

Follow Highway 19 beyond the town Campbell River, crossing the river of the same name, to reach **Painter's Lodge** (1625 MacDonald Dr., 250/286-1102 or 800/663-7090, www.painterslodge.com, late April-mid-Dec., $269-389), an impressive oceanfront fishing lodge offering all the amenities needed by keen anglers, including a marina, guided fishing trips, and fish-cleaning services. Families and non-anglers are also well-catered to, with facilities including an outdoor swimming pool, two hot tubs, tennis courts, a fitness room, a water shuttle to spa services on Quadra Island, and a waterfront restaurant with lots of outdoor seating. The modern guest rooms are offered in a number of different configurations, including standard Garden View rooms; two-story, family-friendly lofts; and private cabins. Many packages are offered that include a variety of fishing options, such as two nights of lodging and two guided fishing trips ($600-800 pp).

South of downtown along the same ocean-hugging highway as the Big Rock Motel recommended above is the **Ramada by Wyndham Campbell River** (462 S. Island Hwy., 250/923-4231 or 866/252-1532, www.wyndhamhotels.com, $280-400 s or d), with a wide range of facilities, including a courtyard with a barbecue for guest use, a hot tub, mini golf, and breakfast included.

Camping

A few commercial campgrounds dot the coastline around Campbell River, but although they're close to the water, the surroundings are generally nothing special. One of the closest to downtown is **Thunderbird RV Park** (2660 Spit Rd., 250/286-3344, www.thunderbirdrvpark.com, hookups $58-52, cottages $228-328 s or d), a 10-minute walk north of downtown. Amenities include full hookups, heated restrooms, and fish-cleaning stations.

A less commercial option, but with limited facilities, is **Elk Falls Provincial Park** (May-mid-Oct., $22), three kilometers (two miles) west of town on Highway 28. The 122 unserviced sites are south of the highway, with many right alongside the Quinsam River. The campground has flush toilets, drinking water, and a playground. Campsites can be reserved through **BC Parks** (519/858-6161 or 800/689-9025, https://camping.bcparks.ca).

Farther out and in a more rustic setting is **Loveland Bay Provincial Park** (mid-May-Sept., $22), on a northern arm of Campbell Lake 20 kilometers (12 miles) west of town. The 31 sites are close to the water and shaded by a second-growth forest. To get there, follow Snowden Camp Road beyond the Elk Falls day-use turnoff and turn west (left) onto Brewster Lake Road; the campground is around 12 kilometers (7.5 miles) from Elk Falls.

INFORMATION AND SERVICES

Park in the large parking lot of **Tyee Plaza,** along the waterfront in downtown Campbell River, and you're within easy walking distance of the information center and all services. At the front of the parking lot is **Campbell River Visitor Centre** (1235 Shopper's Row, 250/830-0411, 8:30am-5pm summer, 9am-5pm Mon.-Fri. fall-spring). Aside from providing tons of brochures and information on both the city and northern Vancouver Island, the knowledgeable staff can answer just about any question on the area you could think up. For other information, contact **Campbell River Tourism** (250/286-1616, www.campbellrivertourism.com).

Other plaza tenants include banks, a big-box grocery store, a laundromat, and various family-style eateries. Across from the plaza is the **post office** (1251 Shopper's Row) and **On Line Gourmet** (970 Shopper's Row, 250/286-6521, 8am-4pm Mon.-Sat.), where you can check your email for a small charge. **North Island Hospital** (375 2nd Ave., 250/287-7111) is south of downtown.

GETTING THERE AND AROUND

Although Campbell River is only 260 kilometers (162 miles) north of Victoria, you should allow over three hours for the trip by road, and at least another three hours to reach Port Hardy, 235 kilometers (146 miles) farther north, as the roads this far north are very windy and the going is often slow when stuck behind logging trucks.

Campbell River Airport (YBL), off Erickson Road 20 kilometers (12 miles) south of downtown, is served by **Pacific Coastal** (800/663-2872) and **Central Mountain Air** (888/865-8585) from Vancouver. **Campbell River Airport Shuttle** (250/914-1010) meets all scheduled flights and charges $15 pp for door-to-door drop-off in town.

From Victoria, **Islandlink Bus** (509 13th Ave., 250/287-7151) operates four or five buses daily to Campbell River; in summer, at least one daily continues north to Port Hardy, timed to link with the ferry departing for Prince Rupert. Get around town by **Campbell River Transit System** (250/287-7433, $2 per sector, $4.50 day pass), which departs from Tyee Plaza via Shopper's Row along eight routes. Rental car agencies in Campbell River include **Budget** (250/923-4283) and **National** (250/923-1234), both with airport desks (but make reservations in advance).

Offshore Islands

QUADRA ISLAND

A 10-minute ferry ride across Discovery Passage from downtown Campbell River takes you to Quadra Island (pop. 2,400), which blends beautiful scenery, First Nations culture, and upscale fishing lodges to create a unique and worthwhile detour from your up-island travels. The ferry docks in the south of the island, where most of the population resides. This narrow peninsula widens in the north to an unpopulated area where provincial and marine parks protect a wealth of wildlife. Marinelife around the entire shoreline is widespread; orcas cruise Discovery Passage, and seals and sea lions are commonly spied in surrounding waters.

Captain Vancouver may have been the first European to step onto the island when he made landfall at **Cape Mudge** in 1792, but the island had been inhabited by the Kwakwaka'wakw people for many centuries before.

Sights

Take Green Road south from the ferry dock to reach **Nuyumbalees Cultural Centre** (34 Weway Rd., 250/202-7707, call ahead to check hours, adults $10, seniors $8, children $6), a waterfront complex dedicated to the Kwakwaka'wakw people. Many artifacts on display have been returned to the island by museums from around the world after being taken by early European explorers. Highlights include the Sacred Potlatch Collection and an outdoor workshop where First Nations artists can be seen at work during summer. Ask for directions to petroglyphs (rock carvings) scattered around the grounds and beyond.

Continuing south, at the island's southwestern tip, **Cape Mudge Lighthouse** was built in 1916 to prevent shipwrecks in the wild surging waters around the point that marks the southern entrance to the treacherous Discovery Passage. You can drive right up to the lighthouse.

Rebecca Spit Marine Provincial Park

Around 9 kilometers (5.5 miles) north along Heriot Bay Road from the ferry dock on the island's east coast is Rebecca Spit Marine Provincial Park, which protects a 2-kilometer-long (1.2-mile) beach-lined peninsula. A road leads around halfway up the peninsula, from where a two-kilometer hiking trail loops up and around the end of the spit (allow 40 minutes round-trip). However, there are many access points to the beach, and it's just as enjoyable walking along the sand as the trail, especially on the east side, which is piled high with driftwood. The park's only facilities are restrooms and picnic areas.

Heriot Bay and the North

On the east coast is **Heriot Bay,** the name of both a cove and the island's largest community (population 500). This is the place to get gas, stock up on groceries, and, if time allows, jump aboard a ferry for Cortes Island (see below).

Take Hyacinthe Bay Road north from Heriot Bay and look for Walcan Road leading off to the left after six kilometers (four miles); a short drive along this side road leads to the trailhead for a three-kilometer (two-mile) hiking trail to the summit of **Chinese Mountain,** from where views extend east across Cortes Island to the mainland of British Columbia. Allow at least two hours for the round-trip.

From around 9 kilometers (5.5 miles) north of Heriot Bay, the main road up the island divides: Village Bay Road spurs left to the east coast, and Granite Bay Road continues north. The road to the coast also leads past

Main Lake Provincial Park, a 3,530-hectare (8,720-acre) tract of the interior, protecting the largest freshwater lake system in any of the Gulf or Discovery Islands. Some of the nine lakes are connected by natural canals, while others require a portage to access—regardless, this wilderness area is a great place for an overnight canoe adventure. The main launch point is Mine Lake, along Village Bay Road, from where a number of backcountry campsites can easily be accessed in a few hours of paddling.

Food

At Quathiaski Cove, near where ferries dock from Campbell River, **Aroma Café** (685 Heriot Bay Rd., 250/285-2404, 8am-1pm daily, breakfast $10-16) has tables inside and out. It's the headquarters for a small roasting operation that distributes to stores and cafés around the island and beyond. It has healthy yet delicious cooked breakfasts, including a couple of choices using local salmon. In the vicinity, **Island Farm to Table** (685 Harper Rd., 780/972-6000, 7am-3pm Mon.-Sat., lunch $12-16) does a wonderful job of creating delicious sandwiches, soups, and salads from locally grown produce. Across the island at Heriot Bay, **Java Bay Cafe** (1536 W Rd., 250/285-2833, 8am-5pm Tues.-Sun., lunch $7.50-12) pours coffee as good as any on the main island and is a full-service café with a few outdoor tables.

Herons Restaurant (Heriot Bay Inn, off Heriot Bay Rd., 250/285-3322, breakfast, lunch, and dinner daily in summer, $18-39) has as many tables outside on the harborfront deck as it does inside. The dinner menu includes lots of island produce and seafood, including butter-poached halibut. Also at the inn is the more casual **HBI Pub** (11:30am-10pm daily, $19-22), also with water views.

At Cape Mudge Resort in the south of the island, **Hama?Elas** (1 Lighthouse Rd., 250/250-830-2299, 7:30am-8:30pm daily May-Sept., $24-30) has sweeping ocean views from tables inside and out. Over the years, the emphasis on traditional foods has lessened, although the salmon soup garnished with seaweed and served with a side of bannock bread is a delight. For mains, there's the usual steak, pork, and chicken choices, or stay with the local theme and order grilled salmon.

Accommodations and Camping

Since the 1890s, **Heriot Bay Inn** (off Heriot Bay Rd., 250/285-3322 or 888/605-4545, www.heriotbayinn.com, rooms $119-129 s or d, cabins $265-305 s or d) has been the social hub of the island's largest community. Separated from the water by a wide swath of landscaped garden, the lodge has 10 small but comfortable guest rooms (some with water views) and three kitchen-equipped wooden cabins.

Near Cape Mudge Lighthouse is ★ **Cape Mudge Resort** (1 Lighthouse Rd., 250/820-2299, www.capemudgeresort.com, May-Sept., $169-349 s or d), built by the local Kwagiulth people. The centerpiece of this magnificent waterfront lodge is the foyer, built in the style of a Big House (a traditional meeting place) using locally milled woods. Each of the 35 spacious rooms is decorated in a Pacific Northwest theme, and each has a private balcony with water views. Rates start at a reasonable $169 s or d, with meal packages available. The more expensive units are two-bedroom cottages. The lodge coordinates fishing charters and cultural activities, and its restaurant specializes in First Nations foods.

Campers have two good options. **Oceanfront RV Park** (Cape Mudge Resort, 250/820-2299, www.capemudgeresort.com, May-Sept., $50-55) is part of the Cape Mudge Resort property on the island's southern tip. It has 13 sites, most of which are right on the ocean, as well as full hookups, wireless Internet, and hot showers. The other choice is the charming **We Wai Kai Campsite** (250/285-3111, www.wewaikai.

com, mid-May-early Oct., $35-45), set along a pleasant sandy beach at the head of Heriot Bay and close to Rebecca Spit Marine Provincial Park. Amenities include basic hookups, showers, and a laundromat.

Getting There

BC Ferries (250/386-3431, www.bcferries. com) offers services from Campbell River to the island, every hour on the hour 6am-11pm daily; round-trip fare is adults $9.10, children $4.55, vehicles $21.10.

CORTES ISLAND

Accessible by ferry from Quadra Island, Cortes Island (pronounced cor-TEZ—it was named by a Spanish explorer in 1792 for Hernán Cortés, a Spanish conquistador) is a relatively remote place at the top of the Strait of Georgia, closer to the mainland of British Columbia than to Vancouver Island. Few visitors venture out here, but those who do are rarely disappointed. The island's year-round population is just 1,000 people, many of whom live in three small communities.

The island has no official visitors center. You can get an idea of island life by checking out the online version of the local newspaper (www.cortesisland.com), which has everything you'll need to know for a visit.

Sights

South of the ferry dock, Manson's Landing Provincial Park is a beautiful little spot sandwiched between a large tidal lagoon and the forested shoreline of Hague Lake. The park is named for the Manson brothers, who emigrated from Scotland in 1887 and became the island's first European settlers. Learn about their history at Cortes Island Museum (957 Beasley Rd., 250/935-6340, 10am-4pm Tues.-Sun. summer, noon-4pm

Fri.-Sat. the rest of the year, donation), which is housed in a former general store and surrounded by a garden planted with the same species of vegetables and herbs used by early settlers. South of Manson's Landing, Smelt Bay Provincial Park is a quiet spot for beachcombing and taking in the unique island environment.

Accommodations and Camping

Accommodations on the island are limited, so unless you plan to camp, make reservations before coming over. Close to the ferry dock on a protected waterway, ★ Gorge Harbour Marina Resort (Hunt Rd., Gorge Harbour, 250/935-6433, www.gorgeharbour.com, tent sites $33, hookups $44-54, motel rooms $192 s or d) is set across a sprawling acreage sloping down to the water. Amenities include an oceanfront outdoor swimming pool, kayak and boat rentals, fishing charters, a waterfront restaurant (noon-9pm Mon.-Sat., 10am-9pm Sun. June-mid-Sept., $14-23) with fantastic fish-and-chips, and a general store. Smelt Bay Provincial Park, 15 kilometers (9 miles) from the ferry terminal, offers a few campsites (no services, mid-May-Sept., $20), but you will need a reservation to ensure a spot (519/858-6161 or 800/689-9025, https://camping.bcparks.ca).

Getting There

The ferry trip between Heriot Bay on Quadra Island and Whaletown on Cortes Island takes 40 minutes. BC Ferries (250/386-3431, www. bcferries.com) operates scheduled service between the two islands six times daily, with the first departing Quadra Island at 9am and the last departing Cortes Island at 5:50pm. Peak round-trip fare is adults $10.70, children $5.35, vehicles $24.65.

1: hiking trail through Strathcona Provincial Park 2: dense forests of Quadra Island 3: the world's largest burl in Port McNeill 4: MV *Uchuck III* in Friendly Cove

World's Largest Burl
Port McNeill, B.C.

Highway 28

Running from the east coast to the west coast through the northern section of magnificent **Strathcona Provincial Park,** Highway 28 is another island road worth traveling for the scenery alone. Beyond Elk Falls Provincial Park, the highway parallels Upper Campbell Lake for 20 kilometers (12 miles) before splitting, with the main highway continuing west to Gold River and a side road following the east shore of Buttle Lake into Strathcona Provincial Park.

STRATHCONA PROVINCIAL PARK

circumnavigated the world in the 1570s (some believe he would have sighted the peak from his ship). The park's other superlative natural features include 440-meter (1,440-foot) **Della Falls,** one of North America's highest waterfalls, and a 1,000-year-old, 93-meter-tall (300-foot) Douglas fir, British Columbia's tallest known tree. Douglas fir and western red cedar carpet the valley, and wildflowers—lupine, Indian paintbrush, moss campion, and kinnikinnick—cover the high slopes. Resident mammals include black bears, wolves, cougars, marmots, deer, and most of the island's 3,000 elk. Cutthroat trout, rainbow trout, and Dolly Varden fill the park's lakes, and all kinds of birds soar the skies here, including the provincial bird, the Steller's jay.

Sights and Recreation

You'll get a taste of Strathcona's beauty along Highway 28, but to get into the park proper, turn south off Highway 28 halfway between Campbell River and Gold River. This access road hugs the eastern shore of **Buttle Lake,** passing many well-marked nature walks and hiking trails. One of the first is the short walk (10 minutes one-way) to **Lupin Falls,** which are more impressive than the small creek across from the parking lot would suggest. Continuing south along the lakeshore past

driftwood-strewn beaches, you'll come to the 2-kilometer (1.2-mile) loop **Karst Creek Trail** (allow 40 minutes), which passes through a karst landscape of sinkholes and disappearing streams. At the lake's southern end, where the road crosses Thelwood Creek, a six-kilometer (four-mile) trail (2.5 hours one-way) climbs a steep valley to **Bedwell Lake** and surrounding alpine meadows.

As the road continues around the lakeshore, look for **Myra Falls** across the water. After passing through the Boliden-Westmin Resources mining operation, the road ends on the edge of an old-growth forest. From this point, explore on foot by taking the three-kilometer (two-mile) **Upper Myra Falls Trail** (1 hour one-way) to a lookout point above the aforementioned falls.

Camping

Apart from numerous day-use areas along the shore of Buttle Lake, the only facilities within the park are two campgrounds. **Buttle Lake Campground** (May-Sept., $20) is on the west side of Buttle Lake, just west of the junction of Highway 28 and the park access road. **Ralph River Campground** (May-Sept., $20) is 35 kilometers (22 miles) farther south, on the shore of Buttle Lake. Both have pit toilets, picnic tables, and fire rings, but no hookups. For reservations, contact **BC Parks** (519/858-6161 or 800/689-9025, https://camping.bcparks.ca).

GOLD RIVER AND THE REMOTE NORTHWEST COAST

Those looking for a glimpse of Vancouver Island away from the touristy east coast will find the 90-kilometer (56-mile) drive west from Campbell River to Gold River (pop. 1,200) along Highway 28 both enjoyable and interesting. Beyond the western boundary of Strathcona Provincial Park, Highway 28 descends along the Heber River to its confluence with the Gold River, where the town lies. Built in 1965 to house employees of a pulp mill, it was the first all-electric town in Canada. The orderly streets seem a little out of place amid the surrounding wilderness, which is why most residents and visitors alike are drawn to the area.

The big attraction for visitors to this part of the island is cruising Nootka Sound from Muchalat Inlet, 14 kilometers (9 miles) south of town (see below), but the town is also a base for anglers and a jumping-off point for travel along the maze of logging roads to the west. Meanwhile, golfers rave about the forest-lined fairways of **Gold River Golf Course** (250/283-7266, $25) simply because it's there.

Upana Caves

The natural highlight of Gold River is **Upana Caves,** but unless you're a spelunker, chances are you've never heard of them. The cave system, accessed 16 kilometers (10 miles) west of town along Head Bay Road (this road eventually leads to Tahsis), has at least 15 entrances and over 500 meters (1,500 feet) of passages to explore, including a river that flows underground for 150 meters (500 feet) through eroded limestone bedrock. Unlike Horne Lake Caves near Qualicum Beach, there are no guides or services at Upana. That said, a well-traveled trail leads through the forest to the main cave. You'll need warm and waterproof clothing, hiking boots, and a reliable light source.

Accommodations and Camping

Rooms at the **Ridgeview Motor Inn** (395 Donner Court, 250/283-2277, www.ridgeview-inn.com, $135-175 s or d) were slightly nicer than expected, and each comes with a fridge and a small TV. A light breakfast is included in the rates. The adjacent pub-restaurant serves decent food and has an outdoor eating area with fantastic valley views.

One of the island's premier sporting lodges, ★ **The Lodge at Gold River** (100 Muchalat Dr., 250/283-2900, www.thelodgeatgoldriver. ca, $375 s or d) is across the river to the south

side of town on the road out to Muchalat Inlet. Although set up with anglers in mind, everyone is welcome to soak up the wilderness setting of this striking riverside log structure. Added bonuses include a fully equipped tack room, a pond to practice fly-casting, a small fitness room, and spa services. Packages including transportation from Campbell River, lodging, and three memorable meals per day are $725 s, $1300 d.

Gold River Municipal Campground (Muchalat Dr., 250/283-2202, $12), five kilometers (three miles) south of town, is beside the Gold River along the road out to Muchalat Inlet. Facilities include fire pits, picnic tables, and restrooms, but no hookups. With similar amenities is **Muchalat Lake Campground** (Gold River Mainline Rd., May-Sept., $12), eight kilometers (five miles) northwest of town, the preferred spot for anglers looking to hook into rainbow or cutthroat trout.

Information

At the entrance to town, stop at the **Gold River Visitor Centre** (Muchalat Dr., 250/283-2418, www.goldriver.ca, 10am-6pm Fri.-Sun. mid-May-June, 10am-6pm daily July-Aug.).

★ CRUISING NOOTKA SOUND

The best reason to travel west from Campbell River is to take a cruise along the spectacular Muchalat Inlet to Nootka Sound, passing uninhabited islands, abundant marinelife, and remote First Nations villages. **Get West Adventure Cruises** (250/283-2515, www. getwest.ca) operates the MV *Uchuck III,* a converted World War II minesweeper, which departs from the dock at the end of Highway 28, which is 14 kilometers (9 miles) south from Gold River. The vessel's primary purpose is dropping supplies at remote west coast communities, logging camps, and fishing lodges, but interested visitors are welcome and are made to feel comfortable by the hardworking crew. Amenities include a lounge, a small coffee shop, restrooms, and a viewing deck.

At 9am every Tuesday, the MV *Uchuck III* sets out on its run around Nootka Sound and as far west as Yuquot (adults $86, seniors $81, children $50), returning to port between 6pm and 8pm. At 10am on Wednesday and Saturday in summer, it's off to Yuquot (also known as Friendly Cove) for a six-hour round-trip (adults $102, seniors $97, children $57). Now a small village of just 25 First Nations people, Yuquot was visited by Captain James Cook but is best known as the site of the only Spanish settlement established in Canada. It was this settlement that led to the Nootka Sound Conventions, a series of negotiations between Great Britain and Spain that were attended by George Vancouver and Juan Francisco de la Bodega y Quadra at this remote outpost in 1792. The longest sailing departs at 7am every Thursday March-October, heading out to the open ocean and up the coast to the remote First Nations village of **Kyuquot.** This is a two-night trip, with meals and accommodations at local lodgings included in the fare ($1,325 s or d).

TAHSIS

The remote village Tahsis, at the head of Tahsis Inlet, an arm of Nootka Sound, is accessible by logging road (known locally as Head Bay Rd.), 63 kilometers (40 miles) from Gold River; allow at least one hour. Along the way, look for the **Three Sisters Falls,** which tumble down from Malaspine Peak a short distance after the road leaves Head Bay. Originally a forestry town, the sawmill closed in 2001, and although the population has dropped from over 2,000 to just 300 people, it's a popular destination for travelers looking to experience a side of Vancouver Island that is a world away from the busy east coast.

The best Tahsis lodging is at **Moutcha Bay Resort** (Head Bay Rd., Moutcha Bay, 250/337-8962, www.moutchabay.com, camping $79-99, yurt $379-699 s or d, lodge room $399 s or d), halfway between Gold River and Tahsis. This modern waterfront fishing lodge has a range of overnight options, including luxurious yurts with wraparound decks. The resort is a destination for kayakers and anglers—you can fish right off the dock for trophy-size fish, or take a charter into Nootka Sound. The resort restaurant enjoys sweeping ocean views.

ZEBALLOS

Gold was discovered in this region as early as the late 1700s, but it was more than a century later, in 1924, that mining began on the Zeballos River. The mining took place inland, but the township grew on the ocean, where supplies were dropped off and the ore shipped out. Mining continued until 1948, but a road linking Zeballos to the outside world wasn't completed until 1970. Although a very rough logging road links Tahsis to Zeballos, the easiest way to get there by road is to head south from Zeballos Junction, located along Highway 19, about 150 kilometers (94 miles) west of Campbell River and 84 kilometers (53 miles) southeast of Port Hardy. From this junction, travel is south for 46 kilometers (29 miles) along an unpaved logging road to reach the remote community.

Today, Zeballos is a quiet backwater, a base for commercial and recreational fishing boats, and home to basic visitor services. The same range of activities enjoyed elsewhere on Vancouver Island is possible, including walking along short oceanfront walking trails, sea kayaking, ocean fishing, and even surfing.

At the north end of the village, **Cedars Inn** (203 Pandora Ave., 250/761-4044, www.zeballosexpeditions.com, $125-145 s or d) is a converted hospital, but don't let this put you off, as the 13 guest rooms are warm and inviting. The in-house **Blue Heron Restaurant** (7am-10am and 5pm-8:30pm daily, $14-25) has a varied menu, including West Coast seafood and Italian. The inn is affiliated with a local tour operator, so it makes a good base for looking to rent kayaks, hire a fishing guide, or take a water taxi to one of the nearby villages.

A short walk from the center of town is **Cevallos Campsite** (250/761-4229, $10), on the Zeballos River. It has toilets, drinking water, and free firewood. For pre-trip planning, visit www.zeballos.com.

Port McNeill and Vicinity

Highway 19, covering the 235 kilometers (146 miles) between Campbell River and Port Hardy, is a good road with plenty of straight stretches and not much traffic. Passing through relatively untouched wilderness (with only logged hillsides to remind you of the ugliness humanity can produce with such ease), it's almost as though you've entered another world, or at least another island. Stop at all of the frequent lookouts for the best views of endless forest, deep blue mountains, white peaks, sparkling rivers and lakes, and cascading waterfalls.

PORT MCNEILL

After taking a convoluted inland route for 130 kilometers (81 miles), Highway 19 returns to the coastline at **Port McNeill** (population 2,100), a logging town that dates to the 1930s. Port McNeill is a good base for visiting Malcolm Island and Alert Bay, and is also home of the world's largest burl (and the world's second largest).

Head beyond the main street along Broughton Boulevard and you'll find the **Ronning Burl,** the world's largest burl, which was cut from a 350-year-old Sitka spruce in 2005. A burl is a rounded outgrowth—a kind of deformation—found in some tree trunks. Most burls are plate-size, but this one is estimated to weigh 30 tons and is around 18 meters (60 feet) in circumference. The world's second-largest burl (it held title of world's biggest until 2005) is back up on the main highway, 2 kilometers (1.2 miles) north of town at the entrance to a logging company office; this one weighs an estimated 20 tons.

Practicalities

Campbell Way leads down off the highway to the waterfront, and along this road, you'll find services such as grocery stores and gas stations. Opposite Cedar Street, **Black Bear Resort Hotel** (1812 Campbell Way.,

250/956-4900 or 866/956-4900, www.port-mcneill-accommodation.com, from $170 s or d) is a sprawling complex of 40 modern motel rooms and a row of compact kitchen-equipped cabins, a barbecue area, an indoor pool and hot tub, a fitness room, and a laundry. Rates include a light breakfast.

Continuing north from the Black Bear Resort Hotel are a few places to eat, including **Tia's Cafe** (1705 Campbell Hwy., 250/956-2379, 8am-6pm Mon.-Fri., 10am-2pm Sat.-Sun., lunch $9-15), which has grab-and-go breakfasts, soups, salads, sandwiches, and a few Mexican-inspired dishes. If you're staying overnight, consider dinner at **Archipelagos Bistro** (1703 Broughton Blvd., 250/956-4553, 8am-1:30pm and 4pm-7pm Wed.-Mon., $17-28), a small, casual dining room with filtered water views. The menu has something for everyone, but the local seafood, simply prepared and presented, is your best choice.

Port McNeill Visitor Centre (1594 Beach Dr., 250/956-3131, www.portmcneill.net, 9am-4pm daily summer, 9am-4pm Mon.-Fri. fall-spring) is along the waterfront near the ferry terminal.

MALCOLM ISLAND

This largish island, immediately offshore from Port McNeill, is home to around 600 people, most of whom live in the village of **Sointula** on Rough Bay. The first European settlers were of Finnish descent and had been toiling in the coal mines of Nanaimo. Led by Finnish philosopher Matti Kurikka, who had written a book on creating a Finnish utopia, they arrived in 1901, having reached an agreement with the British Columbia government to take possession of Malcolm Island. Meaning "harmony" in Finnish, Sointula evolved as a utopian community in which everyone shared everything and everyone was equal. The ideals of a peaceful existence didn't last long: in 1903, a fire destroyed the community hall and killed 11 residents, and then in 1904, Kurikka left the island with a massive debt, forcing the community into bankruptcy. Although ownership of the island was then returned to the government, remaining residents were allowed to retain their homes and businesses. Today, to some extent, utopian ideals continue, with Finnish descendants operating the general store and gas station as British Columbia's oldest cooperative, allowing profits to remain in the community.

Sights and Recreation

In town, wander along the residential streets and admire the trim homes and well-tended gardens, then visit **Sointula Museum** (280 1st St., noon-4pm daily summer, donation), in a renovated school building three blocks north of the ferry dock. Then walk the three-kilometer (two-mile) Mateoja Heritage Trail from the north end of 3rd Street to a popular swimming and bird-watching spot, **Big Lake,** passing the remains of an original Finnish homestead along the way. The best ocean access is at **Bere Point Regional Park,** on the north side of the island overlooking Queen Charlotte Strait. The beach in front of the park comprises rounded pebbles, and occasionally in summer, orca whales will come close to shore to rub their bellies on the smooth rocks (a purpose-built whale-watching platform is a short walk west from the day-use area). **Beautiful Bay Trail** heads out east from the park for five kilometers (three miles) to Malcolm Point.

Accommodations and Camping

On the downtown waterfront one block from the ferry dock, the **Oceanfront Hotel** (210 1st St., 250/230-6722, www.theoceanfronthotel.ca, $149-249 s or d) is a rambling old hotel with 20 comfortable guest rooms. All have TVs and Internet access, and many have ocean views (the more expensive ones have private decks). Guests have use of a communal lounge and kitchen. **Orca Lodge** (500 1st

St., 250/230-6722, www.orcalodge.ca, $250 s or d) comprises two self-contained suites in a renovated 1915 boathouse. Both units have ocean-facing decks, full kitchens, barbecues, and laundry facilities.

One of the many upscale fishing lodges scattered throughout this part of the world is ★ **Sointula Lodge** (250/973-6381, www.sointulalodge.com, May-Sept., US$4,000 for 3 nights with meals and fishing), located on a beautiful waterfront property east of Sointula. It is everything a luxurious fishing lodge should be, but it is a completely unpretentious family-run operation. Inside the spacious guest cabins you'll find super-comfortable beds, log furniture, top-notch baths, and original art. Guests stay as part of all-inclusive packages, which include memorable meals and as much guided fishing as you can handle.

Drive across the island three kilometers (two miles) to **Bere Point Regional Park Campsite** (250/956-3301, May-Sept., $20-24), where 22 campsites overlook Queen Charlotte Strait, but there are no hookups or drinking water.

Other Practicalities

Stop by the **Sointula Cooperative Store** (175 1st St., 250/973-6912, 9:30am-5:30pm Tues.-Sat.) for groceries, gas, liquor, and the island's only ATM. At funky **Coho Joe's** (145 1st St., 250/230-2233, 9am-2:30pm Wed.-Sun., lunch $8-14), across from the downtown waterfront, soups, sandwiches, cinnamon buns, and fish tacos are made daily, and there is a good choice of coffee drinks. One block north, everything at **Upper Crust Bakery** (180 1st St., 250/973-6333, 7am-3:30pm Mon.-Sat.) is made daily from scratch.

Although the island has no official visitors center, the **Sointula Resource Centre** (165 1st St., 250/973-2001, 10am-2:30pm Tues.-Sat.) has lots of local information, or go to www.sointulainfo.ca for a taste of island life.

Getting There

The easiest way to reach Malcolm Island is with **BC Ferries** (250/386-3431), which makes the short run across Broughton Strait from Port McNeill to Sointula around eight times daily. The round-trip fare is adults $10.70, children $5.35, vehicles $24.65.

★ ALERT BAY

This fascinating village is the only settlement on crescent-shaped **Cormorant Island,** which lies in Broughton Strait 45 minutes by ferry east from Port McNeill. The island's population of 700 is evenly split between First Nations and those of European descent.

Alert Bay holds plenty of history. Captain Vancouver landed there in the early 1790s, and it's been a supply stop for fur traders and gold miners on their way to Alaska, a place for ships to stock up on water, and home base to an entire fishing fleet. Today, the village is one of the region's major fishing and marine service centers, and it holds two fish-processing and packing plants. Half the island is owned by the Kwakiutl people, whose powerful art draws visitors to Alert Bay.

Sights

All of the island's numerous attractions can be reached on foot or by bicycle. Start by wandering through the village to appreciate the early-1900s waterfront buildings and the colorful totems decorating **Nimpkish Burial Ground.**

For an outstanding introduction to the fascinating culture and heritage of the Kwakiutl people, don't miss the **U'Mista Cultural Centre** (1 Front St., 250/974-5403, 9am-5pm daily summer, 9am-5pm Tues.-Sat. fall-spring, adults $15, seniors $12, students $5). Built to house a ceremonial potlatch collection confiscated by the federal government after a 1921 ban on potlatches, the center contains masks and other Kwakiutl art and artifacts. Take a guided tour through the center, and then wander at your leisure past the photos and colorful displays to watch two award-winning films produced by the center—one explains the origin and meaning of the potlatch. The

center also teaches local children First Nations languages, culture, song, and dance. It's a 10-minute walk north along the waterfront from the ferry dock.

Along the road to the cultural center, you pass the century-old **Anglican Church.** Also on the north end of the island you'll find the **Indian Big House,** with one of the world's tallest totem poles out front (it's 53 meters/174 feet high; the tallest is in Victoria). To get here, walk uphill from the cultural center; the towering totem pole soon comes into view.

Away from the waterfront, grab an island map to find your way to **Alert Bay Ecological Park** (allow around 40 minutes from downtown). Surrounded by moss-draped forests, the park protects an open area of ghostly black-water spring-fed swamps, home to ravens, bald eagles, and other birds.

Food and Accommodations

Pass N Thyme (4 Maple Rd., 250/974-2670, noon-8pm Tues.-Sat., $12-23) is the bright red building across from the waterfront. Inside, you'll find a friendly, casual ambience, and a menu of seafood, pasta, burgers, and salads.

Along the waterfront and within easy walking distance of the ferry dock, **Alert Bay Lodge** (549 Fir St., 250/974-2410 or 800/255-5057, www.alertbaylodge.com, $145-165 s or d) is a beautiful cedar building that was originally a church. Today, it offers four simple rooms where rates include wireless Internet access and a cooked breakfast.

Information

Turn right after leaving the ferry dock to reach **Alert Bay Visitor Centre** (118 Fir St., 250/974-5024, www.alertbay.ca, 9am-5pm daily summer).

Getting There

BC Ferries (250/386-3431) runs to the island from Port McNeill a few times daily. The round-trip fare is adults $10.70, children $5.35. A vehicle is $24.65 round-trip, but there's no real point taking one over because everything on the island is reachable on foot.

1

2

If you would like to combine a visit to Alert Bay with a trip to Malcolm Island, check the ferry schedule in advance, as some sailings make a direct link between the two islands.

TELEGRAPH COVE

Most visitors come to Telegraph Cove to go whale-watching on Johnstone Strait, but the spot is well worth the eight-kilometer (five-mile) detour from the highway just east of Port McNeill. Built around a deep sheltered harbor, it's one of the last existing "boardwalk" communities on Vancouver Island. Many of the buildings stand on stilts and pilings over the water, linked by a boardwalk.

Fewer than 20 people live here year-round, but the population swells enormously during late spring and summer when whale-watching, diving, and fishing charters do a roaring trade; canoeists and kayakers arrive to paddle along Broughton and Johnstone Straits; and the campground opens for the season.

Whales are occasionally spotted from the cove, but to enjoy the full whale-watching experience, you'll need to join a boat tour. In the village itself, it's easy to spend at least an hour exploring the colorful boardwalk. Here you'll find the **Whale Interpretive Centre** (250/928-3129, 10am-5pm daily May-Sept., adults $5, children $3), a historic fishing shed that has been given a modern makeover and is now filled with interpretive panels and lots of whale bones. Also on the boardwalk is an art gallery, a couple of cafés, the Old Saltery Pub, and a store selling groceries and fishing tackle. Beside the boat ramp, **North Island Kayak** (250/928-3114, www.kayakbc.ca, 8am-5pm daily) has two-hour guided sea kayaking tours for $80, overnight trips, and rentals.

TOP EXPERIENCE

★ Whale-Watching

More than 50 whale-watching operations have sprung up around Vancouver Island in the last three decades, but the opportunity to view orcas (killer whales) close up in Johnstone Strait is unparalleled. These magnificent, intelligent mammals spend the summer in the protected waters around northern Vancouver Island, but are most concentrated in **Robson Bight,** 20 kilometers (12 miles) east of Telegraph Cove, where they rub on the gravel beaches near the mouth of the Tsitka River, an area that has been established as a sanctuary for the whales.

Prince of Whales (250/383-4884 or 888/383-4884, www.princeofwhales.com, adults $140, children $90) was one of British Columbia's first commercial whale-watching companies and continues to lead the way in responsible whale-watching. The company offers two options: a rigid-hulled inflatable boat that gets visitors out to the best whale-watching spots quickly, and a boat with three different viewing places, including a covered area where complimentary hot drinks are served. Both vessels depart 2-5 times daily from Telegraph Cove on 3- to 3.5-hour cruises from mid-May to September. The experienced crew takes you along the coastline to view the whales in their natural habitat and to hear their mysterious and beautiful sounds through a hydrophone (underwater microphone). Reservations are required, and you should call ahead as far as possible to ensure a spot. Dress warmly, and don't forget your camera for this experience of a lifetime.

Kayaking is a popular way for experienced wilderness-lovers to enjoy the whales of Johnstone Strait. **Telegraph Cove Sea Kayaking** (250/756-0094, www.tckayaks.com) makes planning a trip easy, with sea kayak rentals ($60-95 per day for single and double kayaks), GPS and VHF radio rentals, and a water taxi service to popular wilderness campsites along the strait. They also offer one-day tours that include boating out to the best whale-watching spots and then taking to the water by kayak, as well as multinight kayaking trips.

1: carved mask near entrance of U'Mista Cultural Centre in Alert Bay **2:** Alert Bay Ecological Park

Food

Head to ★ **Sally's Food Bar** (250/928-3155, 7am-8pm mid-May-Sept., $9-18) for choices such as burgers with fries cut and cooked to order, which can be enjoyed on the sprawling patio. Breakfasts are mostly under $10, including delicious breakfast burritos.

At the end of the boardwalk, the **Killer Whale Café** (250/928-3155, lunch and dinner May-Sept., $16-38) is in yet another restored building, this one a saltery, where fish were once salted before being transported to market. Although extensively renovated, the building retains many historic elements, including exposed beams, copper tables, and stained-glass windows. The food is a little pricey, but portions are huge and the watery locale can't be beaten.

Accommodations and Camping

Many of the buildings on the boardwalk and around the bay have been converted to guest accommodations and can be rented by the night (reserve well in advance) May through mid-October. For reservations at any of the following options, contact **Telegraph Cove Resort** (250/928-3131 or 800/200-4665, www.telegraphcoveresort.com, May-Sept.). The units range from extremely basic cabins ($150 s or d) spread along the boardwalk to three-bedroom self-contained homes ($350) overlooking the cove. About the only thing they have in common is the incredible setting. We stayed in the three-bedroom **Okura House,** which has a deck with harbor views and is linked to the boardwalk by a private stairway.

Built over the water beside the main boardwalk, the self-contained suites at **Dockside Suites** (250/928-3131 or 800/200-4665, www.telegraphcoveresort.com, May-Oct., $225 s or d) don't have balconies and are not particularly spacious, but each is filled with modern conveniences, including a full kitchen with full-size fridge.

A 10-minute walk from the village is **Forest RV Campground** (250/928-3131 or 800/200-4665, www.telegraphcoveresort.com, May-Sept., $36-45), with 100 campsites spread through towering stands of old-growth forest. Amenities include showers, a laundromat, and an abundance of firewood. The campground is also linked to the oceanfront by a forested trail.

Telegraph Cove

The Grizzly Bears of Knight Inlet

grizzly bear eating mussels at low tide

Beyond the maze of uninhabited islands between northern Vancouver Island and the mainland of British Columbia is Knight Inlet, a remote wilderness that is a sought-after destination for bear-lovers the world over. The inlet extends some 125 kilometers (78 miles) inland, but it is one particular bay, Glendale Cove, around halfway up the fjord, that is the focus for bear-watching. Here, from mid-May to mid- to late August, grizzly (brown) bears come down to the shoreline at low tide to feed on seaweed, crabs, and mussels. From late August to mid-October, the bears move to the lower reaches of the salmon-rich Glendale River. From the bear-viewing platforms located along the river, it's possible to see up to 15 bears feasting on salmon at any one time.

The least expensive way to reach the inlet is with Tide Rip Grizzly Adventures (250/928-3090, www.grizzlycanada.com), which has bear-watching tours departing Telegraph Cove daily mid-May-September. For the first two months, when the bears come down to the waterline to feed, the boat doesn't dock, but from mid- or late August onward, the tour includes two hours spent at a bear-viewing platform. The tour cost is $380 pp and lasts around nine hours.

Knight Inlet Lodge (250/337-1953, www.grizzlytours.com, call for rates) is on the edge of Glendale Cove, and offers the ultimate grizzly bear-viewing experience. Tours start with a float-plane ride from Campbell River and include modern accommodations for 2-6 nights, all meals, and bear-viewing excursions.

BROUGHTON ARCHIPELAGO

Broughton Archipelago Provincial Marine Park, British Columbia's largest marine park, protects a group of 30 remote islands at the entrance to Knight Inlet northeast of both Telegraph Cove and Port McNeill. Those with their own boats are the most frequent arrivals, but there are also water taxis from Port McNeill, and it is possible to paddle all the way from Telegraph Cove in two or three days.

Simoom Sound

Some of the islands of Broughton Archipelago have been settled at different times in the last 100 years. One such settlement was at Simoom Sound. Most of the buildings floated on logs and, somewhat confusingly, the town was towed by barge to Echo Bay, on Gilford Island, but it's still known as Simoom Sound. Here you'll find **Echo Bay Marina** (www.kwaxwalawadi.com), a popular gathering point for yachties and kayakers. The marina has two self-contained suites ($225-250 s or d), boat tours, a restaurant, a grocery store, Internet access, and a laundromat. Check their website for a list of flight operators and water taxi services that link the resort to the outside world.

Also in the sound is **Paddlers Inn** (250/230-0088, www.paddlersinn.ca, June-Sept., from $300 s or d), an eclectic combination of buildings both on the shore and floating in the bay. Originally a floating church, the largest lodging sits on logs and sleeps up to 10 in four smallish double rooms and two single rooms, and has a communal cooking and dining room. The Floathouse Cabin ($300) affords more privacy and has its own kitchen and sauna, while on dry land, the Shoreline Cabin ($500), which sleeps six, has a deck with sweeping ocean views.

Getting There

Silver King Ventures (250/956-4047, www.silverkingventures.com) is a water-taxi service originating in Port McNeill that serves Simoom Sound (the trip over from Port McNeill takes around two hours), or charter their boat for up to eight people for a three-hour wildlife viewing boat tour through the archipelago. **Telegraph Cove Sea Kayaking** (Telegraph Cove, 250/756-0094, www.tckayaks.com) rents kayaks for $60-95 per day and provides transportation to the archipelago in a boat specially built for landing on remote beaches.

Port Hardy and the Far North

Port Hardy (pop. 4,100) lies along sheltered Hardy Bay, 235 kilometers (146 miles) north of Campbell River and 495 kilometers (308 miles) north of Victoria. It's the largest community north of Campbell River and the terminus for ferries sailing the Inside Passage to and from Prince Rupert. The ferry is the main reason most people drive this far north, but Port Hardy is also a good base from which to explore the wild and untamed northern tip of the island or fish for salmon in the sheltered waters of "King Coho Country."

SIGHTS AND RECREATION

As you enter the Port Hardy area, take the scenic route to town via Hardy Bay Road. You'll pass several original chainsaw wood carvings and skirt the edge of peaceful Hardy Bay before entering downtown via Market Street. Turn left to reach **Port Hardy Museum** (7110 Market St., 250/949-8143, 10am-noon and 1pm-5pm Tues.-Sat., donation), which holds a predictable collection of pioneer artifacts.

The Gwa'sala-'Nakwaxda'xw people have called this region home for over 12,000 years, and their culture is displayed throughout town, including at **Tsulquate Park,** along the waterfront, where you can appreciate their carvings (and maybe see bald eagles resting in the trees or swooping about over the water). **K'awat'si Tours** (250/949-8525, kawatsitours.ca) offers a variety of tours and cultural experiences, including cedar weaving, storytelling, and boat tours. Check the websites for dates and pricing.

Fishing

At the **Quatse Salmon Centre** (8400 Byng Rd., 250/949-9022, 10am-5pm daily June-Sept., adults $6, seniors and students $4), on the scenic Quatse River south of town,

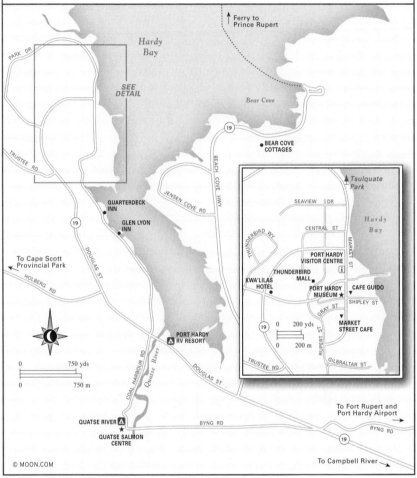

Port Hardy

you can observe incubation and rearing fa-cilities for pink, chum, and coho salmon, as well as steelhead. Good fishing on the river attracts droves of anglers year-round, but most of the fishing action takes place in the offshore tidal waters, with chinook and coho salmon, halibut, lingcod, snapper, and tuna all caught through the March to October season. A well-respected company offering charters is **Tides & Tales** (250/949-0641, www.tidesandtales.com), which charges around $1,200 for an eight-hour fishing trip for up to three anglers.

FOOD

Port Hardy doesn't offer a large variety of dining options. Wander around town and you'll soon see what there is. **Café Guido** (7135 Market St., 250/949-9808, 7am-5pm Tues.-Fri., 8am-5pm Sat., 9am-4pm Sun., lunch $6.50-9.50) pours the best coffee this far north, with savory rolls, paninis, and

Nanaimo bars the best option for food. Downstairs is a bookstore. South one block is **Market Street Café** (7030 Market St., 250/949-8110, 8am-3pm Tues.-Sat., $6.50-9), where the emphasis is on freshly baked breads and pastries (the cinnamon buns are delicious), as well as soups and sandwich lunchtime specials.

Uphill from the waterfront, in the Kwa'lilas Hotel at 9040 Granville Street, are the best two dining options in town. Here you'll find the **Nax'id' Pub** (250/849-8886, 11:30am-10pm daily, $15-24), with the same chic setting as the hotel. The food is all excellent and well-priced, including cooked breakfasts, dishes to share such as cauliflower tempura and smoked salmon dip, and full meals like buffalo sausage stew and halibut-and-chips. **Ha'me Restaurant** (855/949-8525, 6am-10am and 5pm-8pm daily, $19-32) has a wider range of First Nations dishes in a more formal setting and at slightly higher prices. This is the place to try cedar-planked baked salmon, grilled octopus, or salmon chowder with traditional bread. The hotel also has a café (855/949-8525, 6:30am-1pm), offering a wide range of hot drinks, snacks, and grab-and-go meals.

Dine at the **Quarterdeck Pub** (Quarterdeck Inn, 6555 Hardy Bay Rd., 250/902-0455, noon-10pm daily, $14-28), south of downtown in the lodging of the same name, for the opportunity to see bald eagles feeding right outside the window. The menu is fairly standard but well priced, with many seafood choices, including fish tacos and baked salmon.

ACCOMMODATIONS

Lodgings in Port Hardy are limited and often fill up, especially on the night prior to ferry departures.

Around 1 kilometer (0.6 mile) south of downtown, two hotels overlook Port Hardy's busy harbor from the marina. **Glen Lyon Inn** (6435 Hardy Bay Rd., 250/949-7115 or 877/949-7115, www.glenlyoninn.com, $199-299 s or d) has 44 rooms in two wings, many

with balconies overlooking the harbor. Facilities include a laundry room, a restaurant, and a pub. The adjacent **Quarterdeck Inn** (6555 Hardy Bay Rd., 250/902-0455 or 877/902-0459, www.quarterdeckresort.net, $189-219 s or d) offers larger, more modern rooms, many with harbor views. Facilities include a fitness room, a sauna, and a laundry room. Relative to the other town motels, this place is a good value, especially the suites, which are only $20-30 more than standard rooms.

Built and owned by the Gwa'sala-'Nakwaxda'xw people, the ★ **Kwa'lilas Hotel** (9040 Granville St., 855/949-8525, www.kwalilashotel.ca, $219-279 s or d) is a magnificent cedar building shaped like a traditional Big House, and is the pick of lodging in town. First Nations artwork and craftsmanship dominates the property, with displays in public areas and 85 stylish guest rooms decorated with modern interpretations of traditional designs. Rooms are spacious and have luxurious bathrooms and comfortable beds. The hotel also has a restaurant, pub, and café, and is the starting point for cultural tours (book through the hotel).

At **Bear Cove Cottages** (6715 Bear Cove Hwy., 250/949-7939 or 877/949-7939, www.bearcovecottages.ca, $205 s or d), you'll need to reserve well in advance. Located right near the ferry terminal, 10 kilometers (6 miles) out of town, they sit in a neat row high above the ocean with stunning water views. Each modern unit comes with a compact but well-designed kitchen, fireplace, a bath with jetted tub, and private deck. While summer rates are $205 s or d, the price drops to as low as $700 per week in the off-season.

Camping

Both of Port Hardy's commercial campgrounds are south of town, halfway around Hardy Bay to the ferry terminal. The pick of the two is **Quatse River Campground**

1: starfish at San Josef Bay **2:** welcome to Port Hardy sign

(8400 Byng Rd., 250/949-2395, www.quat-secampground.ca, late May-Sept., $35-44, three-night minimum), which is adjacent to the Quatse Salmon Centre. Sites are shaded by a lush old-growth forest, and you can fish in the river right off the camping area—then move over to the communal fire pit and recall stories of the one that got away. In the vicinity is **Port Hardy RV Resort** (8080 Goodspeed Rd., 250/949-8111 or 855/949-8118, www.porthardyrvresort.com, $29-46, cabins $205), also on the Quatse River. Facilities include a barbecue shelter, modern baths, firewood and fire rings, and a small store.

INFORMATION

The staff at the downtown **Port Hardy Visitor Centre** (7250 Market St., 250/949-7622, www.visitporthardy.com, 9am-5pm daily mid-June-Aug., 9am-4pm Mon.-Fri. Sept.-mid-June) will fill you in on everything there is to see and do in Port Hardy and beyond.

GETTING THERE

Most visitors who drive to Port Hardy do so to catch a ferry to points farther north. From Campbell River, 235 kilometers (146 miles) to the south, allow 2.5-3 hours. From Victoria, 495 kilometers (308 miles) south, allow 6 hours without stops.

Port Hardy Airport (YZT), 12 kilometers (7.5 miles) south of town, is served by **Pacific Coastal** (604/273-8666 or 800/663-2872) from Vancouver. It's a spectacular flight, with stunning views of the Coast Mountains for passengers seated on the plane's right side. Airport facilities include parking, a National rental car outlet, and a small café.

Ferry Service

Most people arriving in Port Hardy do so with the intention of continuing north with **BC Ferries** (250/386-3431 or 888/223-3779, www.bcferries.com) to Prince Rupert and beyond. The ferry terminal is at Bear Cove,

10 kilometers (6 miles) from downtown Port Hardy. In summer, northbound ferries depart at least once every two days, with the run to Prince Rupert taking 13 hours. The service runs year-round, but departures are less frequent outside summer. Peak one-way fare is adults $179, children $89.50, vehicles $407.80. These peak-season fares are discounted up to 40 percent outside summer. Cabins are available.

★ CAPE SCOTT PROVINCIAL PARK

Cape Scott Provincial Park encompasses 22,566 hectares (55,760 acres) of rugged coastal wilderness at the northernmost tip of Vancouver Island. It's the place to go if you really want to get away from everything and everyone. Rugged trails, suitable for experienced hikers and outdoorspeople, lead through dense forests of western red cedar, hemlock, and Sitka spruce to 23 kilometers (14 miles) of beautiful sandy beaches and rocky promontories and headlands. Wildlife, including black bears, cougars, raccoons, black-tailed deer, and otters, is prolific.

Hiking

To get to the park boundary, you have to follow 67 kilometers (42 miles) of logging roads (remember that logging trucks always have the right-of-way) leading west from Port Hardy through the logging town of Holberg, and then hike in. The classic park hike to **Cape Scott Lighthouse** (23 kilometers/14 miles; about eight or nine hours one-way) is relatively level, but you'll need stout footwear. A cove east of the cape was once the site of an ill-fated Danish settlement. Around 100 Danes moved to the area in 1896, cutting themselves off from the rest of the world and forcing themselves to be totally self-sufficient. By 1930, the settlement was deserted, with many of the residents relocating to nearby Holberg.

A shorter alternative to the long trek out to the cape is the trail to beautiful **San Josef**

Bay at the southern boundary of the park (2.5 kilometers/1.6 miles; 45 minutes one-way), which has a sandy stretch of beach.

Practicalities

Needless to say, services and facilities within the park are extremely limited. Near the end of the road leading to the park entrance is road-accessible **San Josef River Recreation Site** (primitive campsite $8). You can also camp on one of the pads at Eric Lake, a short distance along the trail to Cape Scott, or on any park beach ($10 pp).

Before setting off for the park, go by the **Port Hardy Visitor Centre** (7250 Market St., 250/949-7622, www.visitporthardy.com, 9am-5pm daily mid-June-Aug., 9am-4pm Mon.-Fri. Sept.-mid-June) and pick detailed logging-road maps for the area.

RAFT COVE PROVINCIAL PARK

South of Cape Scott Provincial Park is Raft Cove Provincial Park. To get here, turn south onto Ronning Main Road 7 kilometers (4 miles) before the park, following a rough 12-kilometer (7.5-mile) logging road to a slight rise where the road ends. From this point, a narrow and rough walking trail leads 2 kilometers (1.2 miles) through a lush old-growth forest to a crescent-shaped sandy beach. From this point, it's a similar distance south along the beach to the mouth of the Macjack River. The cove has become popular with surfers in recent years, but the park is worth searching out for its wilderness values alone. Although there are no designated campsites, camping is allowed at the back of the beach (free), where there are pit toilets and food caches.

Background

The Landscape

Vancouver Island lies on Canada's west coast, in British Columbia, the third largest of Canada's provinces (behind Ontario and Quebec). At 460 kilometers (290 miles) long, up to 80 kilometers (50 miles) wide, and with a total area of 31,284 square kilometers (12,100 square miles), it is Canada's 11th largest island and the largest island on North America's west coast. The island confusingly shares its name with the province's largest city, which lies on the mainland 50 kilometers (30 miles) to the east.

At the southern tip, Victoria is the island's largest city and is also

the provincial capital of British Columbia. By a quirk of history, it lies south of the 49th parallel, the dividing line between the rest of Canada and the United States. Separating Vancouver Island from mainland British Columbia is the Strait of Georgia, an island-studded waterway rich in wildlife and always busy with passenger, freight, and pleasure vessels.

Islands

Vancouver Island's deeply indented coastline is dotted with over 1,000 smaller islands. Between the mainland and Vancouver Island, 200 islands dot the Strait of Georgia, some of which are populated and all of which are protected from the wind- and wave-battering action of the Pacific Ocean by Vancouver Island. While most of the islands along the remote west coast are uninhabited (and some even unexplored), the larger islands of Georgia Strait, including the **Southern Gulf Islands** and **Quadra Island,** are populated year-round and have all the services required for both residents and visitors.

Mountains

The interior of Vancouver Island is dominated by the **Vancouver Island Range,** a north-south ridge of mountains that extends the entire length of the island. The high point of the island is 2,200-meter (7,200-foot) **Mount Golden Hinde** in Strathcona Provincial Park, west of Campbell River.

CLIMATE

Vancouver Island boasts the mildest climate of all Canadian regions, but that comes with one drawback—it rains a lot. Most precipitation, though, falls in winter, and summers are relatively dry. Overall, the main contributing factor to the climate is the Pacific Ocean. The warm waters of the Japan Current radiate heat across the island and beyond, a natural heat conduction system that warms winters, while the ocean keeps summer temperatures mild. Victoria, for example, has half the temperature range of Canada's inland prairies.

Precipitation is strongly influenced by the lay of the land, which means there is a large variation in rainfall across the island. In general, the east side of the island is drier than the interior and west coast. For example, in the far south of Vancouver Island, rainfall in Victoria averages just 610 millimeters (24 inches) annually, whereas Port Renfrew, 100 kilometers (62 miles) to the west, averages 3,670 millimeters (144 inches). Differences in rainfall are similar as you move north, with Quadra Island averaging under 1,000 millimeters (40 inches) of precipitation annually and Tofino, over the Vancouver Island Ranges on the west coast, averaging 3,300 millimeters (130 inches). The highest rainfall ever in Canada was recorded just down the coast from Tofino in Ucluelet on October 6, 1967, when 489 millimeters (19 inches) fell in a 24-hour period. Along the east coast, where most of the population lives, precipitation falls almost entirely as rain, although it does snow in downtown Victoria every year or so (and then melts fairly quickly).

The Seasons

Summer is by far the most popular time to visit Vancouver Island. Daytime temperatures along the east coast in July and August average a pleasant 23°C (73°F). During the last week of June 2021, heat records were shattered on consecutive days across the island. This heat wave culminated with the hottest day on record in Victoria, on June 28, at 39.4°C (103°F). In summer, city paths and parks come alive with cyclists, joggers, and in-line skaters; island beaches with anglers, surfers, and sunbathers; and the parks with anglers, campers, and hikers.

Spring starts early on Vancouver Island: Victoria gardens burst with color in March, and daffodils bloom as early as late February.

Previous: Vancouver Island coastline.

Temperatures throughout both spring and fall are, naturally, cooler than in summer, but in many ways these are prime travel periods. Aside from the June 2021 heat wave, June and September are especially pleasant, because crowds are minimal. The average daytime temperature for Victoria during both April and October is 14°C (57°F).

Vancouver Island's biggest wintertime attraction is that it doesn't feel like winter (well, to other Canadians anyway). For retirees from across Canada, this mild climate is a major draw, with many hotels renting rooms by the month and visitors only needing a sweater (and rain jacket) on all but the coldest days. Although snow is rare along the east coast, higher elevations are blanketed in snow for most of the winter and early spring. The alpine resort at Mount Washington, west of Courtenay, averages 1,150 centimeters (38 feet) of snow annually. In Victoria, the January average high is 8°C (46°F), and on occasion, the temperature in Victoria does not drop below freezing throughout the entire winter.

ENVIRONMENTAL ISSUES

Humans have been exploiting Vancouver Island's abundant natural resources for thousands of years. Indigenous people hunting and fishing obviously had little effect on ecological integrity, but over time, the clearing of land for agriculture and development by Europeans did. Today, the trend is to minimize the effects of logging operations, global warming, fish farming, and offshore oil and gas exploration that are hot-button environmental issues for many island residents.

As rising island population numbers have put ever-increasing demands on the region's plentiful natural resources, conservation measures have become necessary. The province has imposed fishing and hunting seasons and limits, a freeze on rezoning agricultural land, and mandatory reforestation regulations, and has restrained hydroelectric development to protect salmon runs. By preserving its superb physical environment, the island will continue to attract outdoor enthusiasts and visitors from around the world, ensuring a steady stream of tourism revenues. But the ongoing battle between concerned conservationists and profit-motivated developers continues.

Forestry

The issue of forestry management in British Columbia, especially on Vancouver Island, is very complex and beyond the scope of this guidebook. In a province where three companies control an industry worth $17 billion annually, many forestry decisions have as much to do with politics as they do with good management of the natural resource. The most talked-about issue for decades has been **clear-cutting,** where entire forests are stripped down to bare earth, with the practice in Vancouver Island's ever-diminishing old-growth forests especially contentious. The effect of this type of logging goes beyond just the removal of ancient trees; often salmon-bearing streams are affected. Clayoquot Sound, on the west coast of Vancouver Island, is synonymous with the environmentalists' fight against the logging industry. The sound is home to the world's largest remaining coastal temperate forest. More recently, it has been the local logging industry itself raising concern about government policies that have increased the amount of raw lumber being exported, which has led to the closure of sawmills and pulp mills across the island.

You will see the logging throughout British Columbia when you arrive, but to see just how extensive the clear-cutting is, visit Google Maps (http://maps.google.com) and click on the "Satellite" link. Then zoom in on the interior of Vancouver Island.

Contacts

For more information on any of these issues, contact the following local environmental organizations: **Canadian Parks and Wilderness Society** (www.cpaws.org), Greenpeace (www. greenpeace.ca), SPEC (Society Promoting Environmental Conservation) (www.spec. bc.ca), Strathcona Wilderness Institute (www.strathconapark.org), and Valhalla Wilderness Society (www.vws.org).

Plants and Animals

When the first Europeans sailed into the Strait of Georgia in the late 1700s, most of what is now Vancouver Island was covered in a temperate rainforest dominated by hemlock, western red cedar, and Sitka spruce, with forests of Douglas fir thriving in drier areas. The only remaining tract of these ancient forests in settled areas can be found in Victoria's Goldstream Provincial Park.

PLANTS

Two colors invariably jump to mind when you say "Vancouver Island": green and blue. Just about everywhere you travel on the island you see trees, trees, and more trees—well over two-thirds of the island is forested. But the types of trees differ in each geographic and climatic region. The west coast is dominated by temperate rainforest, which requires at least 1,000 millimeters (40 inches) of rain annually and is predominantly evergreens. This biome is extremely rare: at the end of the last ice age, it is estimated that 0.2 percent of the world's land area was temperate rainforest. Only 10 percent of these forests remain, and much of this small percentage is on Vancouver Island. This forest is mostly hemlock, western red cedar, and Sitka spruce. Unfortunately, the vast majority of magnificent **Douglas fir** that once dominated the interior forests have been decimated by logging over the last 100-plus years, but a few areas have been protected. Best known of these are within **Cathedral Grove** between Nanaimo and Tofino, where the biggest trees are 75 meters (250 feet) high and up to 800 years old.

Arbutus (known as Pacific madrone in the United States) is an evergreen hardwood distinctive for its red bark and glossy oval-shaped leaves. It grows near saltwater at the southern end of Vancouver Island and on the Southern Gulf Islands.

The official provincial floral emblem is the **Pacific dogwood,** a small tree sporting huge clusters of cream-colored flowers in spring, and bright foliage and red berries in autumn. Its range on Vancouver Island is south from Port Hardy. The tree is a protected plant in British Columbia; it's a punishable offense to pick from it or destroy it.

In summer, Vancouver Island turns on a really magnificent floral display. Wildflowers in every color of the rainbow pop up on the roadsides: white-and yellow-daisies, purple lupines, pale pink and dark pink wild roses, blood-red Indian paintbrush, orange-and-black lilies, bright pink fireweed, and yellow buttercups, to name but a handful. And if you venture off the beaten track and up into the alpine meadows, the floral beauty is hard to believe. You can pick up a wildflower guide at almost any local bookshop, and most of the park visitor centers stock brochures on wildflower identification.

LAND MAMMALS

Vancouver Island is one of the best places in Canada for viewing wildlife, with highlights being whale- and bear-watching.

Bears

Of the three species of bears present in North America, only **black bears** are officially present on Vancouver Island (although there have been grizzly sightings in recent years at the island's north end).

Black bears are widespread and abundant across the island, with the population estimated to be at least 7,000, among one of the densest in the world. Black bears are not

always black. They can be brown or cinnamon, causing them to be confused with the brown grizzly. Their weight varies considerably (the larger ones are found in coastal areas), but males average 150 kilograms (330 pounds) and females 100 kilograms (220 pounds). Their diet is omnivorous, consisting primarily of grasses and berries but supplemented by small mammals. They are not true hibernators, but in winter, they can sleep for up to a month at a time before changing position. Young are born in late winter, while the mother is still asleep.

The Deer Family

Although the island's **black-tailed deer** are smaller than their mainland cousins, they are similar in appearance, with the exception of a black tip on their tails. Their color varies with the season but is generally light brown in summer, turning dirty gray in winter. It inhabits open forests throughout Vancouver Island as well as the islands of Georgia Strait.

Vancouver Island's 3,000 **Roosevelt elk** are the largest of four elk subspecies present in North America. The animal has a tan body with a dark-brown neck, dark-brown legs, and a white rump. This second-largest member of the deer family weighs 250-450 kilograms (550-990 pounds) and stands 1.5 meters (5 feet) at the shoulder. Pockets of elk inhabit most parts of Vancouver Island, but they tend to spend the summer at higher elevations in the interior. One of the more reliable places to view these animals during summer is Strathcona Provincial Park, although the bulk of the island's elk live north of Campbell River.

Wild Cats and Dogs

Cougars (called mountain lions, Mexican lions, pumas, and catamounts elsewhere in the world) are relatively common on Vancouver Island, where it is estimated the population

numbers between 600-800. Because hunting of these large cats is now prohibited, numbers are increasing, along with human-cougar encounters—there are at least one or two nonfatal attacks recorded annually on the island. The vast majority of cougars live on the northern half of the island, but they are present throughout, including within Victoria city limits. Adult males can grow to over 2 meters (6.5 feet) in length and weigh up to 90 kilograms (200 pounds). The fur generally ranges in color from light brown to a reddish-tinged gray. Their athletic prowess puts Olympians to shame. They can spring forward more than 8 meters (26 feet) from a standstill, leap 4 meters (13 feet) into the air, and safely jump from a height of 20 meters (66 feet). These solitary animals are versatile hunters whose acute vision takes in a peripheral span in excess of 200 degrees.

The **Vancouver Island wolf** is a subspecies of the grey wolf, which is widespread through mainland British Columbia. It is estimated that the entire population of the subspecies is just 150 to 180 animals. Vancouver Island wolves weigh up to 60 kilograms (135 pounds), stand up to a meter (3 feet) high at the shoulder, and resemble large huskies or German shepherds. Wolves range in color from snow-white to brown or black, but those on Vancouver Island tend to be lighter shades of gray and brown. Unlike other predators, they are not solitary but are intriguing animals that adhere to a complex social order, living in packs of 5 to 20 animals and roaming over hundreds of kilometers of northern and western Vancouver Island in search of prey.

Marmots

In subalpine meadows of the Vancouver Island Ranges, chocolate-colored **Vancouver Island marmots** sun themselves on boulders in rocky areas. They are stocky creatures, weighing 4-9 kilograms (9-19 pounds). When danger approaches, these large rodents emit a shrill whistle to warn their colony. Marmots are active only for a few months each summer, spending up to nine months a year in

1: ferns in the temperate rainforest of the west coast 2: the shoreline of Vancouver Island 3: a black bear 4: a seal around Vancouver Island

hibernation. By 1998, it was estimated that just 30 Vancouver Island marmots remained in the wild, making the species one of the world's most endangered animals. Since then, a huge amount of time and money has been spent to ensure the longtime survival of the species, and today there are 200-300 marmots living in colonies south of Port Alberni and in the Mount Washington area. **Comox Valley Visitor Centre** has a display dedicated to this endangered species (children can even climb into a marmot burrow), or visit the website of the **Marmot Recovery Foundation** (www.marmots.org) for updates.

Other Small Mammals

One of the animal kingdom's most industrious mammals is the **beaver.** Growing to a length of 50 centimeters (20 inches) and tipping the scales at around 20 kilograms (44 pounds), it has a flat, rudder-like tail and webbed back feet that enable it to swim at speeds up to 10 km/h (6 mph). The exploration of western Canada can be directly attributed to the beaver, whose pelt was in high demand in fashion-conscious Europe in the early 1800s. The beaver was never entirely wiped out from Vancouver Island, and today, the animals inhabit almost any forested valley with flowing water. Beavers build their dam walls and lodges of twigs, branches, sticks of felled trees, and mud. They eat the bark and smaller twigs of deciduous plants and store branches underwater, near the lodge, as a winter food supply.

The weasel family, comprising 70 species worldwide, is large and diverse, but in general, all members have long slim bodies and short legs, and all are carnivorous and voracious eaters, consuming up to one-third of their body weight each day. The most common member of the species on Vancouver Island is the **short-tailed weasel,** which grows to a length of just 30 centimeters (12 inches). It is widespread across the island.

Weighing just 1 kilogram (2.2 pounds) is the **mink,** once highly prized for its fur. At home in or out of water, it feeds on other smaller mammals and fish. Mink numbers on

Vancouver Island are low; the best chance of viewing them is to rise early and quietly stalk out the edges of rivers and freshwater lakes in forested areas.

MARINE MAMMALS

Whale-watching is a major draw on Vancouver Island, but many other species of marine mammals inhabit these same waters, including seals, sea lions, sea otters, dolphins, and porpoises.

The ubiquitous **harbor seal** is common around the entire Vancouver Island coast and often seen by casual observers from the shoreline, including in Victoria's busy Inner Harbour.

Sea lions are present year-round in the waters around Vancouver Island. Although often confused with seals, it is sea lions that haul out onto rocky outcrops and are seen in places like Active Pass by ferry travelers. Two species are present, the more common **Steller sea lions** and **California sea lions,** only in summer around southern waters.

Whales

Once nearly extinct, today an estimated 20,000-24,000 **gray whales** swim the length of the Vancouver Island coast twice annually between Baja, Mexico, and the Bering Sea. The spring migration (Mar.-Apr.) is close to the shore, with whales stopping to rest and feed in places along the west coast such as Clayoquot Sound. **Orcas,** best known as **killer whales,** are not actually whales but the largest member of the dolphin family. Adult males can reach 10 meters (33 feet) in length and up to 10 tons in weight, but their most distinctive feature is a dorsal fin that protrudes more than 1.5 meters (5 feet) from their back. Orcas are widespread in oceans around the world, but they are especially common in the waters between Vancouver Island and the mainland, especially **Robson Bight,** which is accessible from Telegraph Cove. Three distinct populations live in local waters: resident orcas feed primarily on salmon and travel in pods of up to 50; transients travel by themselves or in

Wildlife and You

The abundance of wildlife is one of Vancouver Island's biggest drawing cards. To help preserve this unique resource, obey fishing and hunting regulations, and use common sense.

• Do not feed the animals. Animals such as deer and marmots may seem tame, but feeding them endangers yourself, the animal, and other visitors. Animals become aggressive when looking for handouts.

• Store food safely. When camping, keep food in your vehicle or out of reach of animals. Just leaving it in a cooler isn't good enough.

• Keep your distance. Although it's tempting to get close to animals for a better look or a photograph, it disturbs the animal and, in many cases, can be dangerous.

• Drive carefully. The most common cause of premature death for larger mammals is being hit by cars.

BEARS AND COUGARS

Black bears and cougars can be dangerous, and while human encounters happen regularly on Vancouver Island, the infamous reputation of both animals far exceeds the actual number of attacks that occur (since 1970, cougar attacks have accounted for three fatalities, and there have been no black bear-attack fatalities on Vancouver Island). That said, common sense is your best weapon against an attack. First and foremost, keep a safe distance, particularly if bear cubs are present—the protective mother will not be far away. Never harass or attempt to feed wildlife, and resist the temptation to move in for an award-winning close-up photo; they are wild animals and are totally unpredictable.

Before heading out on a hike, ask local park staff about the likelihood of encountering bears or cougars in the area, and heed their advice. Travel in groups, never by yourself; the vast majority of cougar attacks are against children playing outside by themselves or who have wandered off into the forest. Out on the trail, watch for signs of recent activity, such as fresh footprints or scat, and again, keep children close by. Make noise when traveling through forested areas (take a noisemaker—a few rocks in a soft-drink can or a bell—or let out a loud yell every now and again to let wildlife know you're coming). Bear spray is popular, but don't trust your life to it by taking unnecessary risks. Cougars are opportunistic hunters; in most attacks, the victim doesn't see the animal coming. Bears, on the other hand, will usually avoid you.

Bear and cougar talk is a favorite topic among outdoor enthusiasts on Vancouver Island, and everyone who has ever spent time in the wilderness has their own theory about the best course of action in the event of an encounter. On a few things, everyone agrees: stay in a group and back away slowly, talking firmly the whole time; do not run—both cougars and bears can easily outrun a human. If a black bear or cougar attack seems imminent, the general consensus is to try to fight the animal off.

very small groups, feeding on marine mammals such as seals and whales; and offshore orcas live in the open ocean, traveling in pods and feeding only on fish.

BIRDS

Bird-watching is popular in on Vancouver Island, thanks to the approximately 200 resident bird species and the hundreds of thousands of migratory birds that pass through each year. All it takes is a pair of binoculars, a good book detailing species, and patience.

British Columbia's official bird is the often-cheeky, vibrant blue-and-black Steller's jay, found throughout the island, but most often seen along the driftwood-strewn beaches of the west coast.

Raptors

Many species of raptors are present on Vancouver Island—some call the region home year-round, while others pass through during annual spring and fall migrations. **Bald eagles** soar over all of Vancouver Island, gathering in large numbers during herring and salmon runs; mature birds can be distinguished from below by their white head and tail. **Golden eagles** are present on Vancouver Island, but relatively rare. They are often confused with immature bald eagles.

Ospreys spend only part of the year in the region, generally from April to October, nesting high up in large dead trees, on telephone poles, or on rocky outcrops, but always overlooking water. They feed on fish, hovering up to 50 meters (160 feet) above water, watching for movement, then diving into the water, thrusting their legs forward and collecting prey in their talons.

Distinct from the previously listed species is a group of raptors that hunts at night. Best known as owls, these birds are rarely seen because of their nocturnal habits, but 12 species have been recorded on Vancouver Island. Most common is the **barred owl,** a grayish-brown bird with dark strips running down its whiter breast. Also present is the **great horned owl,** identified by its prominent "horns," which are actually tufts of feathers. Another is the **great gray owl,** the largest of the owls, which grows to a height of 70 centimeters (27 inches).

FISH

Of the 50 species of fish on around Vancouver Island, many are considered sport fish. The three varieties most sought after by anglers are salmon and halibut—found in tidal waters along the coast—and trout, inhabiting the island's interior freshwater lakes.

Salmon

Five species of salmon are native to the tidal waters of Vancouver Island. All are anadromous; that is, they spend their time in both freshwater and saltwater. The life cycle of these creatures is truly amazing. Hatching from small red eggs often hundreds of miles upriver from the ocean, the fry find their way to the ocean, undergoing massive internal changes along the way that allow them to survive in saltwater. Depending on the species, they then spend 2-6 years in the open water, traveling as far north as the Bering Sea. After reaching maturity, they begin the epic journey back to their birthplace, to the exact patch

Bald eagles are common on Vancouver Island.

of gravel on the same river from where they emerged. Their navigation system has evolved over a million years, relying on, it is believed, a sensory system that uses measurements of sunlight, the earth's magnetic field, and atmospheric pressure to find their home river. Once the salmon are in range of their home river, scent takes over, returning them to the exact spot where they were born. When they reach freshwater, salmon stop eating. Unlike other species of fish (including Atlantic salmon), Pacific salmon die immediately after spawning; hence the importance of returning to their birthplace, a spot the salmon instinctively know gives them the best opportunity for their one chance to reproduce successfully.

Largest of the five salmon species is the chinook, which grows to 30 kilograms (66 pounds) in Vancouver Island waters. Known as king salmon in the United States, chinooks are a prized sport fish most recognizable by their size but also by black gums and silver-spotted tails.

Averaging 2-3 kilograms (4.5-6.5 pounds), sockeye (red salmon) are the most streamlined of the Pacific salmon. They are distinguished from other species by a silvery-blue skin and prominent eyes. While other species swim into the ocean after hatching, the sockeye remain inland, in freshwater lakes and rivers, for at least a year before migrating into the Pacific. When it's ready to spawn, the body of the sockeye turns bright red and the head a dark green.

Chum (dog) salmon are very similar in appearance to sockeye, and their bodies also change dramatically when spawning; a white tip on the anal fin is the best form of identification. Bright, silver-colored coho (silver) average 1.5-3 kilograms (3-6.5 pounds). This species can be recognized by white gums and spots on the upper portion of the tail.

Smallest of the Pacific salmon are the pinks, which rarely weigh over four kilograms (nine pounds) and usually average around two. Their most dominant feature is a tail covered in large oval spots. They are most abundant in northern waters in even-numbered years and in southern waters in odd-numbered years.

Freshwater Fish

Trout are part of the same fish family as salmon, but, with one or two exceptions, they live in freshwater their entire lives. Interestingly, the trout of Vancouver Island are more closely related to Atlantic salmon than to any of the species of Pacific salmon detailed here. The predominant species is the rainbow trout. It has an olive-green back and a red strip running along the center of its body. Many subspecies exist, such as the steelhead, an ocean-going rainbow, which inhabits lower reaches of northern Vancouver Island rivers flowing into the Pacific Ocean. The trout species native to the island is the cutthroat, found in higher elevation lakes, that are named for a bright red dash of color that runs from below the mouth almost to the gills.

History

THE EARLIEST INHABITANTS

Although the forested wilderness they encountered seemed impenetrable to the first Europeans who sighted Vancouver Island, it had been inhabited by humans since becoming ice-free some 12,000 years earlier. The ancestors of these earliest inhabitants had migrated from northeast Asia across a land bridge spanning the Bering Strait. During this time, the northern latitudes of North America were covered by an ice cap, forcing these people to travel south down the west coast before fanning out across the ice-free southern latitudes. As the ice cap receded northward, the people drifted north also, perhaps only a few kilometers in an entire generation. They settled in areas with an abundance of natural resources, such as Vancouver Island, and over thousands of years, three distinct groups evolved, each with their own language: the Coast Salish people lived along the southern coasts of Vancouver Island, including the area occupied today by Victoria; the Nuu-chah-nulth people lived on the west coast around Nootka Sound and were the first aboriginal people on the west coast of North America to come into contact with Europeans; and the Kwakwaka'wakw (often referred to as Kwakiutl) people lived on the island's northeast coast and its nearby islands.

These earliest inhabitants lived a very different lifestyle from the stereotypical plains dwellers—they had no bison to depend on, they didn't ride horses, nor did they live in tepees, but instead developed a unique and intriguing culture that revolved around the ocean and its bountiful resources. The three groups all hunted in the water and on the land—harvesting salmon in the rivers, collecting shellfish such as clams and mussels along the tide line, and hunting bears, deer, and elk in the forest. They formed highly specialized societies and a distinctive and highly decorative artistic style featuring animals, mythical creatures, and oddly shaped human forms believed to be supernatural ancestors. Like other nations along the West Coast, they emphasized the material wealth of each chief and community, displayed to others during special events called potlatches.

The potlatch ceremonies were held to mark important moments in society, such as deaths, marriages, puberty celebrations, and totem-pole raisings. The wealth of a community became obvious when the chief gave away enormous quantities of gifts to his guests—the nobler the guest, the better the gift. The potlatch exchange was accompanied by dancing, entertainment, feasting, and speech-making, all of which could last many days. Stories performed by hosts garbed in elaborate costumes and masks educated, entertained, and affirmed each clan's historical continuity.

Within the three distinct nations were many bands. At the southern end of Vancouver Island, for example, the groupings were less distinct but are now divided cleanly into three groups by linguistics: the Songhees, the Saanich, and the Sooke.

The oldest archaeological sites discovered on Vancouver Island are ancient middens of clam and mussel shells, which accumulated as garbage dumps for villages. They date to at least 8,000 years old and are concentrated on the east coast of the island's northern end, near Port Hardy.

EUROPEAN EXPLORATION

The first Europeans to venture along North America's west coast north of the 49th parallel were in search of a northwest passage to the Orient. This fabled route across the top of the continent was first attempted from the east by Martin Frobisher in 1576, but the route wasn't attempted from the west until the 1770s. Numerous Spanish expeditions and a fourth led by Captain James Cook, with George Vancouver as navigator, sailed past the entrance to the Strait of Georgia, but none of these ships entered the waters upon which the city of Victoria now lies. The Spanish expeditions originated at San Blas (along the Pacific coast of what is now Mexico), and in the process of searching out the fabled passage, Spanish commander Juan Francisco Bodega y Quadra claimed the Pacific Northwest, including Vancouver Island, for Spain in 1779.

A decade later, Spain attempted to reaffirm its claim by sending explorer Esteban José Martínez to Nootka Sound to establish a settlement, but the arrival of two British trading vessels led to a confrontation that saw the eventual establishment of the Nootka Convention, a political accord signed by George Vancouver a few years later. Vancouver had returned to the area as Captain Vancouver in 1792, leading an expedition sent to chart the waters of the strait. In the process, Vancouver encountered a Spanish expedition, and in spite of diplomatic issues

Traveling throughout the Pacific Northwest, you can't help but notice all the totem poles that decorate the landscape, and many can be found on Vancouver Island. All totem poles are made of red (or occasionally yellow) cedar painted black, blue, red, white, and yellow, using colored pigment derived from minerals, plants, and salmon roe. They are erected as validation of a public record or documentation of an important event. Six types of poles are believed to have evolved in the following order: house posts (an integral part of the house structure), mortuary posts (erected as a chief's or shaman's grave, often with the bones or ashes in a box at the top), memorial posts (commemorating special events), frontal posts (a memorial or heraldic pole), welcome posts, and shame posts. None is an object of worship; each tells a story or history of a person's clan or family. The figures on the pole represent family lineage, animals, or a mythical character.

Since a government ban on potlatch ceremonies—of which the raising of totem poles is an integral part—was lifted in 1951, the art form has been revived. Over the years, many totem poles have been relocated from their original sites. Both historical and more modern poles can be viewed on Vancouver Island.

In Victoria, **Thunderbird Park** holds a small collection of historical totem poles close to the Inner Harbour. To see totem poles that stand where they were originally raised, plan on traveling up Vancouver Island to tiny **Alert Bay,** a Kwakiutl village on Cormorant Island. Here poles rise from the local burial ground and from beside a traditional big house. The best place to view a large concentration of modern poles is **Duncan,** which has around 80 scattered throughout the city.

between the two countries, the vessels sailed north together, surveying the entire Strait of Georgia. Vancouver then continued around the island to the west coast harbor of Nootka Sound, where he arrived in November 1792.

Another Spanish expedition, this one led by Juan Francisco Bodega y Quadra, was also in the sound that winter, and the two commanders put their political differences aside to name the island **Quadra and Vancouver Island.** Within a couple of years, Spain abandoned all claims to Vancouver Island and the Pacific Northwest, after which Vancouver set out to survey Vancouver Island more extensively than had been done on previous expeditions. As Spanish influence in the region waned, British cartographers were quick to shorten the name to simply Vancouver Island. The legacy of Spanish exploration remains in names dotted through the region, including Galiano Island, Cortes Island, Quadra Island, and Estevan Point.

The Fur Trade

The first wave of Europeans to arrive on the west coast of North America came overland in search of fur-bearing mammals. The first to reach the coast was Simon Fraser, who was sent west by the North West Company to establish a coastal trading post. In 1806, he reached the coast across the Strait of Georgia from Vancouver Island via the river that was later named for him, and in 1808, he built a trading post east of today's Vancouver. In 1827, the Hudson's Bay Company established its own trading post, Fort Langley, on the Fraser River 48 kilometers (30 miles) east of present-day downtown Vancouver. Neither of these two outposts spawned a permanent settlement.

Fort Victoria

Needing to firmly establish a permanent British presence on the continent's west coast, the Hudson's Bay Company built Fort Victoria—named after Queen Victoria—on the southern tip of Vancouver Island in 1843 (at the foot of what is now Fort Street in downtown Victoria). The fort quickly became the headquarters for the Hudson's Bay Company trade empire west of the Canadian Rockies. Three years later, the Oregon Treaty fixed the U.S.-Canadian boundary at the 49th parallel, with the proviso that the section of Vancouver Island lying south of that line would be retained by Canada. To forestall any claims that the United States may have had on the area, the British government gazetted the entire island as a Crown colony and leased it back to the Hudson's Bay Company (HBC), on the condition that the HBC would establish a settlement within five years. Gradually, land around Fort Victoria was opened up by groups of British settlers brought to the island by the company's subsidiary, Puget Sound Agricultural Company. Several large company farms were developed, and Esquimalt Harbour became a major port for British ships.

Growth

Although mostly content to leave the island in the hands of the Hudson's Bay Company, the British nevertheless sent **Richard Blanshard** out from England to become the island colony's first governor. Blanshard soon resigned and was replaced in 1851 by **James Douglas,** chief trader of the Hudson's Bay Company. Douglas had long been in control of the island, and his main concerns were to maintain law and order and to purchase land from the indigenous people. In the early 1850s, he made treaties in which the land became the "entire property of the white people forever." In return, the First Nations people retained use of their village sites and enclosed fields and could hunt and fish on unoccupied lands. Each indigenous family was paid a pitiful compensation—often a just a few blankets and a small amount of coins.

In the early 1850s, as animal populations were decimated by trapping and hunting, the fur trade dwindled in importance throughout the western region of North America, and although development continued, the original fort had been torn down. Around this same time, a gold rush in California created a demand for lumber, and a number of sawmills began operation on the southern end of the island. In 1852, coal was discovered near Nanaimo, and English miners were imported to develop the deposits. Around the same time, loggers began felling the enormous timber stands along the Alberni Canal, and the Puget Sound Agricultural Association (a subsidiary of Hudson's Bay Company) developed several large farms in the Victoria region. In the late 1850s, gold strikes on the mainland's Thompson and Fraser Rivers brought thousands of gold miners into Victoria, the region's only port and source of supplies. Overnight, Victoria became a classic boomtown, but with

Fort Rupert

Coal was discovered on northern Vancouver Island in 1835, and by 1849, a small mine had begun operation. Mine workers were brought to the region from Scotland, including Robert Dunsmuir, who would go on to make his fortune mining coal in Nanaimo and eventually become one of the island's most prominent residents. To trade with the Kwakiutl people, who inhabited northern Vancouver Island, and also to protect mine workers from a perceived threat by these same indigenous people, a crude fortified trading post was established just east of present-day Port Hardy on Beaver Harbour in 1849. Named for Prince Rupert, the first governor of the Hudson's Bay Company, it was constructed of 6-meter-high (18-foot) logs sunk vertically into the ground. The first commander was William Henry McNeill, an HBC employee who had previously established a site for Fort Victoria, at the other end of Vancouver Island.

The coal at Fort Victoria proved to be of poor quality, and after just one year of operation, the mine was closed. Even without an operating mine, the fort remained open as a trading post until 1873. Initially, the Kwakiutl people were drawn to Fort Rupert to trade for European goods, but eventually, they settled permanently around Beaver Harbour, remaining after the trading post closed and still living in the area. The only sign of the original fort today is the crumbling remains of a brick chimney.

a distinctly British flavor; most of the company men, early settlers, and military personnel firmly maintained their homeland traditions and celebrations. Even after the gold rush ended, Victoria remained an energetic bastion of military, economic, and political activity and was officially incorporated as a city in 1862. Douglas, who had a great influence on the direction of Victoria's development, left his post in 1864.

Confederation

By the 1860, the town of Victoria, with its moderate climate and fertile soil, had developed into an agreeable settlement of 2,000 residents. Farming settlements had been established at Duncan and the Comox Valley by this time, and these were followed by sawmills at Chemainus and Port Alberni later that same decade. In 1866, the colonies of Vancouver Island and mainland British Columbia were united as the Colony of British Columbia, and two years later Victoria was made capital. The next big political issue to concern residents of the newly amalgamated British Columbia was confederation. The eastern colonies had become one large dominion, and British Columbia was invited to join. The British government wanted British

Columbia to join, to assist in counterbalancing the mighty U.S. power to the south. After much public debate, the westernmost colony entered the Confederation as the Province of British Columbia in July 1871—on the condition that the west coast be connected to the east by railway.

Esquimalt & Nanaimo Railway

The original 1873 plan approved by the federal government showed the Pacific terminus of the transcontinental railway at Esquimalt on Vancouver Island, with the line reaching the west coast of the mainland at the mouth of Bute Inlet. From this point, the proposed rail line crossed to Sonora and Quadra Islands and then crossed Seymour Narrows to reach the island near present day Campbell River. Although the government went so far as to ship rails to Vancouver Island from England, the federal government eventually saw the folly in their plan, and realigned the line to end in Vancouver.

By the time the transcontinental railway had been completed by the Canadian Pacific Railway (CPR) to Vancouver, Nanaimo coal baron Robert Dunsmuir had petitioned the federal government to take over the island portion of the original proposal, eventually coming to an agreement that included receiving land grants for over 10 percent of the entire island in return for taking on the expensive project. The original rail line built by Dunsmuir was completed in 1886 and linked Esquimalt, west of downtown Victoria, with Nanaimo. Two years later, the line was extended to Dunsmuir's Nanaimo coal-mining operation. In 1905, Dunsmuir sold the rail line to the CPR, with spur lines completed to Port Alberni in 1911, Lake Cowichan in 1912, and Courtenay in 1940. As island highways improved, there was less demand for freight and passenger service, and ownership in the rail line changed, including in 1978, when the operation was purchased by VIA Rail. Passenger service was discontinued in 2011, and although there have been plans to restart rail service, the line up the island sits unused.

Modern Times

By the time scheduled ferry service between mainland British Columbia and Vancouver Island commenced in 1903, the population of Victoria was around 25,000 and the population of the entire island was 50,000. Throughout the two world wars, the city of Victoria continued to grow, reaching a population of 120,000 by 1941, and more than doubling in the decades since. As the island road network was improved, industries such as logging, mining, farming, and fishing continued to thrive.

Improved transportation also created a thriving tourism industry. Sportfishing was the original draw, with Painter's Lodge at Campbell River opening in the 1920s and soon attracting worldwide attention from celebrity guests that included Bob Hope and Bing Crosby. The island's mild climate attracted a distinct countercultural movement in the 1960s and 1970s, especially on the Gulf Islands and in the west coast town of Tofino, which was linked to the outside world by road only as recently as 1961. By the time Victoria hosted the 1994 Commonwealth Games, the

population of Greater Victoria had exceeded 250,000.

The People Today

Today, the total island population is 850,000. Islanders are concentrated on the southern portion of Vancouver Island, with the population of Victoria being 370,000, making it Canada's 12th largest city. Most of this growth has occurred on the western side in Victoria and along the east coast in places such as Nanaimo and the Comox Valley, where the mild climate and attractive lifestyle are major draws for mainland Canadians from across the country. The island's other major population centers are Nanaimo (92,000), Comox Valley (66,000), and Campbell River (35,000). The island's overall population density is just 24 people per square kilometer (61 per square mile).

Place of origin statistics for the island's residents are hard to come by, but around 34 percent of British Columbians are of British origin, followed by 30 percent of other European lineage, mostly French and German. To really get the British feeling, just spend some time in Victoria—a city that has retained its original English customs and traditions from days gone by. First Nations make up 5.9 percent of the provincial population. While the First Nations of Vancouver Island have adopted the technology and the ways of the Europeans, they still remain a distinct group, contributing to and enriching the culture of the island.

English is the mother tongue for 90 percent of Vancouver Island residents. Although the main language spoken is English, almost 8 percent of the population also speaks French, Canada's second official language. All federal government information is written in both English and French throughout Canada.

1: Many former railway stations have been converted to museums, including the Duncan Railway Station. 2: statue of Captain James Cook on Victoria's Inner Harbour 3: Commercial fishing is a major island industry.

Government and Economy

GOVERNMENT

Canada is a constitutional monarchy. Its system of government is based on England's, and the British monarch is also king or queen of Canada. However, because Canada is an independent nation, the British monarchy and government have no control over the political affairs of Canada. An appointed **governor general** based in Ottawa represents the Crown as head of state, as does a **lieutenant governor** in each province. Both roles are mainly ceremonial, but their "royal assent" is required to make any bill passed by legislators into law.

Elected representatives debate and enact laws affecting their constituents. The head of the federal government is the **prime minister,** and the head of each provincial government is its **premier.** The **speaker** is elected at the first session of each parliament to make sure parliamentary rules are followed. A bill goes through three grueling sessions in the legislature—a reading, a debate, and a second reading. When all the fine print has been given the royal nod, the bill then becomes a law.

Provincial Politics

The provincial capital of British Columbia is **Victoria,** which is home to the waterfront **Parliament Buildings.** Also in Victoria is **Government House,** the official residence of the lieutenant governor, whose role is at the top of the provincial ladder. Under the governor are the members of the **Legislative Assembly** (MLAs). Assembly members are elected for a period of up to five years, though an election for a new assembly can be called at any time by the lieutenant governor or on the advice of the premier. In the Legislative Assembly are the premier, the cabinet ministers and backbenchers, the leader of the official opposition, other parties, and independent members. All Canadian citizens and

BC residents 19 years old and over can vote, providing they've lived in the province for at least six months.

Provincial politics in British Columbia have traditionally been a two-party struggle. The province was the first in Canada to hold elections on a fixed date every four years. The laws of British Columbia are administered by the cabinet, premier, and lieutenant governor; they are interpreted by a **judiciary** made up of the Supreme Court of BC, Court of Appeal, and County or Provincial Courts. For information on the provincial government, its ministries, and current issues, visit www.gov.bc.ca.

ECONOMY

The economy of Vancouver Island is no different than other major coastal regions of North America, although the lack of manufacturing in Victoria makes the capital more reliant on tourism. Aside from tourism, much of the industry located on Vancouver Island revolves around natural resources.

Fishing

Commercial fishing, historically Vancouver Island's principal resource-based industry, has seen a massive decline in salmon stock over the last few decades, so much so that the fishery was closed for a period of time in 2021. Sockeye stocks have declined by around 90 percent in the last 50 years, affecting the 2,000 registered fishing boats that rely on tidal waters around the island for their livelihood. Other species harvested include herring, halibut, cod, sole, and shellfish, such as crabs. Canned and fresh fish are exported to markets all over the world—the waters around Vancouver Island are considered one of the most productive fishing regions in Canada. Japan is the largest export market, followed by Europe and the United States. The fishery industry also includes aquaculture (fish farming), which revolves around Atlantic salmon.

Tourism

Tourism has rapidly ascended in economic importance; it's now the second-largest industry on Vancouver Island, worth $1.8 billion dollars annually to the local economy and is the region's largest employer (more than 80,000 islanders are directly employed in the industry). Like the rest of the world, the pandemic affected many local businesses, but tourism remains strong. With Canadians unable to travel internationally, domestic travelers have been flocking to the island.

Destination BC promotes British Columbia to the world, while **Tourism Vancouver Island** (www.vancouverisland. travel) is a nonprofit that advocates for the island's tourism industry.

Forestry

Over two-thirds of Vancouver Island is forested, primarily in coniferous softwood (hemlock, Douglas fir, and western red cedar). The provincial government owns around 80 percent of the forestland, and private companies and the federal government own the remaining 20 percent. While private companies log much of the provincially owned forest under license from the government, the forestry industry has been decimated in recent years by a number of factors, including the increased export of raw lumber. At the turn of this century, the forestry industry directly employed 25,000 islanders, but as dozens of major sawmills and pulp mills have closed, this number has dipped to 7,000, decimating the economy of many smaller towns in the north of the island. Surging lumber prices across North America in recent years have been offset by timber supply issues and U.S. tariffs.

Essentials

Getting There and Around

Vancouver Island's only international airport is **Victoria International Airport** (YYJ, www.victoriaairport.com), while the smaller **Comox Valley Airport** (YQQ, www.comoxairport.com) is the other island gateway for air travelers. Many island-bound travelers fly into **Vancouver International Airport** (YVR, www.yvr.ca), from where they jump aboard a short connecting flight to Victoria, or catch the ferry across to Swartz Bay, a short drive from Victoria.

For those without their own transportation, regular bus-ferry combos link downtown Vancouver with downtown Victoria. If

you're traveling up to Vancouver Island from Washington State, you can miss Vancouver altogether by jumping aboard one of ferries that ply the protected waters of Juan de Fuca Strait and sail directly into Victoria's Inner Harbour.

AIR

In addition to a number of regional airlines, Vancouver Island is served by **Air Canada** (604/688-5515 or 888/247-2262, www.aircanada.com), one of the world's largest airlines, and **WestJet** (604/606-5525 or 800/538-5696, www.westjet.com), Canada's second-largest airline.

Vancouver to Vancouver Island

Both **Air Canada** and **WestJet** fly between Vancouver and Victoria. The distance between these two airports is just 64 kilometers (39 miles); official gate-to-gate flight time is just 24 minutes. All flights depart from Vancouver's domestic terminal, with both airlines generally operating 50-seat Dash 8s that require walking out onto the tarmac for boarding.

Aside from the big two, **Pacific Coastal** (604/273-8666 or 800/663-2872, www.pacificcoastal.com) departs from **Airport South** (also called the South Terminal)—which is linked to the main domestic and international terminals at Vancouver International Airport by a free shuttle bus—to Victoria, Nanaimo, Tofino, Comox, Campbell River, and Port Hardy.

The floatplanes operated by **Harbour Air** (250/274-1277 or 800/665-0212, www.harbourair.com) provide a handy direct link between Vancouver and Victoria, departing from the downtown Vancouver waterfront and landing on Victoria's Inner Harbour (access from Wharf St.).

From Elsewhere in Canada

In addition to Vancouver, **Air Canada** offers direct flights to Victoria from Calgary, Edmonton, and Toronto, and to Comox from Vancouver, Calgary, and Edmonton. Travel with Air Canada to Victoria from other Canadian airports requires a plane change in Vancouver or Calgary.

Direct **WestJet** flights to Victoria originate in Vancouver, Kelowna, Calgary, Edmonton, and Toronto, and to Comox from Vancouver, Calgary, and Edmonton. Vancouver has WestJet flights from Hamilton, Ottawa, Regina, Saskatoon, Thunder Bay, Toronto, Montreal, and as far east as St. John's, Newfoundland, with easy connections made in Vancouver for Victoria.

From the United States

The easiest way to travel between Seattle and Victoria is with **Kenmore Air** (425/486-1257 or 866/435-9524, www.kenmoreair.com), which has scheduled floatplane flights between the north end of Lake Washington and Victoria's Inner Harbour, Nanaimo, and the Southern Gulf Islands.

No Canadian airlines have direct flights from the U.S. to Victoria, but **Alaska Airlines** (800/252-7522, www.alaksaair.com) flies in multiple times daily from Seattle, and **United Airlines** (800/241-6522, www.united.com) daily from San Francisco.

All other flights from the U.S. require a plane change in Vancouver, including those offered by Air Canada from Los Angeles, San Francisco, Las Vegas, Denver, Phoenix, Chicago, Washington DC, New York, and Orlando. Vancouver is also served by the following U.S. carriers: **Alaska Airlines** (800/252-7522, www.alaksaair.com), **American Airlines** (800/433-7300, www.aa.com), **Delta Air Lines** (800/221-1212, www.delta.com), and **United** (800/864-8331, www.united.com).

Previous: BC Ferries provide a link between the island and the mainland.

From Outside North America

The only way to access Vancouver Island by air from outside North America is by making transfers through the major hub of Vancouver International Airport. From the South Pacific, Air Canada operates nonstop flights from Sydney, taking around 14 hours. Air New Zealand (866/351-9528, www.airnewzealand.com) offers nonstop flights between Vancouver and Auckland.

Vancouver is the closest West Coast gateway from Asia, more than 1,200 kilometers (750 miles) closer to Tokyo than Los Angeles is. The city is well served by most Asian carriers from across the Pacific, in addition to Air Canada's Asian destinations. From Europe, Air Canada flies directly from London and Frankfurt to Vancouver, and from other major European cities via Toronto. In addition to Air Canada, British Airways (www.britishairways.com) also flies this route daily. Air Canada flights between Vancouver and continental Europe are routed through Toronto, but KLM (www.klm.com) has a daily nonstop flight to Vancouver from Amsterdam, and Lufthansa (www.lufthansa.com) flies from Frankfurt. Air Canada's flights originating in the South American cities of Buenos Aires, São Paulo, Lima, and Bogotá are routed through Toronto, where you'll need to change planes for Vancouver.

FERRY

Ferries ply eight different routes between the mainland and Vancouver Island year-round. Three of these routes link the city of Vancouver to the island, one sails between Powell River (north of Vancouver) and Comox, three provide a link between Washington state and the southern end of the island, and the eighth route sails between the northern tip of the island and Prince Rupert (Northern British Columbia), a terminus for the Alaska Marine Highway System.

From Vancouver

BC Ferries (250/386-3431 or 888/223-3779, www.bcferries.com) operates a year-round ferry service between Vancouver and Vancouver Island, taking around 90 minutes one-way. Ferries from Vancouver depart Tsawwassen, south of Vancouver International Airport, and terminate on Vancouver Island at Swartz Bay, 32 kilometers (20 miles) north of downtown Victoria, and at Nanaimo, the first major population center north of the capital. From Horseshoe Bay, on Vancouver's North Shore, ferries sail across the Strait of Georgia to Nanaimo.

The one-way fare on all routes is adults $17.60, ages 5-11 $8.80, and vehicles $59.50. Vehicle reservations (604/444-2890 or 888/724-5223, www.bcferries.com) cost $15 per booking. In high season (late June-mid-Sept.), the ferries run about once an hour 7am-10pm. If you don't have a reservation, expect a wait in summer and on weekends, particularly if you have an oversize vehicle.

From Powell River (Sunshine Coast)

BC Ferries sails up to four times daily between Powell River and Comox, providing access to a loop route that allows island visitors to avoid backtracking down to Nanaimo or Victoria to cross back to the mainland. In summer, the one-way fare for this 75-minute sailing is adults $13.80, children $6.90, vehicles $43.15.

From Washington State

Three companies provide a ferry link between Washington State and Vancouver Island. Clipper Navigation (800/888-2535, www.clippervacations.com, adults US$200-260, children $100-130 round-trip) has a passenger-only service departing Seattle's Pier 69 for Victoria's Inner Harbour up to five times daily in summer and less frequently fall-spring.

A daily year-round link between Port Angeles and Victoria is made by the MV Coho (250/386-2202 or 360/457-4491, www.cohoferry.com, adults US$21, children US$10.50, vehicles with driver US$70, reservation fee US$11-16), which has been sailing this route

Alaska Marine Highway System

The Alaska Marine Highway System (907/465-3941 or 800/642-0066, www.dot.state.ak.us/amhs) is an extensive network of government-run ferries through Alaska's Inside Passage and along the British Columbia coast between Vancouver Island and the mainland. Although these ferries don't stop at Vancouver Island, their main southern terminus is just a short hop away at Bellingham, in Washington State. Because of international border regulations, the only Canadian port of entry used by the ferry system is Prince Rupert in northern British Columbia.

From the southeastern Alaska town of Ketchikan, an alternative to the nonstop two-day trip to Bellingham is to catch an Alaska Marine Highway ferry to Prince Rupert, then a BC Ferries vessel to Port Hardy, at the northern tip of Vancouver Island, from where it's a scenic drive down to Nanaimo or Victoria for the short hop across the Strait of Georgia to Vancouver with BC Ferries. This is a great way to include Vancouver Island in your northern itinerary without backtracking, and at a similar cost.

since 1959. Onboard the 1,000-passenger ship is a café, a gift shop, and a variety of indoor and outdoor observation decks for viewing the journey.

Washington State Ferries (206/464-6400, www.wsdot.wa.gov/ferries, adults US$21, seniors and children US$10.50, vehicles with driver US$65) link Anacortes, north of Seattle, with Sidney, 32 kilometers (20 miles) north of Victoria.

From Northern British Columbia

The **BC Ferries** service between Prince Rupert and Port Hardy, on the northern tip of Vancouver Island, departs every two days in summer (less frequently fall-spring) and takes around 13 hours one-way. Although not cheap (adults $179, children $89.50, vehicles $407.80, discounted up to 40 percent outside summer), the route is popular with travelers heading to or from Alaska with the **Alaska Marine Highway System.** Alternatively, if your road travels have taken you through northern British Columbia, this link avoids backtracking through the mainland to get back down to the southwest portion of the province.

RAIL

Although the idea of linking Vancouver Island to the mainland by tunnel is floated

every decade or so, the western terminus of the transcontinental rail line is today in the same place it was when completed in 1886: the eastern edge of downtown Vancouver. Today, rail travel has many fans, and it is a viable way of traveling from points east across Canada to Vancouver's **Pacific Central Station** (1150 Station St.), from where an inexpensive bus-ferry combination ticket will get you across the Strait of Georgia to Victoria. For more information on Canadian rail travel, contact **VIA Rail** (888/842-7245, www.viarail.ca).

BUS
From Vancouver

For those without a vehicle, **BC Ferries Connector** (866/986-3466, www.bcfconnector.com) offers regularly scheduled buses between Vancouver International Airport and downtown Victoria's **Capital City Station** (721 Douglas St.). The trip takes 3.5 hours and the fare is a reasonable $60.50 pp including ferry fare.

CAR

Traveling by car is the best way to enjoy the wonders of Vancouver Island beyond Victoria. Either bring your own vehicle across to the island by ferry (see above), or pick one up from one of the many rental locations scattered in Victoria and at all airports (see below).

Driving in Canada

U.S. and International Driver's Licenses are valid in Canada. All highway signs give distances in kilometers and speeds in kilometers per hour. Unless otherwise posted, the maximum speed limit on the highways is 100 km/h (62 mph).

Use of safety belts is mandatory, and motorcyclists must wear helmets. Infants and toddlers weighing up to 9 kilograms (20 pounds) must be strapped into an appropriate child's car seat. Use of a child car seat for larger children weighing 9-18 kilograms (20-40 pounds) is required of British Columbia residents and recommended to nonresidents. Before venturing north of the 49th parallel, U.S. residents should ask their vehicle insurance company for a Canadian Non-Resident Inter-Province Motor Vehicle Liability Insurance Card (also known as a Yellow Card), which may or may not be requested by Canadian authorities in the event of an accident or traffic infraction. You may also be asked to prove vehicle ownership, so carry proof of vehicle registration. If you're involved in an accident with a BC vehicle, contact the nearest Insurance Corporation of British Columbia (ICBC) office (800/663-3051, www.icbc.com).

If you're a member in good standing of an automobile association, take your membership card—the Canadian Automobile Association provides members of related associations full services, including free maps, itineraries, excellent tour books, road and weather conditions information, accommodations reservations, travel agency services, and emergency road services. For more information, contact the **British Columbia Automobile Association** or visit their Victoria office (1644 Hillside Ave., 250/414-8320, www.bcaa.com, 9:30am-5:30pm Mon.-Sat., 11am-5:30pm Sun.), east of downtown in the Hillside Shopping Centre.

Drinking and driving (with a blood-alcohol level of 0.05 percent or higher) in British Columbia can get you imprisoned for up to 10 years and will cost you your license for at least 12 months.

GETTING AROUND

The easiest way to get around Vancouver Island is with a vehicle, either your own or a rental. All major roads are paved, and over the last few decades, the major highway between Victoria and Campbell River has been rerouted to bypass many towns, making the trip up the island much quicker. The total distance between Victoria in the south and Port Hardy in the far north is 495 kilometers (308 miles), but even with road improvements, you should allow at least six or seven hours.

The major public bus systems are operated by **VI Connector** (866/986-3466, www.viconnector.com), which has service to island cities and towns as far north as Campbell River from the Victoria depots on the 700 block of Douglas Street.

Car Rental

All major car rental companies are represented on Vancouver Island. If you are flying into Victoria, it makes sense to rent a vehicle at that airport, but if your flight terminates at Vancouver, an interesting option is to rent a vehicle at that airport, and use the BC Ferries network to explore the island, making a loop by crossing from Comox to Powell River by ferry and driving down the Sunshine Coast back to Vancouver. There are no restrictions on taking rental vehicles on any of Vancouver Island's ferries.

Regardless of whether you rent a vehicle on the island or on the mainland, try to book in advance, especially in summer. Expect to pay from $80 per day and $400 per week for a small economy car with unlimited kilometers.

Vehicles can be booked for Canadian pickup through parent companies in the United States or elsewhere using the Internet or toll-free numbers. **Island Rent A Car** (402 Esquimalt Rd., 250/384-4881, www.islandrentacar.ca) is a local company whose vehicles are kept in service a little longer than those at the other major companies, but rates are excellent—even through summer—especially if booked in advance. Although allowing only 200 kilometers (124 miles) for each single rental day, weekly summer rentals are around $400 and include unlimited mileage. Other companies represented on Vancouver Island and at Victoria International Airport include **Avis** (800/352-7900, www.avis.ca), **Budget** (800/268-8900, www.budget.com), **Enterprise** (844/307-8008, www.enterprise.ca), **Hertz** (800/654-3131, www.hertz.ca), **National** (844/307-8014, www.nationalcar.com), **PractiCar** (800/327-0116, www.practicar.ca), and **Thrifty** (800/334-1705, www.thriftycanada.ca).

Camper and RV Rental

None of the major North American rental companies have RVs (recreational vehicles) or offices on Vancouver Island. Instead, **RV Rent Vancouver Island** (778/426-8292, www.rvrentvancouverisland.com) has a fleet of 19- to 30-foot motorhomes that cost from $1,000 per week in midsummer, inclusive of 100 free kilometers (62 miles) daily. The company offers free pickups from the Victoria airport and Sidney ferry dock. Based at Nanaimo, **Island RV Rentals** (250/616-0636, www.islandrv.ca) is a little different from most rental companies in that they deliver an RV or travel trailer to your campground of choice, along with extras such as camp chairs and a barbecue. Weekly costs start at $900 plus a towing fee

of $150-900 to get the unit to the campground of your choice.

An alternative to renting on the island is to pick up a camper or RV in Vancouver. The two largest Canadian agencies, both with Vancouver depots, are **Canadream** (403/259-5447 or 800/347-7126, www.canadream.com) and **Cruise Canada** (604/946-5775 or 800/334-4110, www.cruisecanada.com). In summer, expect to pay from $200 per day for your own home-on-wheels. The one-way fare for all vehicles between Vancouver and Vancouver Island is $59.50 for the first 20 feet and then $6.75 per additional foot.

Gas Stations

All towns on Vancouver Island have gas stations. Gasoline is sold in liters (3.79 liters equals one U.S. gallon) and is generally $1.40-1.60 cents per liter for regular unleaded, rising to $1.80 on the northern part of the island or on one of the outlying islands. Gas station hours vary greatly, but along the main island highway, they are generally open 6am-10pm.

All gas purchases in British Columbia are pre-pay, meaning you must pay at the pump prior to filling up, or, in the case of visitors with non-Canadian credit cards, go inside and leave your credit card with the clerk.

Visas and Officialdom

ENTRY FOR U.S. CITIZENS

Citizens and permanent residents of the United States are required to carry a passport for both entry to Canada and for reentry to the United States. At press time, the U.S. government was developing alternatives to the traditional passport. For further information, see the website http://travel.state.gov/. For current entry requirements to Canada, check the Citizenship and Immigration Canada website (www.cic.gc.ca).

Entry for Other Foreign Visitors

All other foreign visitors entering Canada must have a valid passport and may need a visitor permit or Temporary Resident Visa, depending on their country of residence and the vagaries of international politics. At present, visas are not required for citizens of British Commonwealth countries or Western Europe. The standard entry permit is for six months, and you may be asked to show onward tickets or proof of sufficient funds to last you through your intended stay. Extensions are available from the Citizenship and Immigration Canada office in Vancouver. This department's website (www.cic.gc.ca) is the best source of the latest entry requirements.

CLEARING CUSTOMS

You can take the following into Canada duty-free: reasonable quantities of clothes and personal effects, 50 cigars and 200 cigarettes, 200 grams of tobacco, 1.14 liters of spirits or wine, food for personal use, and gasoline (normal tank capacity). Pets from the United States can generally be brought into Canada, with certain caveats. Dogs and cats must be more than three months old and have a rabies certificate showing date of vaccination. Birds can be brought in only if they have not been mixing with other birds, and parrots need an export permit because they're on the endangered species list.

Handguns, automatic and semiautomatic weapons, and sawn-off rifles and shotguns are not allowed into Canada. Visitors with firearms must declare them at the border; restricted weapons will be held by Customs and can be picked up on exit from the country. Those not declared will be seized, and charges may be laid. It is illegal to possess any firearm in a national park unless it is dismantled or carried in an enclosed case. Up to 5,000 rounds of ammunition may be imported but should be declared on entry.

On reentering the United States, if you've been in Canada more than 48 hours, you can bring back up to US$400 worth of household and personal items, excluding alcohol and tobacco, duty-free. If you've been in Canada fewer than 48 hours, you may bring in only up to US$200 worth of such items duty-free.

For further information on all customs regulations, contact **Canada Border Services Agency** (204/983-3500 or 800/461-9999, www.cbsa-asfc.gc.ca).

Recreation

The great outdoors: Vancouver Island certainly has plenty of it. The island encompasses some 32,000 square kilometers (12,700 square miles) of land area and a convoluted coastline totaling 3,400 kilometers (2,140 miles). With spectacular scenery around every bend, over 100 provincial and marine parks, and an abundance of wildlife both above and below the water, the island is an outdoors-enthusiast's fantasy come true. Hiking, fishing, boating, canoeing, kayaking, paddleboarding, surfing, swimming, golfing, and even skiing and snowboarding—it's all here.

HIKING

Just about everywhere you go on Vancouver Island, you'll find good hiking opportunities, from short easy walks in Victoria's city parks to the famous long-distance West Coast Trail.

The Southern Gulf Islands are a great place for shorter wilderness hikes. Here, trails lead to high viewpoints, unspoiled beaches, and intriguing coastal rock formations. Along the interior Vancouver Island Ranges, trails lead through old-growth forests to high alpine meadows, past turquoise lakes, and up to snow-dusted peaks providing breathtaking views. One of the best interior destinations for hiking is **Strathcona Provincial Park,** west of Campbell River. The best-known hiking lies along the wild and remote west coast of Vancouver Island; backpackers return time and again to the **West Coast Trail,** an unforgettable 75-kilometer (47-mile) trek through Pacific Rim National Park. For the less ambitious, easy hiking opportunities abound in **Juan de Fuca Provincial Park** and the region of coastline between Ucluelet and Tofino protected by **Pacific Rim National Park.**

To get the most out of a hiking trip, peruse the hiking section of any local bookstore—many books have been written on island hiking trails, but some are regional editions not widely available off the island.

CYCLING AND MOUNTAIN BIKING

Cycling is a great way to explore Vancouver Island. The casual pace allows riders time to stop and appreciate the smaller towns, scenery, wildlife, and wildflowers that can easily be overlooked at high speeds. Some of the most popular areas for cycling trips are the Southern Gulf Islands, accessible by ferry from north of Victoria (quiet, laid-back, loads of sunshine, rural scenery, and lots of artists) and the Oceanside region of the east coast (following the Strait of Georgia past lazy beaches and bustling towns).

For information on touring, tour operators, bicycle routes, rental shops, and handy tips, visit online sources such as those provided by Cycling BC (604/737-3034, www.cyclingbc. net). The Vancouver Island Backroad Mapbook, available at most outdoor retailers and island gas stations, has a section dedicated to bike-accessible trails.

ON THE WATER

Kayaking and Paddleboarding

The convoluted coastline of Vancouver Island is prime sea kayaking territory. You can rent a single or double kayak, or a stand-up paddleboard (SUP) at most coastal communities, but if you bring your own, you can slip into any body of water whenever you please, taking in the coastal scenery and viewing marinelife such as seals and whales from water level. You can choose from the calm but busy waters of Victoria's Inner Harbour, or set out on a multiple-night wilderness expedition along the west coast.

The Southern Gulf Islands are ideal for kayakers of all experience levels, while destinations such as the Broken Group Islands and Broughton Archipelago are the domain of experienced paddlers. Most outfits offering kayak rentals also rent stand-up paddleboards, provide lessons, and offer tours.

One such Vancouver Island operation is Ocean River Sports (400 Swift St., 250/381-4233 or 800/909-4233, www.oceanriver.com). Tofino, on the island's west coast, is a magnet for sea kayakers. Tofino Sea Kayaking Company (320 Main St., 250/725-4222, www.tofinoseakayaking.com) rents kayaks and leads tours through local waterways.

River Rafting and Tubing

The best and easiest way to experience a white-water rafting trip is on a half- or full-day trip with a qualified guide. The main Vancouver Island operator is Destiny River Adventures (250/287-4800, www.destinyriver.com), which operates on the Campbell River, near the town of the same name.

Tubing is fun for all ages, and although it can be enjoyed on many island rivers, on the Cowichan River it's almost a lifestyle, with literally hundreds of people each hour taking off from a purpose-built dock, with rentals and shuttles available onsite.

Boating

The sheltered, island-dotted Strait of Georgia, between Vancouver Island and the mainland, is a boater's paradise. Along it are sheltered coves, uninhabited islands, sandy beaches, beautiful marine parks, and facilities specifically designed for boaters—many accessible only by water. One of the most beautiful marine parks is Broughton Archipelago, east of Port McNeill.

Many coastal communities have marinas with boat rental companies, but for bareboat yacht charters, you will need to contact Cooper Boating (1832 Mast Tower Rd., Granville Island, Vancouver, 604/683-6837 or 800/667-9833, www.cooperboating.com), which boasts Canada's largest sailing school and also holds the country's biggest fleet for charters. They also have boats for rent at the main marina in Sidney (9835 Seaport Pl., 604/683-6837). For those with experience, Cooper's rents yachts (from $1,000 per day) for a day's local sailing, or take to the waters of the Strait of Georgia on a bareboat charter.

Scuba Diving

Some of the world's most varied and spectacular cold-water diving lies off the coast of Vancouver Island in the Strait of Georgia. Diving is best in winter, when you can expect up to 40 meters (130 feet) of visibility. The diverse marinelife includes sponges, anemones, soft corals, rockfish (china, vermilion, and canary), rock scallops, and cukes. Plenty of shipwrecks also dot the underwater terrain. The most popular dive sites are off the Southern Gulf Islands, Ogden Point in Victoria, and Nanaimo (for wreck diving). Victoria, Sidney, and Nanaimo have dive shops with gear rentals and air tanks, and many can put you in touch with charter dive boats and guides. In the capital, **Rockfish Divers** (19 Dallas Rd., 250/516-3483, www.divevictoria.com) is a full-service dive shop offering rentals, sales, organized diving trips, and PADI dive-certification courses throughout the year. British Columbia-based *Diver* magazine (www.divermag.com) is another good source of information; its Links page lists retail stores, resorts, charter boats, and other services.

FISHING

The tidal waters of Vancouver Island offer some of the world's best fishing, with remote lodges scattered along the coast catering to all budgets. And although most keen anglers will want to head farther afield for the best fishing opportunities, many top ocean fishing spots can be accessed without a boat along the coast (a massive pier at **Campbell River,** which promotes itself as the "salmon fishing capital of the world," has been purpose-built for anglers), while inland lakes teem with freshwater species.

Fishing guides, tours, and lodges (from rustic to luxurious) are concentrated on the west coast and around northern Vancouver Island. Expect to pay $1,000-1,200 per day for a four-person charter boat, and up to several thousand dollars for several days at a luxury lodge with all meals and guided fishing included.

Tidal

The five species of Pacific salmon are most highly prized by anglers. The chinook (king) salmon in particular is the trophy fish of choice. They commonly weigh over 10 kilograms (22 pounds) and are occasionally caught at over 20 kilograms (44 pounds); those weighing over 13.5 kilograms (30 pounds) are often known as "tyee." Other salmon present are coho (silver), pink (humpback), sockeye (red), and chum (dog).

Although halibut are associated with fishing farther north and in Alaska, Port Hardy, at the north end of the island, is a hotbed of halibut fishing. Halibut are caught on the sandy flats close to town, although the biggest fish, up to 90 kilograms (200 pounds), lurk in the deeper waters of Quatsino Sound. Other species sought by Vancouver Island anglers include lingcod, rockfish, tuna, and snapper.

Seasons vary, but along the tidal waters of northern Vancouver Island, between Campbell River and Port Hardy (one of the world's best-known salmon-fishing destinations), the most popular catches and their seasons are: chinook (July-Sept.), pink (mid-July-Sept.), coho (July-Oct.), sockeye (mid-July-Aug.), chum (mid-Sept.-Nov.), halibut (May-Aug.), lingcod (June-Aug.), and snapper (May-Sept.).

A tidal-water sportfishing license for residents of Canada, good for one year from March 31, costs $22 (over age 64 $11.50); for nonresidents, the same annual license costs $106, or $7.30 for a single-day license, $19.80 for three days, and $32 for five days. A **salmon conservation stamp** is an additional $6.25. Licenses are available online through **Fisheries and Oceans Canada** (www.pac.dfo-mpo.gc.ca), from sporting stores, gas stations, marinas, and charter operators. When fish-tagging programs are on,

---

1: a backpacker on Vancouver Island
2: Island beaches are busy throughout summer.
3: overlooking Victoria with friends from the top of Mount Douglas on Vancouver Island

you may be required to make a note of the date, location, and method of capture, or to record on the back of your license statistical information on the fish you catch.

The **Sport Fishing Institute of British Columbia** (www.sportfishing.bc.ca) has an online database of charter operators and fishing lodges, and details license requirements.

Freshwater

The island's freshwater anglers fish primarily for trout—mostly rainbow trout, kokanee, cutthroat trout, smallmouth bass, and perch. One particular type of rainbow trout, the large anadromous **steelhead,** is renowned as a fighting fish and considered by northern Vancouver Island locals to be the ultimate fishing challenge; winter fishing for steelhead is excellent in the Elk and Quatse Rivers.

Fishing licenses are required for freshwater fishing, and prices vary according to your age and place of residence. British Columbia residents pay $36 for an adult license, good for one year. All other Canadians pay $20 for a one-day license, $36 for an eight-day license, or $55 for a one-year. Nonresidents pay $20 for a one-day license, $50 for an eight-day license, or $80 for a one-year. For more information, contact the **Ministry of Environment** (www.env.gov.bc.ca) and download the *Freshwater Fishing Regulations Synopsis.*

The website www.gofishbc.com is a good source of freshwater fishing information, including reports for which lakes have been stocked with which species.

GOLFING

Relative to the rest of Canada, Vancouver Island's climate is ideal for golfing, where the sport can be enjoyed year-round. Many of the island's 50-plus golf courses are in spectacular forest, ocean, or lake settings.

They range from ultra-private 100-year-old courses such as **Victoria Golf Club** to modern resort courses like the Jack Nicklaus-designed **Bear Mountain** to friendly nine-holers where payment is made on an honor system. Municipal courses offer the lowest greens fees, generally $30-60, but the semiprivate, private, and resort courses usually boast the most spectacular locations. At these courses, greens fees can be as high as $200. At all but the smallest rural courses, club rentals, power carts, and lessons are available, and at all but the most exclusive Victoria courses, nonmembers are welcomed with open arms. The mild climate and abundance of water create ideal conditions for the upkeep of golf courses in the south of the island—you'll be surprised at how immaculately manicured most are.

SKIING AND SNOWBOARDING

When islanders want a winter holiday, they generally head over to the mainland to Whistler, but Vancouver Island does have two lift-serviced resorts. Island slopes are best suited to beginner- and intermediate-level skiers and boarders. The price of lift tickets is generally reasonable, and you never have to spend half your day lining up for the lifts.

The best-known Vancouver Island resort is **Mount Washington** (www.mountwashington.ca), near Courtenay, which has a sprawling base village of residential units, hotels, and restaurants. The resort has six lifts, a vertical rise of 500 meters (1,500 feet), and averages over 11 meters (33 feet) of snow annually. Farther north, community-operated **Mount Cain** (www.mountcain.com) is also legendary for high snowfalls, as well as its out-of-the-way location between Campbell River and Port Hardy.

Accommodations and Camping

The most comprehensive guide to Vancouver Island lodgings is online at the Tourism BC website (www.hellobc.com; click on the "Plan Your Trip" tab), with an easy-to-navigate breakdown of different lodging types. It contains no ratings, simply listings with facilities and rates.

All rates quoted in this book are for a standard guest room in the high season (July-Aug.). In general, expect to pay less outside of the busy summer period. Although there are a limited number of chain motels on the island, those that are represented use dynamic pricing, so depending on demand, you may or may not get a bargain at any time of year.

HOTELS AND MOTELS

Don't let the rates quoted in this book scare you away from staying in downtown Victoria or resort towns like Tofino. Although the rates quoted are for a standard guest room in the high season (July-August), almost all accommodations are less expensive outside these busy months, some cutting their rates by as much as 50 percent. You'll enjoy the biggest seasonal discounts at properties that rely on summer tourists. The same applies to weekends: Many Victoria hotels rely on business travelers to fill the bulk of their rooms outside summer, so when the end of the week rolls around, meaning Friday, Saturday, and sometimes Sunday nights, the hotels are left with rooms to fill at discounted rates.

If you're after a regular motel room, rates fluctuate greatly across the island, but pockets of well-priced properties do exist, including around the outskirts of Victoria and on the north side of downtown Nanaimo.

BED-AND-BREAKFASTS

Bed-and-breakfast accommodations are found throughout Victoria and across Vancouver Island. Styles run the gamut from restored heritage homes to modern townhouses. They are usually private residences, with up to six guest rooms, and as the name suggests, breakfast is included. Rates fluctuate enormously. In Victoria, for example, they range $90-380 s or d. Amenities also vary greatly—the "bed-and-breakfast" may be a single spare room in an otherwise regular family home or a full-time business in a purpose-built home. Regardless, guests can expect hearty home cooking, a peaceful atmosphere, personal service, knowledgeable hosts, and conversation with like-minded travelers.

Reservation Agencies

Most bed-and-breakfasts have their own website, although not all are set up for online reservations, so you'll need to call them directly. **Accredited BC Accommodations** (www.accreditedaccommodations.ca) represents bed-and-breakfasts across the province, including Vancouver island, but doesn't take bookings. **Bed and Breakfast Online** (www.bbcanada.com) doesn't take bookings either, but links are provided and a search engine helps you find the lodging that best fits your needs.

VACATION RENTALS

The two main vacation rental websites, **Vrbo** (www.vrbo.com) and **Airbnb** (www.airbnb.com), have listings for properties throughout Vancouver Island. The main difference between these two companies is that Vrbo only rents out entire units, while Airbnb also represents owners looking to rent a room or just part of their property.

BACKPACKER ACCOMMODATIONS

Budget travelers have a few options on Vancouver Island, but most backpackers gravitate to the stability of Hostelling International properties, of which four are located on the island. Either way, staying in what have universally become known as "backpacker hostels" is an enjoyable and inexpensive way to travel through the region. Generally, you need to provide your own sleeping bag or linens, but most hostels supply extra bedding (if needed) at no charge. Accommodations are in dormitories (2-10 beds) or private rooms. Each also offers a communal kitchen, a lounge area, Internet access, and laundry facilities, while some have bike rentals and organized tours.

You don't *have* to be a member to stay in an affiliated hostel of Hostelling International, but membership pays for itself after only a few nights of discounted lodging. Aside from lower rates, benefits of membership vary from country to country but often include discounted air, rail, and bus travel; discounts on car rental; and discounts on some attractions and commercial activities. For Canadians, the membership charge is $25 annually, or $175 for a lifetime membership. For more information, contact **HI-Canada** (613/237-7884, www.hihostels. ca). Joining the Hostelling International affiliate of your home country entitles you to reciprocal rights in Canada, as well as around the world; click through the links on the Hostelling International website (www.hihostels.com) to your country of choice.

CAMPING

With a season that extends from April to October, camping is very popular on Vancouver Island. If you're planning on camping on weekends or any time during July and August, you should make reservations as far in advance as possible. This is especially true at the most popular beaches along the east coast, on any of the Gulf Islands, or at Tofino, where you will need reservations up to a year in advance.

Most provincial parks have campgrounds, with facilities ranging from primitive to full-service. Regardless of the park, you should make reservations. At the time of publication, provincial park reservations could be made up to two months in advance through **BC Parks** (519/858-6161 or 800/689-9025, https://camping.bcparks.ca), but the booking window may change, so check the website for details early in the year. Camping fees are $15-$35 per night, and the reservation fee is $6 per night to a maximum of $18 per booking.

The three campgrounds in Gulf Islands National Park are open mid-May to September, while out on the west coast, Pacific Rim National Park campgrounds are open May to mid-October. All national park campsites are booked through the **Parks Canada Reservation Service** (877/737-3783, www. reservation.pc.gc.ca) for a nonrefundable $12 reservation fee. Reservations begin in January for the upcoming summer (check exact date online), and in some cases, campgrounds will fill for the entire summer within an hour or two of the system opening.

Commercial and municipal campgrounds operate throughout the island. They mostly provide full hookups and have showers, but generally lack the natural surroundings found in national and provincial parks. At the most popular destinations, like Tofino, you will need to book a full year in advance and pay upwards of $100 for an oceanfront site.

Travel Tips

EMPLOYMENT AND STUDY

Vancouver Island is especially popular with young workers from across Canada looking to spend time in a warmer climate, but also with international travelers.

International visitors wishing to work or study in Canada must obtain authorization *before* entering the country. Authorization to work will only be granted if no qualified Canadians are available for the work in question. Applications for work and study are available from all Canadian embassies and must be submitted with a nonrefundable processing fee. The Canadian government has a reciprocal agreement with Australia for a limited number of holiday work visas to be issued each year. Australian citizens aged 30 and under are eligible; contact your nearest Canadian embassy or consulate. For general information on immigrating to Canada, contact Citizenship and Immigration Canada (www.cic.gc.ca).

VISITORS WITH DISABILITIES

A lack of mobility should not deter you from traveling to Vancouver Island, but you should definitely do some research before leaving home.

If you haven't traveled extensively, start by doing some online research. Government of Canada has a section of their website for those with disabilities planning on travel within and between Canadian cities (https://travel.gc.ca). The website also has a lot of general travel information for those with disabilities. Destination BC (www.hellobc.com) has a wealth of information on accessible travel, including regular blog posts on accessible destinations. The Canadian National Institute for the Blind (800/563-2642, www.cnib.ca)

offers a wide range of services across the country. Although it's based in Vancouver, Spinal Cord Injury BC (604/324-3611, https://sci-bc.ca) is a good source of information on island resources.

The Society for Accessible Travel and Hospitality (212/447-7284, www.sath.org) supplies information on tour operators, vehicle rentals, specific destinations, and companion services. For frequent travelers, the annual membership fee (adult US$49, senior US$29) is well worthwhile. *Emerging Horizons* (www.emerginghorizons.com) is a U.S. online quarterly magazine dedicated to travelers with special needs.

LGBTQ+ TRAVELERS

Victoria and Vancouver Island are very inclusive and accepting. The Vancouver Island Queer Resource Collective (www.viqueercollective.com) is a volunteer-run organization that maintains an online database of resources and support for all of the island through the Local Connections link on their website. The Victoria Pride Society (www.victoriapridesociety.org) provides similar resources, along with an LGBTQ+ business directory, as does the Nanaimo Pride Society (www.nanaimopride.ca).

The International LGBTQ+ Travel Association (IGLTA) (954-776-2626, www.iglta.org) is the trade association for the LGBTQ+ travel industry, and offers an online directory of LGBTQ-friendly travel businesses around the world.

TRAVELING WITH CHILDREN

Regardless of whether you're traveling with toddlers or teens, you will come upon decisions affecting everything from where you

Coronavirus in British Columbia

At the time of writing in 2022, Canada was had mostly stabilized from the effects of the coronavirus, but the situation was constantly evolving.

Now more than ever, Moon encourages its readers to be courteous and ethical in their travel. Be respectful to residents and mindful of the evolving situation when planning your trip.

TRAVEL CHECKLIST

- Check websites (listed below) for local restrictions and the overall health status of British Columbia and your point of origin. If you're traveling to or from an area that is currently a COVID-19 hotspot, you may want to reconsider your trip.

- Only fully vaccinated travelers are permitted entry into Canada, and you must provide proof of a negative COVID-19 test by an accepted agency (rapid antigen tests are not accepted). Use ArriveCAN (www.travel.gc.ca/travel-covid) to submit proof of vaccination and your negative test up to 72 hours in advance of your arrival. If traveling by air, you may also be required to be tested upon arrival in Canada. Use ArriveCAN to register for this test. When doing so, you are required to submit a proposed quarantine plan in the event you test positive.

- If you plan to fly into Canada, check with your airline for updated travel requirements. Some airlines may be taking more steps than others to help you travel safely, such as limited occupancy; check their websites for more information before buying your ticket, and consider a very early or very late flight, to limit exposure. Flights may be more infrequent, with increased cancellations.

stay to your choice of activities. Luckily for you, Vancouver Island is very family-friendly, with a variety of indoor and outdoor attractions aimed specifically at the younger generation.

Admission and tour prices are generally reduced for children ages 6-16. For two adults and two or more children, always ask about family tickets. Children under age 6 nearly always get in free. Most hotels and motels will happily accommodate children, but always try to reserve your room in advance and let the reservations desk know the ages of your kids. Children stay free in major hotels, and in the case of some major chains—such as Holiday Inn—eat free also. Generally, bed-and-breakfasts aren't suitable

for children, and in some cases don't accept kids at all; ask ahead.

As a general rule when it comes to traveling with children, let them help you plan the trip, looking at websites and reading up on the province together. To make your vacation more enjoyable, if you'll be spending a lot of time on the road, rent a minivan (all major rental agencies have a supply). Don't forget to bring along favorite toys and games from home—whatever you think will keep your kids entertained when the joys of sightseeing wear off.

The websites of Destination British Columbia (www.hellobc.com) and Tourism Victoria (www.tourismvictoria.com) have sections devoted to children's activities.

- Pack hand sanitizer, a thermometer, and plenty of face masks. Consider packing snacks, bottled water, a cooler, or anything else you might need to limit the number of stops along your route, and to be prepared for possible closures and reduced services over the course of your travels.

- Assess the risk of entering crowded spaces, joining tours, and taking public transit.

- Expect general disruptions. Events may be postponed or cancelled, and some tours and restaurants may require reservations, enforce limits on the number of guests, be operating during different hours than the ones listed, or be closed entirely.

RESOURCES

- Government of Canada: www.travel.gc.ca/travel-covid

- BC response to COVID: www2.gov.bc.ca/gov/content/covid-19/info/response

- BC Centre for Disease Control: www.bccdc.ca

- Island Health Authority: www.islandhealth.ca

- City of Victoria: www.victoria.ca

Health and Safety

Compared to other parts of the world, Vancouver Island is a relatively safe place to visit. That said, wherever you are traveling, carry a medical kit that includes bandages, insect repellent, sunscreen, antiseptic, antibiotics, and water-purification tablets. Good first-aid kits are available at most camping shops. Health care in Canada is mostly dealt with at a provincial level.

Taking out a travel-insurance policy is a sensible precaution because hospital and medical charges start at around $1,000 per day. Copies of prescriptions should be brought to Canada for any medicines already prescribed.

HIKING SAFETY

When venturing out on the hiking trails that lace Vancouver Island, using a little common sense will help keep you from getting into trouble. First, don't underestimate the forces of nature; weather can change dramatically anywhere on the island, but especially along the west coast and in the rugged interior mountains. That clear, sunny sky that looked so inviting during breakfast can turn into a driving storm within hours. Go prepared for all climatic conditions (always carry food, a sweater, a waterproof jacket, and matches), and take plenty of fresh water—it's not always safe to drink from streams.

Most visitor centers have detailed information on local hiking trails and can keep you informed on weather conditions. Extra measures should be taken when heading out into remote areas of the island or on overnight excursions; most importantly, let someone know where you're going and when you expect to return.

CRIME

Although Victoria is generally safer than U.S. cities of the same size, the same safety tips apply as elsewhere in the world, especially in the downtown core, which has a high population of homeless people and transients. Tourists, unused to their surroundings and generally carrying valuables such as phones and cameras, tend to be easy targets for thieves. You can reduce the risk of being robbed by using common sense. Wherever you are, avoid traveling or using ATMs at night, try to blend in with the crowd by walking with a purpose (be discreet if reading a map out in public), and don't wear expensive jewelry.

GIARDIA

Giardiasis, also known as beaver fever, is a real concern for those heading into the backcountry of Vancouver Island. It's caused by an intestinal parasite, *Giardia lamblia,* that lives in lakes, rivers, and streams. Once ingested, its effects, although not instantaneous, can be dramatic; severe diarrhea, cramps, and nausea are the most common symptoms. Preventive measures should always be taken, including boiling all water for at least 10 minutes, treating all water with iodine, or filtering all water using a filter with a pore size small enough to block the *Giardia* cysts.

WINTER TRAVEL

Travel to Victoria in winter is relatively easy, with snowfall only very rarely falling in the downtown area. Traveling beyond the capital to inland areas during winter months should not be undertaken lightly. Before setting out in a vehicle, check antifreeze levels, and always carry a spare tire and blankets or sleeping bags. **Frostbite** is a potential hazard in the mountains of central and northern Vancouver Island, especially when cold temperatures are combined with high winds (a combination known as **wind chill**). Most often, frostbite leaves a numbing, bruised sensation, and the skin turns white. Exposed

Currency Exchange

As of 2022, the Canadian dollar has been holding steady in value against the U.S. dollar. At press time, exchange rates (into CDN$) for major currencies are:

- US$1 = $1.27
- AUS$1 = $0.93
- €1 = $1.44
- HK$10 = $1.61
- NZ$1 = $0.87
- UK£1 = $1.68
- ¥100 = $1.11

On the Internet, check current exchange rates at www.xe.com.

All major currency can be exchanged at banks in Victoria, at the Victoria International Airport, or at the airport in the gateway city of Vancouver. Many Canadian businesses will accept U.S. currency, but you will get a better exchange rate from the banks.

areas of skin, especially the nose and ears, are most susceptible.

Hypothermia occurs when the body fails to produce heat as fast as it loses it. It can strike at any time of the year but is more common during cooler months. Cold weather, combined with hunger, fatigue, and dampness, creates a recipe for disaster. Symptoms are not always apparent to the victim. The early signs are numbness, shivering, slurring of words, dizzy spells, and, in extreme cases, violent behavior, unconsciousness, and even death. The best way to dress for the cold is in layers, including a waterproof outer layer. Most important is to wear headgear. The best treatment is to get the victim out of the cold, replace wet clothing with dry, slowly give hot liquids and sugary foods, and place the victim in a sleeping bag. Warming too quickly can lead to heart attacks.

Information and Services

MONEY

As in the United States, Canadian currency is based on dollars and cents. Coins come in denominations of 5, 10, and 25 cents, and 1 and 2 dollars. The $1 coin is the gold-colored "loonie," named for the bird featured on it. The unique $2 coin is silver with a gold-colored insert. Notes come in $5, $10, $20, $50, and $100 denominations.

All prices quoted in this book are in Canadian dollars unless noted. American dollars are accepted at many tourist-oriented businesses, but the exchange rate is more favorable at banks. Currency other than U.S. dollars can be exchanged at most banks, airport money-changing facilities, and foreign exchange brokers in Victoria. All major credit and charge cards are honored at Canadian banks, gas stations, and most commercial establishments. Automatic teller machines (ATMs) can be found in almost every town.

Costs

The cost of living on Vancouver Island is similar to that of all other Canadian major cities, but higher than in the United States. If you will be staying in hotels or motels, accommodations will be your biggest expense.

Tipping charges are not usually added to your bill. You are expected to add a tip of 15-20 percent to the total amount for restaurant servers, barbers and hairdressers, taxi drivers, and other such service providers. Bellhops, door attendants, and porters generally receive $1 per item of baggage.

Taxes

A 7 percent Provincial Sales Tax is applied to almost all purchases made within British Columbia (basic groceries are exempt), and a 5 percent goods and services tax (GST) is applied across Canada.

TOURIST INFORMATION

Before leaving home, you should visit the Destination British Columbia website (www.hellobc.com). Other regional tourism websites are Tourism Victoria (www.tourismvictoria.com) and Tourism Vancouver Island (www.vancouverisland.travel). Upon arrival on the island, you will find visitor centers in all major towns and most smaller centers. In general, these are open daily in summer, and weekdays only during the rest of the year. In the capital, Victoria Visitor Centre (812 Wharf St., 250/953-2033 or 800/663-3883) is open 8:30am-8:30pm daily May to September and 9am-5pm daily October to April.

COMMUNICATIONS
Postal Services

Canada Post (www.canadapost.ca) issues postage stamps that must be used on all mail posted in Canada. First-class letters and postcards sent within Canada are $1.07, to the United States $1.30, to foreign destinations $2.71. Prices increase along with the weight of the mailing. You can buy stamps at post offices found in almost every town and village across Vancouver Island, including the main Victoria Post Office (709 Yates St., 866/607-6301, 9am-5pm Mon.-Fri.).

Phones and Cell Reception

The vast majority of Vancouver Island telephone numbers have the 250 area code, with 236, 672, and 778 as newer additions to the province's numbering plan. Unless otherwise noted, all numbers must be dialed with this prefix, including local calls made from the island. The country code for Canada is 1, the same as the United States.

Cell phone reception is good in populated areas, but reception may be spotty in some areas beyond town boundaries. Currently, there is no reception between Port Alberni and the west coast, and between Campbell River and Port Hardy.

Internet Access

You'll find public wireless Internet networks throughout Vancouver Island. Most lodgings and cafés have free access for guests and customers (the exceptions are lodges in remote locations). BC Ferries has wireless Internet access at all its larger terminals, but not onboard its vessels. The safest way to avoid any surprises on your cell phone bill is to add Canadian roaming to your plan before leaving home.

WEIGHTS AND MEASURES

Like every country in the world (except the United States, Liberia, and Myanmar), Canada is on the metric system, although many people talk about distance in miles, and supermarket prices are advertised by ounces and pounds. Electricity in Canada is 120 volts, 60 hertz, the same as in the United States.

Resources

Suggested Reading

NATURAL HISTORY

Bartley, Glenn. *Birds of Vancouver Island.* Victoria: Glenn Bartley Photography, 2010. A beautifully presented coffee-table book showcasing many of the 350 bird species present on Vancouver Island.

Cannings, Richard, and Russell Cannings. *Birdfinding in British Columbia.* Vancouver: Greystone Books, 2013. Written by a local expert and his son, this field guide covers all of the province, including the unique species of Vancouver Island, as well providing detailed directions to the best viewing spots.

Cannings, Richard. *British Columbia: A Natural History of its Origins, Ecology, and Diversity with a New Look at Climate Change.* Vancouver: Greystone Books, 2015. The natural history of the province divided into 10 chapters, from the earliest origins of the land to challenges of climate change. It includes lots of color photos, diagrams, and maps.

Folkens, Peter. *Marine Mammals of British Columbia and the Pacific Northwest.* Vancouver: Harbour Publishing, 2001. In a waterproof, fold-away format, this small booklet provides vital identification tips and habitat maps for 50 marine mammals, including all species of whales present in the ocean waters surrounding Vancouver Island.

Jennings, Neil. *Popular Wildflowers of Coastal British Columbia and Vancouver Island.* Victoria: Rocky Mountain Books, 2020. A full-color field guide, with detailed descriptions of hundreds of flower species.

Mason, Adrienne. *Long Beach Wild.* Vancouver: Greystone Books, 2012. The unspoiled coastline between Ucluelet and Tofino is one of the most intriguing and seductive destinations on the island. In this book, local resident Mason explores the natural appeal of this region through the stories of those who call the region home.

Nightingale, Ann, and Claudia Copley. *Nature Guide to the Victoria Region.* Victoria: Royal BC Museum, 2012. This pocket-size book is a good introduction to plant and animal species found in and around Vancouver Island's largest city.

Parfit, Michael, and Suzanne Chisholm. *The Lost Whale: The True Story of an Orca Named Luna.* New York: St. Martins, 2013. In 2001, a young orca whale was separated from his family and found a new home in Nootka Sound, much to the delight of visitors and the consternation of conservationists. This is his story.

HUMAN HISTORY

Allen, D. *Totem Poles of the Northwest.* Surrey, BC: Hancock House, 1977. Describes the importance of totem poles to First Nations culture, and totem pole sites and their history. Look for it at used bookstores across the island.

Arima, Eugene, and Alan Hoover. *The Whaling People of the West Coast of Vancouver Island and Cape Flattery.* Victoria: Royal BC Museum, 2019. An in-depth look at the First Nations people of Vancouver Island's west coast, including their culture, customs, and fishing techniques.

Bosher, J. F. *Vancouver Island in the Empire.* Self-published, 2012. Don't be put off by this book being self-published—this extensive tome is the best historical reference to the island's European history currently in print.

Hayes, Derek. *British Columbia: A New Historical Atlas.* Madeira Park: Douglas & McIntyre, 2019. If you love maps, you'll love this massive tome of over 900 maps that showcase work as early as that of ingenious people, to the fine artwork of cartographers.

Humphreys, Danda. *Government Street.* Victoria: Heritage House, 2012. Archival prints, contemporary photos, and meticulous research combine to bring the history of downtown Victoria's main thoroughfare to life.

Layland, Michael. *The Land of Heart's Delight: Early Maps and Charts of Vancouver Island.* Victoria: TouchWood Editions, 2013. Beautifully illustrated with 130 historic maps dating back to 1593, this book provides a complete cartographic history of the island.

MacPherson, Ian. *Reaching Outward and Upward: The University of Victoria, 1963-2013.* Montreal: McGill-Queen's University Press, 2012. A detailed history of one of Canada's most respected universities, beginning from its origins as Victoria College.

Reksten, Terry. *Rattenbury.* Victoria: Sono Nis Press, 1998. The biography of Francis Rattenbury, British Columbia's preeminent architect at the beginning of the 20th century. The histories of his most famous Victoria buildings are given, and the final chapter looks at his infamous murder at the hands of his wife's young lover.

Russell, Nick. *Glorious Victorians.* Kelowna, BC: Sandhill Book Marketing, 2011. A celebration of residential architecture in Victoria, from the oldest pioneer homes to the millionaire mansions of suburban Uplands.

Young, David. *The Uchuck Years: A West Coast Shipping Saga.* Madeira Park, BC: Harbour Publishing, 2012. Authored by the owner of Nootka Sound Service, which operated the *Uchuck* service from Gold River, this book is filled with seafaring tales from the wild west coast of Vancouver Island.

RECREATION

Dombrowski, Theo. *Popular Day Hikes: Vancouver Island.* Victoria: Rocky Mountain Books, 2019. A well-researched guide to trails you can complete in one day, from Victoria in the south to Cape Scott in the north. Includes color photos and maps.

Dombrowski, Theo. *Seaside Walks on Vancouver Island.* Victoria: Rocky Mountain Books, 2014. Escape the touristy areas with this hiking guidebook filled with ideas for beach walks, cliffside strolls, and forest treks. Includes difficulty rating and color maps of each trail.

Kimantas, John. *BC Coastal Recreation Kayaking and Small Boat Atlas.* Vancouver: Whitecap Books, 2012. A detailed guide to coastal waterways, with an excellent map list. Although primarily designed for maritime users, the maps and text are also relevant for those traveling the coastal areas by road.

Kimantas, John. *Wild Places: Vancouver Island.* Vancouver: Whitecap Books, 2021. Over 300 pages of detailed information that will lead you to lesser-known natural areas of Vancouver Island, with lots of practical information, including GPS readings.

Ungstad, Adam. *Secret Lakes of Southern Vancouver Island.* Self-published, 2013. More than just a guide, this handy book includes information on fishing, boating, beaches, swimming spots, and picnic areas.

Windh, Jacqueline. *The Wild Side Guide to Vancouver Island's Pacific Rim.* Madeira Park: Harbour Publishing, 2010. An updated guide to the very best recreational opportunities, accommodations, and restaurants along the west coast between Ucluelet and Tofino.

SCENIC

Jerritt, Boomer, and Peter Grant. *Vancouver Island Imagine.* Lunenburg, Nova Scotia: MacIntyre Purcell, 2014. An inexpensive coffee-table-style book showcasing the stunning photography of Jerritt, one of the island's preeminent photographers.

OTHER GUIDEBOOKS AND MAPS

Backroad Mapbooks. Vancouver Island: Mussio Ventures. This atlas series (www.backroadmapbooks.com) is perfect for outdoor enthusiasts, with detailed maps and highlights such as campgrounds, fishing spots, and swimming holes.

Crockford, Ross. *Victoria: The Unknown City.* Vancouver: Arsenal Pulp Press, 2006. Filled with little-known facts and interesting tales, this book describes how to get the best seats on BC Ferries, where to shop for the funkiest used clothing, the history of local churches, and more.

MapArt. Driving maps for all of Canada, including Vancouver Island. Maps are published as old-fashioned fold-out versions, as well as laminated and in atlas form (www.mapart.com).

Postnikoff, Dawn, and Joanne Sasvari. *Island Eats.* Vancouver: Figure 1 Publishing, 2021. A recipe book celebrating the food culture of Vancouver Island through the use of local seafood, produce, and game. Stunning photography adds to the appeal of the hardcover book.

MAGAZINES

British Columbia. Vancouver. This quarterly magazine depicts the beauty of the province through stunning color photography and informative prose (www.bcmag.ca).

Canadian Geographic. Ottawa: Royal Canadian Geographical Society. Bimonthly publication pertaining to Canada's natural and human histories and resources (www.canadiangeographic.ca).

Explore. Vancouver. Bimonthly publication of adventure travel throughout Canada (www.explore-mag.com).

Western Living. Burnaby. Lifestyle magazine for western Canada. Includes travel, history, homes, and cooking (www.westernliving.ca).

Internet Resources

TRAVEL PLANNING

Destination Canada
www.destinationcanada.com
Official tourism website for all of Canada.

Destination British Columbia
www.hellobc.com
Learn more about the province, plan your travels, and order tourism literature.

Tourism Vancouver Island
www.vancouverisland.travel
A non-profit association that supports the island's tourism industry.

Tourism Victoria
www.tourismvictoria.com
The official tourism site for British Columbia's capital.

PARKS

BC Parks
www.bcparks.ca
A division of the government's Ministry of Environment, this office is responsible for British Columbia's provincial parks. Website includes details of each park, as well as recreation and camping information.

Canadian Parks and Wilderness Society
www.cpaws.org
Nonprofit organization that is instrumental in highlighting conservation issues throughout Canada. The link to the Vancouver chapter provides local information and a schedule of guided walks.

BC Parks Campground Reservations
https://camping.bcparks.ca
Online reservation service for British Columbia provincial park campgrounds.

Parks Canada
www.pc.gc.ca
Official website of the agency that manages Canada's national parks and national historic sites. Website has information on Vancouver Island's two national parks, as well as national historic sites.

Parks Canada Reservation Service
www.reservation.pc.gc.ca
Online reservation service for national park campgrounds, including the West Coast Trail.

Rainforest Conservation Foundation
www.raincoast.org
Conservationists focused on environmental issues affecting the British Columbia coastline.

GOVERNMENT

Citizenship and Immigration Canada
www.cic.gc.ca
Check this government website for anything related to entry into Canada.

Environment Canada
www.weather.gc.ca
Seven-day forecasts from across Canada, including around 30 locations on Vancouver Island. Includes weather archives such as seasonal trends and snowfall history.

Government of British Columbia
www.gov.bc.ca
The official website of the British Columbia government.

Government of Canada
www.gc.ca
The official website of the Canadian government.

TRANSPORTATION AND TOURS

Air Canada
www.aircanada.ca
Canada's largest airline.

BC Ferries
www.bcferries.com
Providing a link between Vancouver and Vancouver Island, as well as access to over a dozen smaller islands.

VI Connector
www.viconnector.com
Provides scheduled bus service throughout Vancouver Island.

Pacific Coastal
www.pacificcoastal.com
Offers scheduled flights between Vancouver and major Vancouver Island centers.

West Coast Trail Express
www.trailbus.com
Makes getting to and from the West Coast Trail easy.

WestJet
www.westjet.com
Canada's second-largest airline.

PUBLISHERS

Abebooks
www.abebooks.com
The world's largest online database of used books had its humble roots in suburban Victoria.

Harbour Publishing
www.harbourpublishing.com
Although based on the mainland, this mid-size publishing house has many nonfiction Vancouver Island books on its title list.

Heritage House
www.heritagehouse.ca
With over 700 nonfiction books in print, this large Vancouver Island publisher is known for its historical and recreation titles covering all of western Canada.

Orca Book Publishers
www.orcabook.com
This Victoria publisher specializes in children's books.

Postelsia Press
www.postelsiapress.com
A small Tofino-based publisher with an eclectic title list of locally themed books.

Whitecap
www.whitecap.ca
Best known for its Canadian coffee table books, this Vancouver publisher also produces respected regional Vancouver Island cooking and recreation titles.

Index

List of Maps

Photo Credits

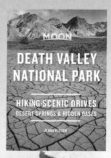

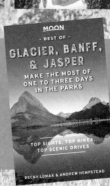

Plan an epic adventure with
Moon USA State by State and
Moon USA National Parks!

ROAD TRIP GUIDES

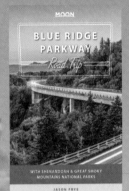

MOON

BLUE RIDGE
PARKWAY
Road Trip

WITH SHENANDOAH & GREAT SMOKY
MOUNTAINS NATIONAL PARKS

JASON FRYE

MOON

CALIFORNIA
Road Trip

SAN FRANCISCO, YOSEMITE, LAS VEGAS,
GRAND CANYON, LOS ANGELES,
& THE PACIFIC COAST HIGHWAY

STUART THORNTON

MOON

NASHVILLE TO
NEW ORLEANS
Road Trip

NATCHEZ TRACE PARKWAY • MEMPHIS •
TUPELO • MISSISSIPPI BLUES TRAIL

MARGARET LITTMAN

MOON

NEW
ENGLAND
Road Trip

SEASIDE SPOTS, MAJESTIC MOUNTAINS &
FALL FOLIAGE, COZY GETAWAYS

MILES HOWARD

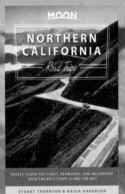

MOON

NORTHERN
CALIFORNIA
Road Trips

DRIVES ALONG THE COAST, REDWOODS, AND MOUNTAINS
WITH THE BEST STOPS ALONG THE WAY

STUART THORNTON & KAYLA ANDERSON

MOON

OREGON
TRAIL
Road Trip

HISTORIC SITES, SMALL TOWNS, AND
SCENIC LANDSCAPES ALONG THE LEGENDARY
WESTWARD ROUTE

KATRINA EMERY

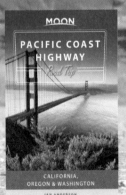

MOON

PACIFIC COAST
HIGHWAY
Road Trip

CALIFORNIA,
OREGON & WASHINGTON

IAN ANDERSON

MOON

PACIFIC
NORTHWEST
Road Trip

OUTDOOR ADVENTURES AND CREATIVE CITIES
FROM THE COAST TO THE MOUNTAINS

ALLISON WILLIAMS

MOON

ROUTE 66
Road Trip

JESSICA DUNHAM

MOON.COM | ROADTRIPUSA.COM

MOON

SOUTH FLORIDA & THE KEYS
Road Trip

WITH MIAMI, WALT DISNEY WORLD, TAMPA & THE EVERGLADES

JASON FERGUSON

MOON

SOUTHERN CALIFORNIA
Road Trip

DRIVES ALONG THE BEACHES, MOUNTAINS, AND DESERTS WITH THE BEST STOPS ALONG THE WAY

IAN ANDERSON

MOON

SOUTHWEST
Road Trip

LAS VEGAS, ZION & BRYCE, MONUMENT VALLEY, SANTA FE & TAOS, AND THE GRAND CANYON

TIM HULL

MOON

U.S. & CANADIAN ROCKY MOUNTAINS
Road Trip

DRIVE THE CONTINENTAL DIVIDE AND EXPLORE 8 NATIONAL PARKS

BECKY LOMAX

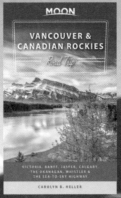

MOON

VANCOUVER & CANADIAN ROCKIES
Road Trip

VICTORIA, BANFF, JASPER, CALGARY, THE OKANAGAN, WHISTLER & THE SEA-TO-SKY HIGHWAY

CAROLYN B. HELLER

MOON

YELLOWSTONE TO GLACIER NATIONAL PARK
Road Trip

JACKSON HOLE, CODY, THE GRAND TETONS & THE ROCKY MOUNTAIN FRONT

CARTER G. WALKER

MOON

BASEBALL
Road Trips

TIMOTHY MALCOLM

THE COMPLETE GUIDE TO ALL THE BALLPARKS, WITH BEER, BITES, AND SIGHTS NEARBY

MOON

the OPEN ROAD

50 BEST ROAD TRIPS in the USA

From Weekend Getaways to Cross-Country Adventures

JESSICA DUNHAM

MOON

Road Trip USA
25TH ANNIVERSARY EDITION

CROSS-COUNTRY ADVENTURES ON AMERICA'S TWO-LANE HIGHWAYS

Jamie Jensen

BAJA

CARTAGENA
& COLOMBIA'S
CARIBBEAN COAST

CHILE

COSTA
RICA

ECUADOR
& THE GALÁPAGOS ISLANDS

TRIP OF A LIFETIME

MACHU
PICCHU

OAXACA

YUCATÁN
PENINSULA

Alaska

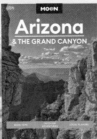

Arizona
& THE GRAND CANYON

Coastal
Maine
WITH ACADIA
NATIONAL PARK

Montana &
Wyoming
WITH YELLOWSTONE, GRAND TETON
AND GLACIER NATIONAL PARKS

New Mexico

NORTH
CAROLINA

TENNESSEE

UTAH

BAHAMAS

DOMINICAN REPUBLIC

JAMAICA

PUERTO RICO

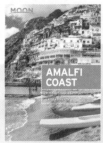

AMALFI COAST

AMSTERDAM BRUSSELS & BRUGES

EGYPT

Greek Islands & ATHENS

ICELAND

WITH A ROAD TRIP ON THE RING ROAD

IRELAND

MOROCCO

NORMANDY & BRITTANY

WITH MONT-SAINT-MICHEL

PRAGUE, VIENNA & BUDAPEST

ROME, FLORENCE & VENICE

Scotland

SOUTHERN ITALY

SICILY, PUGLIA, NAPLES & THE AMALFI COAST

Provinces & Regions

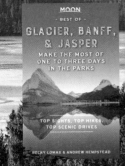

ATLANTIC CANADA

BRITISH COLUMBIA

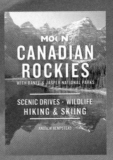

MOON

CANADIAN ROCKIES

WITH BANFF & JASPER NATIONAL PARKS

SCENIC DRIVES · WILDLIFE
HIKING & SKIING

ANDREW HEMPSTEAD

NEWFOUNDLAND & LABRADOR

ANDREW HEMPSTEAD

NOVA SCOTIA
NEW BRUNSWICK & PRINCE EDWARD ISLAND

ANDREW HEMPSTEAD

VANCOUVER

CAROLYN B. HELLER

VICTORIA & VANCOUVER ISLAND

ANDREW HEMPSTEAD

Best Ofs & Road Trips

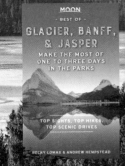

MOON

- BEST OF -
GLACIER, BANFF, & JASPER

MAKE THE MOST OF
ONE TO THREE DAYS
IN THE PARKS

TOP SIGHTS, TOP HIKES,
TOP SCENIC DRIVES

BECKY LOMAX & ANDREW HEMPSTEAD

MOON

PACIFIC NORTHWEST
Road Trip

OUTDOOR ADVENTURES AND CREATIVE CITIES
FROM THE COAST TO THE MOUNTAINS

ALLISON WILLIAMS

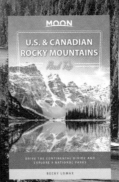

MOON

U.S. & CANADIAN ROCKY MOUNTAINS
Road Trip

DRIVE THE CONTINENTAL DIVIDE AND
EXPLORE 9 NATIONAL PARKS

BECKY LOMAX

MOON

VANCOUVER & CANADIAN ROCKIES
Road Trip

VICTORIA, BANFF, JASPER, CALGARY,
THE OKANAGAN, WHISTLER &
THE SEA-TO-SKY HIGHWAY

CAROLYN B. HELLER

MAP SYMBOLS

Expressway	○ City/Town	✈ Airport	⚲ Golf Course
Primary Road	◉ State Capital	✈ Airfield	🅿 Parking Area
Secondary Road	⊛ National Capital	▲ Mountain	▲ Archaeological Site
Unpaved Road	⊕ Highlight	✛ Unique Natural Feature	Church
Trail	★ Point of Interest		Gas Station
Ferry	• Accommodation	Waterfall	Glacier
Railroad	▼ Restaurant/Bar	⚑ Park	Mangrove
Pedestrian Walkway	■ Other Location	❶ Trailhead	Reef
Stairs	Ⓐ Campground	Skiing Area	Swamp

CONVERSION TABLES

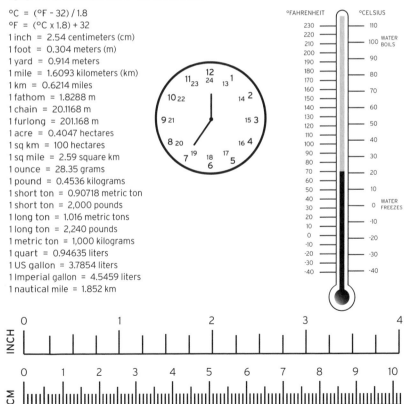

°C = (°F - 32) / 1.8
°F = (°C x 1.8) + 32
1 inch = 2.54 centimeters (cm)
1 foot = 0.304 meters (m)
1 yard = 0.914 meters
1 mile = 1.6093 kilometers (km)
1 km = 0.6214 miles
1 fathom = 1.8288 m
1 chain = 20.1168 m
1 furlong = 201.168 m
1 acre = 0.4047 hectares
1 sq km = 100 hectares
1 sq mile = 2.59 square km
1 ounce = 28.35 grams
1 pound = 0.4536 kilograms
1 short ton = 0.90718 metric ton
1 short ton = 2,000 pounds
1 long ton = 1.016 metric tons
1 long ton = 2,240 pounds
1 metric ton = 1,000 kilograms
1 quart = 0.94635 liters
1 US gallon = 3.7854 liters
1 Imperial gallon = 4.5459 liters
1 nautical mile = 1.852 km

MOON VICTORIA & VANCOUVER ISLAND

Avalon Travel
Hachette Book Group
1700 Fourth Street
Berkeley, CA 94710, USA
www.moon.com

Editor: Kimberly Ehart
Acquiring Editor: Nikki Ioakimedes
Series Manager: Kathryn Ettinger
Copy Editor: Callie Stoker-Graham
Graphics and Production Coordinator:
   Lucie Ericksen
Cover Design: Toni Tajima
Map Editor: Albert Angulo
Cartographers: Erin Greb Cartography and
   Karin Dahl
Indexer: Greg Jewett

ISBN-13: 978-1-64049-674-3

Printing History
1st Edition — 2014
3rd Edition — January 2023
5 4 3 2 1

Front cover photo: orcas at Telegraph Cove,
Vancouver Island © Jeroen Mikkers/GettyImages
Back cover photo: Inner Harbour Victoria ©
Jonghyunkim | Dreamstime.com

Printed in Malaysia for Imago

Avalon Travel is a division of Hachette Book Group,
Inc. Moon and the Moon logo are trademarks of
Hachette Book Group, Inc. All other marks and logos
depicted are the property of the original owners.